THE STAR-SPANGLED REPUBLIC

Jeffersonian America
CHARLENE M. BOYER LEWIS, ANNETTE GORDON-REED,
PETER S. ONUF, ANDREW J. O'SHAUGHNESSY,
AND ROBERT G. PARKINSON, EDITORS

The Star-Spangled Republic

*Political Astronomy and the Rise
of the American Constellation*

Eran Shalev

UNIVERSITY OF VIRGINIA PRESS
Charlottesville and London

The University of Virginia Press is situated on the traditional lands of the Monacan Nation, and the Commonwealth of Virginia was and is home to many other Indigenous people. We pay our respect to all of them, past and present. We also honor the enslaved African and African American people who built the University of Virginia, and we recognize their descendants. We commit to fostering voices from these communities through our publications and to deepening our collective understanding of their histories and contributions.

University of Virginia Press
© 2025 by the Rector and Visitors of the University of Virginia
All rights reserved
Printed in the United States of America on acid-free paper

First published 2025

1 3 5 7 9 8 6 4 2

ISBN 978-0-8139-5384-7 (hardback)
ISBN 978-0-8139-5385-4 (paperback)
ISBN 978-0-8139-5386-1 (ebook)

Library of Congress Cataloging-in-Publication Data is available for this title.

Cover art: Our Banner in the Sky, Frederic Edwin Church, 1861. Oil paint over lithograph on paper, laid down on cardboard. 7½ × 11⅝. (Terra Foundation for American Art, Daniel J. Terra Collection, 1992.27; photography © Terra Foundation for American Art, Chicago)
Cover design: Susan Zucker

To Michal, Yonatan, Yuli, and Ben,
my constellation of ever-shining luminaries

It is the stars, The stars above us, govern our conditions.

—William Shakespeare, *King Lear*

CONTENTS

Acknowledgments	*xi*
Introduction	1
1 | The American Universe: The Conditioning of Political Astronomers	26
2 | From the Sun King to Republican Solar Systems: Planetary Politics from the Revolution to the Civil War	73
3 | The American Constellation: Political Firmaments, Stars, and Flags	117
Epilogue: The American Star	167
Notes	*195*
Index	*229*

ACKNOWLEDGMENTS

I conceived the ideas underpinning this book years ago following a discussion with my colleague Zur Shalev about a paper he wrote on early modern European cosmography. Our conversation made me reflect on the "new American constellation," a curious phrase I kept encountering in late eighteenth-century newspapers. Certain that I would find ample writing on the meaning of American stars and constellations, I was proven wrong. Little did I know that what seemed like an innocent flashing light bulb would spark a long journey of thinking about American political astronomy.

The Star-Spangled Republic has thus been long in the making, and I hope that I have not forgotten some of the many debts I have incurred as I wrote it. David Nirenberg has generously offered his vast intellect to think about ideas far related from his fields of expertise. The great Peter Onuf was always there to help me think afresh about my work, and in the process taught me so much about history and friendship. Alexis McCrossen lent her acute observations, support, and companionship time and again. For the third time, I did not hit the "send" button for a book manuscript without the approval of Carl Richard, a brother I found late in life.

I wholeheartedly thank Nadine Zimmerli for being an engaged, helpful, and enthusiastic editor. The list of friends and colleagues that were there at crucial junctions with first-rate criticisms, suggestions, and support is long. They include, in alphabetical order, David Bell, Barak Biton, Eli Cook, Simon Cook, François Furstenberg, Laura Kalman, Trent MacNamara, Ifat Mizrachi-Harari, Ken Moss, Nathan Perl Rosenthal, Arnaldo Testi, John Vile, Molly Warsh, Avihu Zakai, and Yossi Ziegler. I thank the Israel Science Foundation and the University of Haifa's Research Authority for providing me generous material help.

THE STAR-SPANGLED REPUBLIC

Introduction

Our Banner in the Sky (1861) was painted in oil by Edwin Church, the Connecticut-born landscape artist, in response to the attack on Fort Sumter in Charleston, South Carolina, the first salvo of the Civil War. The modest-sized yet striking painting depicts the American flag as an arrangement of inanimate and meteorological objects, with a tree stump serving as a pole and a transient arrangement of horizontal stripes of cloud formations cast in hues of red and white by the setting sun. Reverberating such fundamental themes of early America national sentiment as destiny and progress, this sublime and sorrowful painting was popular among Northerners in the opening weeks of the war, widely distributed through the chromolithographs published by Goupil & Co. soon after the original was completed.[1] The pathos-filled scene was intended to evoke the proper emotions at this moment of national crisis by way of such elements as the blood-red sky and the looming darkness above. Yet the scene's most striking feature, the unevenly strewn piercing stars that impale the dark-blue firmament on the flag's upper-left corner, communicated a message that today may be easily missed. The shining stars in Church's painting, which do not represent any actual or recognizable star formation, remind us that the stars on the American flag are representations of physical and natural objects and point to a central, if mostly

FIGURE 1. *Our Banner in the Sky,* Frederic Edwin Church, 1861. Oil paint over lithograph on paper, laid down on cardboard. 7½ × 11⅜. (Terra Foundation for American Art, Daniel J. Terra Collection, 1992.27; photography © Terra Foundation for American Art, Chicago)

forgotten, world of astro-political meanings in the formation and self-conception of the pre–Civil War United States.

Church was not alone in viewing the American flag as endowed with celestial meaning, a practice in which numerous American citizens from every region of the United States participated from the Revolution to the Civil War era. Like Senator Robert Hayne of South Carolina, they reveled in a "banner studded all over with *stars*" and would have concurred with the unknown writer from New York struck by the heavenly spectacle of the "constellation of free states . . . moving by well-regulated law, each in its own proper orbit around the brighter star in Washington." Conscious of the cosmic meaning of this symbolism, Americans occasionally expressed their fear of a "brilliant sun, extending its golden rays from the [federal] centre to the extremities," the bright light of which would cause the stars on the flag to disappear.[2]

But why the stars on the American flag in the first place? Simple and deceptively naïve questions occasionally yield weighty rewards. This book arose out of wonder at the frequently encountered metaphor of the United States government as a planetary system, and the common phrase "the new constellation" to denote the Union of American states. Surprised at not finding any ready-to-hand answers as to the origins and meaning of the cosmic images widely encountered by any historian of the early United States, I found myself on a long and fascinating journey in which I was compelled to devise a notion of "political astronomy" to capture this early American discourse, only to find the phrase already deployed in the literature pertaining to other historical contexts and meanings.[3]

The Star-Spangled Republic directs attention for the first time to the cosmic backdrop to the new American nation's political culture and national debates. The book uncovers the ways in which "political astronomy," the discussion and representation of politics through astronomical models, allusions, and metaphors, facilitated a rich and broad public discourse through which American citizens throughout the revolutionary era, the early republic, and the antebellum period justified and found meaning in their concrete modes of governance and buttressed their national sentiment. The system of cosmic images that they elaborated provided modes of expression that made sense of the Revolution and the novel federal republic to which it gave birth. The first decades of the new nation saw statesmen and orators, news reporters and private authors, and middling men and women from every region of the expansive republic repeatedly turn to the starry heavens witnessed in their nightly skies to substantiate this idea of the United States. *The Star-Spangled Republic* traces this unique correlation of universe and revolving night skies with a revolutionary human world. That correlation encouraged citizens of the early United States to merge and match familiar models of the cosmos with a new American model of governance in ways that still reverberate in political discourse of the modern United States and across the globe.

Early American political astronomy reworked a discourse that had originated in early modern European courts, where kings across the continent, including Britain, were depicted as suns around which the nation revolved. The American Revolution turned this Old World monarchical astro-politics on its head, revealing a very different picture in the heavens. In this preindustrial world, in which people were familiar with a night sky that they could see far more clearly without light pollution than can we today, the Americans turned from the sun of the day to the stars and constellations of the night, to discover republicanism imprinted in the firmament that would replace solar monarchy. This novel and distinctly republican reading of the night sky proved a stepping stone to the popular image of the American states as stars, and consequently the United States as a "new constellation," which transformed even as it borrowed from older European discourses of political power in terms of spheres of influence and proper orbits of the respective branches of government. While today such political astronomy remains embedded in still-popular turns of phrase and visual imagery, it is now more commonly found in celebrations of a socially privileged class of humans. While they are many where previously only one sun king dominated his domain, modern society's "stars" and "superstars" share a direct lineage with the political suns and stars of past centuries, as the following pages uncover.

The Star-Spangled Republic identifies, contextualizes, and illuminates a unique and significant worldview that played a crucial role in the formation of American political culture and still retains a bearing on contemporary culture. The study of political astronomy in the early United States, and the worlds of meaning that it has generated, sheds new light on the ways in which we understand central issues in American history and how contemporaries explained their political unions and coped with national anxieties. This book demonstrates, for example, how a novel political view of the heavens (the "political firmament" was the common phrase) enabled the American public to articulate, debate, and make better sense of such great yet fiercely abstract political innovations of the age as republicanism and federalism, which to become accessible, comprehensible, and thus acceptable were frequently dressed in elaborate metaphor for public consumption. Indeed, without recognizing how political astronomy was framed, and so made sense of and likely even helped shape emerging political ideas and debate, we cannot properly understand major currents in American history, among them the perception of the United States as a nation in harmony with the cosmos, and more generally American exceptionalism. Political astronomy was a meaningful and rich mode of expression in the formative decades of the American republic, which enabled contemporaries to communicate their positions regarding state and society, justify and vindicate their political values, and express their doubts regarding the fate of the United States. *The Star-Spangled Republic* presents the ways in which early American political thought fostered a profound public discourse in which cosmic models and symbols represented its central ideas, and illuminates why and how a twenty-first-century nation living under the aegis of its Star-Spangled Banner is still immersed in a culture of American "superstars" that is centuries old.

Scholars have long studied the ways in which humans have interpreted and deciphered the night skies, which they surely have been observing for as long as they have observed anything, finding in what they saw meaning and significance for their individual and collective lives. They have studied how ancient societies engaged in astronomy in conjunction with astrology (two fields of knowledge that emerged in tandem and were categorically separated only relatively recently), employing the methods not only of the sociology of knowledge and the history of science but also standpoints such as archaeoastronomy (the interdisciplinary study of architecture, archaeology, and astronomy), and ethnoastronomy (the study of contemporary practices related to astronomy, particularly among indigenous societies).[4]

The apparent connection of ancient understandings of the cosmos and large-scale human endeavors has been traced to the dawn of history, identifying the symbiotic relationship of astronomy and politics back to Stonehenge and many other Neolithic monuments. The archaeologist Jacquetta Hawkes speculated long ago that even prehuman hominids contemplated their relation to the cosmos, specifically their understanding of the sun as a powerful external force that shaped their lives.[5] Whatever one's beliefs, whether one was a prehistoric hunter-gatherer or the child of the Enlightenment, the cosmos seemed to present a plan that was, in the words of a geographer in the early United States, "inexpressibly magnificent, yet regular beyond the power of invention."[6]

The earliest concrete examples of such contemplation come from Mesopotamian cultures, which like the civilizations before and after them produced "a cosmos in terms of [their] own observation . . . and experience."[7] The fact that they understood human society as an integral part of the cosmos led the late Danish historian Thorkild Jacobsen to label the Mesopotamian polities "cosmic states."[8] These civilizational cities were rumored to harbor "cosmic halls"—supposedly comprised of a rotunda domed like the heavens that revolved about its own axis, which captured the imagination of Western travelers and readers.[9] The world was imagined as a system of cohesive parts, with all earthly things functioning and reflecting the universe. Within this cosmology, the earthly kingdom was a function and reflection of the rule of the sun in the heavens. The king was surrounded by his vassals and satraps in a fashion that reflected the celestial hierarchy: Just as the stars surrounded the sun in the firmament, so the great lords surround the king in his palace. The political astronomy that developed from the late third millennium BCE in Mesopotamia thus constructed an earthly system that was believed to be inseparable from the celestial.[10]

While the phrase "political astronomy" (or the concept or the ideas it stands for) has been used in past studies, it has been by and large applied to ancient or indigenous societies, and only occasionally to early modern culture. Rarely, if at all, was political astronomy studied in the context of the modern societies of the late eighteenth century and after.[11] *The Star-Spangled Republic* thus uncovers a major yet overlooked aspect of the history of the United States from its inception until the mid-nineteenth century and beyond. In identifying, underscoring, and contextualizing the centrality of cosmic concepts to American politics and the political imagination, it tells a distinctly American story, unique in its modernity, but one that has its root in older European modes of thought.[12] Illuminating studies have demonstrated in the past the mechanical characteristics of American politics, and the extent to which Newtonian physics have influenced and shaped American constitutionalism in particular.[13] Yet the *astronomical* and *cosmic* source of these mechanical tropes has yet to be fully acknowledged, and thus we have yet to understand and contextualize these findings within the much broader and extraordinarily rich political astronomy of American politics. Such a perspective brings to the fore political astronomy and analyzes how it has been an established and vital mode of thought for many decades from the founding of the United States.

A mundane phenomenon such as newspaper titles highlights both the pervasiveness of political astronomy and the extent to which it was a distinctly American mode of thought. Newspapers in the early American republic were vastly popular, often vehicles of partisan political rhetoric, and thus the focus of intense scholarly scrutiny.[14] Yet newspapers' major role in the political and cultural life of the early United States notwithstanding, the nomenclature of their titles has been barely noticed. Anyone who scrutinizes these titles is struck by how many are astronomically related. Initially, early American newspaper titles took their cue, as in virtually every other cultural parameter, from their metropolitan counterparts. One should examine with caution those English newspapers with astronomical titles, however, and in particular the dozens (!) of early English newspaper titles including variants of "Mercury." Caution is warranted as it was not the small, scorching planet that these titles referred to but rather Mercury, the wing-footed Roman god of communication (coincidentally after which the closest planet to the sun was named). Only with the publication in London of *The Star* in 1788 does a truly cosmic nomenclature begin, one that would take seed in the British North American colonies and flourish in the early United States.[15]

If Americans took their initial cue from English publications, they soon surpassed them in this practice. The titles of many American newspapers included the word "Mercury," possibly gaining a cosmic connotation in light of the remarkable proliferation of other cosmic titles, and came in a variety of local variants such as the *New-Hampshire Mercury*. *The Sun*, however, was a particularly popular title, which demonstrates the American inclination to endow their newspapers with cosmic titles. That inclination far surpassed the British practice and went far beyond the epithets *Sun* (and its many variants, such as the *Western Sun*, etc.) and *Mercury*. Americans went on to publish papers with titles such as *The Constellation*, the *Weekly Aurora*, the *Federal Galaxy*, and *The Globe*, often with graphic mastheads that complemented the title with astronomical images. It was *The Star*, however, that became perhaps the most pervasive title, with dozens of so-named local publications with a variety of iterations: from the simple *The Star*, to a starry locality such as the *Berkshire Star*, the *American Star*, or *New Star*, *Morning Star*, *Star of Freedom*, and *Republican Star*, among others.

This astronomical nomenclature certainly became fashionable, an

FIGURE 2. Vermont's *Federal Galaxy* was among the many newspapers that made use of the symbolism of the American state-star and the "new constellation" in its title and the graphic representation on its masthead. (Early American Newspapers, Readex)

almost imitative reflex of public speech, yet it was neither hollow talk nor unthinking practice, its meanings opening to a contextualization within the wider discourse of political astronomy of the day. Cosmic titles were mobilized to reflect images of light and illumination and partook in a more general fascination with astronomy and astronomical objects, and particularly in the *political* astronomy of the day.[16] Indeed, contemporary reflection on these names demonstrates that while titles were chosen in imitation of other celestial-named publications, their adoption was carefully considered. The announcement of the soon-to-be-published *Star of Raleigh* (North Carolina) in 1808, for example, discloses the new newspaper's editorial goals and explains its chosen astronomical title. Acknowledging that other newspapers made use of grandiose titles such as "The Sun" and "The Constellation," the new paper assumed but "the more humble epithet 'The Star.'" Though this more modest title admittedly could not "rival the great luminaries" of the aforementioned competitors, the new *Star*'s publishers hoped that "it will not be altogether lost in the brilliancy of their [its rivals'] rays, and twinkle without regard." *The Star*, it was hoped, "will attract the notice of our various astrologers [that is, readers], and contribute something to the general illumination."[17]

The *Federal Orrery* was yet another remarkable and distinctly American newspaper title of a Boston publication that commenced in 1794, during the height of the battles of the First Party System. An orrery was a spectacular, mechanical model of the solar system that demonstrated the relative positions and proper motions of the planets and moons with the aid of intricate systems made of cogwheels.[18] The newspaper's masthead depicted a central sun surrounded by fifteen five-point stars (the Union

FIGURE 3. The *Federal Orrery* borrowed the image of the popular mechanical models of the solar system for its name. (Early American Newspapers, Readex)

included fifteen states in June 1796, the date of the issue displayed in figure 3), and its motto is borrowed from Virgil's Aeneid (VI.640.1), translated from the Latin: They know their own sun, and stars of their own.

A short and remarkable piece, published in the first year of the *Federal Orrery*'s publication, reveals the ways in which political astronomy was part and parcel of the content of those cosmically titled newspapers. Written during the climax of the Whiskey Rebellion (1794), the editorial (if it may be thus called) took the side of the national government vis-à-vis the uprisings and protests against the federal "whiskey tax," mobilizing extraordinary and elaborate astronomical language. Defending the disputed tax, the unnamed author dubbed the unrest in western Pennsylvania a "flaming meteor ... of the sulfur of anarchy" that blazed "with so much fury through the Columbian hemisphere, revolving in the eccentric path of Jacobinism." With what was already becoming by the late eighteenth century a characteristic mixture of astronomy and politics, the author raised the specter of anarchy that "impinged on the orbit of one of the largest planets in the Federal System," Pennsylvania, which, as "all our political astronomers" believed, was expected to "run so near the disc of the sun of [the federal] government." Yet the "political astronomers" were optimistic, confident that the noxious meteor of anarchy "must soon be absorbed by the attraction, and become invisible in the rays of our National Luminary," that is, the only recently ratified federal Constitution. The Union, they were sure, will overcome "the blazing stars of faction, and the fiery tail of rebellion." While this piece was remarkable in the exhaustive detail of its metaphor, it was nevertheless, as we shall come to see in the following chapters, rather characteristic in its modes of relaying political occurrences as astronomical phenomena.[19]

Orbits, meteors, constellations and firmaments, radiancy and light, and, of course, revolutions, were all astronomical occurrences and concepts brought into public, political speech as heuristic tools to explore and figuratively explain social life in terms of the celestial. Political astronomy would sharpen early Americans' deliberative tools and enable them to recognize and validate aspects of their political lives, to find the meanings of earthly institutions through the language of the heavenly firmament. The pervasivness, longevity, and richness of political astronomy attest to the fact that it took part in shaping contemporaries' view of the world and was essential to how they communicated, learned, discovered, and constructed their political universe. Indeed, political astronomy was so vital because key concepts of American political thought were themselves constructed by literally putting it to use. Hence, for example, the image of the Constitution as a sun that holds other institutions or states in their proper orbit, which was among the fundamental figures of American political astronomy, helped contemporaries visualize and imagine, and in turn to expound the abstractions of constitutional power. The constitution-as-sun metaphor thus enabled early Americans, as we shall see, to make sense of and manage their unprecedented postrevolutionary political world.

Humans are creatures of language, shaped and constrained by conceptions that are composed through words. Hence, when considering choices and tactics available to individuals at particular historical moments, one should take note of distinct representations and their relationships in order to account for how historical events were perceived, how pronouncements came about and action was taken. By recognizing and understanding the linguistic and cognitive frameworks within which past communities operated, we are able to better understand specific courses of action and decisions that otherwise may have been misunderstood and misinterpreted. That the pervasive American political astronomy was a metaphorical mode of thought should not make us think less of it; metaphors are at work in and vital to all fields of human endeavor, conditioning or found behind and beneath most thought. Metaphors can specifically help in shaping and constraining action, as Lakoff and Johnson have suggested in their classic study of metaphorical thinking. Humans, who continuously struggle to impose order on their universe, thus make constant use of metaphorical thinking to make sense of the world. Cognitive scientists have recognized their pervasiveness and have come to appreciate metaphors not as mere playful rhetorical tropes whose role is to embellish language. Rather, through their mixing the foreign and unknown with familiar shapes attitudes, beliefs, and actions, metaphors are indispensable to thought.[20]

Aristotle's classic definition of metaphor as "giving the thing a name that belongs to something else" is still effective.[21] Hence, a metaphor juxtaposes two different things and then provides a fresh point of view that underscores new and unexpected similarities. The notion that understanding is perceiving patterns is attributed to the philosopher Isaiah Berlin but is surely much older; in any case, metaphor is more than discovering patterns; it is the creation of patterns. We select information about something with which we are familiar, the metaphor's source—such as, for example, visible star formations—and apply it to what we know about its target, the American Union. Metaphorical thinking thus discovers similarities, such as those shared between a cluster of celestial objects and a group of polities, but at the same time manipulates and invents the likenesses it describes, transforming the Union of American states into a "new constellation," a natural, harmonious and radiant formation of state-stars. Once a metaphor coheres and sticks, it does not merely reflect past opinions of whoever initially coined it but actively helps shape present judgments and actions, priming opinions, attitudes, and beliefs. An effective metaphor needs not hold a certain, or any, truth-value but rather depends on easy accessibility, which is what allows it to become a common organizing principle through which everything pertaining to that idea is seen.[22]

States and nations are the creation of human minds, and as such develop and endure in time due to the sustained faith of numerous men and women in their material existence. Thus, to remain effective and affective, a variety of metaphors have been developed throughout the millennia to render these complex social structures comprehensible and sensible. The classical Greek tradition produced some of the most enduring metaphors for the state, such as the Aristotelian analogy of the family and polity as presented in the *Politics,* and the Platonic "ship of state."[23]

Medieval Christian thought introduced the enduring *corpus politicum*, an organic view that identified the polity with the human body, the "body politic"; and Thomas Hobbes asserted in *Leviathan* (1651), in the context of the English Civil War, that large-scale organized political society was a "leviathan," a huge ocean beast, and an "artificial man." Ever since, polities and their apologists have been keen to collect metaphors and other symbolic and figurative systems, many of which fall on the spectrum between the natural and the artificial.

Scholarly interest in these immensely influential political metaphors has produced some classics of intellectual history, such as Ernst Kantorowicz's *The King's Two Bodies*.[24] Historians of the United States have followed suit and produced remarkable studies of dominant political metaphors.[25] Major studies have focused on political metaphors that derived from nature, such as the analogy through which the political society was likened to a biological organism that was born, matured, decayed, and died. The historian Drew McCoy was among the first to discuss this important metaphor in his eye-opening book *The Elusive Republic*. Viewing the early American republic as a living organism suggested a temporal cycle in which society, like a living creature, inevitably decayed and perished. Although that corporal metaphor was fundamentally pessimistic, its allure was that it implied that the United States was not artificial and thus unacceptable, as its detractors suggested. Rather, if the republic was like a biological organism, it was deemed "natural," and, in turn, whatever was natural was right and good.[26]

More recently, the literary historian Eric Slauter has demonstrated the centrality of the notion of the United States' government as not natural but artificial, a human creation. Slauter points out that the United States, and in particular its novel Constitution, were conceived as "a work of art," a subject fit for observation and criticism. As metaphors tend to compound upon each other, the state-as-art metaphor was made sense of through an additional set of metaphors, such as that of the government as a constructed edifice and state-building as architecture. The architectural metaphor's emergence during the early years of the republic seems to indicate that, as time passed, bodily and biological representations declined, both in use and in conceptual value, replaced by a vision of states and governments as fashioned by and subjected to humans.[27]

Yet the long-term shift from organic to cultural political metaphors, from "nature" to "art," even if it thus occurred, was not straightforward. Rather, several studies of persistent political metaphors in the United States focus not on the republic's artificiality but on images that, while corresponding with nature, were not bodily or organic.

Several historians have by now pointed out how early Americans appealed to the physical, and particularly the mechanical aspects of the American Union.[28] One study, for example, observed that citizens of the early United States were likened to "republican machines" that dutifully fulfilled their civic duties. These civic "machines" demonstrated "orderly, hierarchical structure, harmonious, regular motion, and sheer constructability . . . beautifully epitomized by mechanism's physical qualities and aesthetic appeal."[29] While machines may have been man-made, they reflected the laws governing the physical world, particularly through the reigning paradigm of Newtonian physics. With the universe itself seen as an enormous clockwork, clocks and other mechanical contraptions were seen as representing and echoing important aspects of nature. In this vein, Michael Foley demonstrated in his monographic *Laws, Men and Machines* how Newtonian mechanics provided a central metaphor for the novel American political system. Similarly, Richard Striner specifically focused on the cosmos, and the clockwork as its dominant representation, as the archetypical model for the United States.[30]

The Star-Spangled Republic participates in this significant discussion by demonstrating the centrality and pervasiveness of political astronomy in the early United States. Like the handful of studies that highlighted Newtonian metaphors in the early United States, it underscores a long-term change in ideas about the state through appeals to the cosmos. In tandem with other scholarly works, it suggests a movement away from organic analogies and thus implies that the state was seen as more permanent than a body subject to biological decay. Yet *The Star-Spangled Republic* pushes such arguments further by demonstrating the extent to which the cosmos, and hence a "nature" that while abiding to natural laws was not organic, was vital for making sense of fundamental political concepts. Indeed, political astronomy helped explicate and justify the most fundamental elements of American political thought, such as power and harmony, which were in turn central for imagining the novelty of a federal republic. Such metaphors for presenting political power in natural terms originated in European courts (the sun king being the most recognizable) and served as the basis of the republicanized and more developed political astronomy of the United States. Although often overlooked, American political astronomy, as the following pages establish, was a robust, enduring, and pervasive metaphorical array. Indeed, political astronomy presented the American republic, to paraphrase the great historian Perry Miller, not as nature's nation, but as the universe's nation.

Within the context of the rise of modern nations in the age of revolutions, emerged an "impersonal" state that was autonomous and equally independent from its rulers and its citizens.[31] These transformations were common to many emerging states, but after Independence, Americans confronted a series of momentous decisions regarding the nature of their republican governments and their confederate Union. In particular, they had to resolve how power was organized and sovereignty distributed between the federal center and the states. As these and similar questions were being determined, political astronomy became central to the attempts to rationalize and familiarize the novel American federal republic to broad publics, and ultimately to make the United States an affective force in the lives of its citizens.

Political astronomy displayed significant advantages that enabled it to become prevalent and effective throughout the Revolution, early republic, and the antebellum era. First, it became particularly useful for mediating abstract political notions and ideas due to its accessibility, which rested on the surprisingly widespread knowledge of both vernacular and scientific astronomy. Astronomical metaphors that involved planets, constellations, and comets reverberated so powerfully in large segments of American society because commoners as well as elites, women, and probably even enslaved Black Americans had access to astronomical knowledge that enabled them to decipher and put to use celestial metaphors.[32] Second, the heavens were particularly effective for reenforcing novel political notions because they were associated with two fundamental axioms in America: The cosmos was the supreme creation of divinity; and Newtonian science, particularly mechanical physics, was the tool through which the workings and meaning of the divinely constructed cosmos could be unlocked. In a world that still valued custom and antiquity above any other attribute in evaluating political decisions and conduct, the recently created and conspicuously unprecedented American federal republic was born with significant disadvantage. That political astronomy could associate the United States with towering ideas such as divine design and Newtonian physics endowed it with much-needed legitimacy. Third, political astronomy was so effective since it could readily apply the cosmic harmony of a well-tempered universe to earthly, human political conditions.

Political astronomy was appealing and so potent since the ideas it propagated, such as that of the new American constellation or the United States as a union of state-stars, were perceived as natural and consonant with the cosmos; and because they were natural, they were harmonic. Such thinking about politics in terms of astronomical phenomena participated in an age-old and widespread belief in cosmic harmony that in the West stretched back into antiquity. Harmony was a state of natural equilibrium, sublimity, and beauty in which conflict and dissonance were resolved. Throughout the ages various conventions, such as the idea of the Great Chain of Being, a medieval expression of harmonic thinking that presented a universal model of a good, consonant government, strove toward harmonic politics.[33] Hence, the mischief of Hobbes notwithstanding, by the days of the founding of the United States, English speakers had behind them centuries of advocacy of a balanced and harmonized "natural" polity. Such government was supposed to be in agreement with a cosmological framework and provided what the historian James Daly called a "political theory of order."[34] American readers and writers inherited this tradition, in which *harmony* named something good, orderly, and fundamentally true. Most agreed throughout the middle of the nineteenth century that their national Union provided the best guarantee of the people's liberty and happiness, and political astronomy was a mode of supporting and strengthening this Union and the attachment to it by articulating and manifesting its supposedly harmonic nature and thus godly sanction.

Political harmony proved particularly important in the discordant world of early American politics. The historian Kirsten Wood effectively demonstrated how sung performances in the eighteenth century, vocal

Introduction

and choral recitals, attempted to overcome corruption and constitute virtuous government. Such belief compelled Americans to conceive the conflict between the factions and parties that pervaded the early republic not as existential ruptures but as "temporary dissonances encompassed within a harmonic framework."[35] We should understand and contextualize political astronomy within this striving for a harmonic ideal in republican politics. Its early practitioners hoped that the American constellation of state-stars would emerge after Independence along the lines of the proverbial city upon a hill, as a Patriot in South Carolina (of all places) proclaimed after the conclusion of the war with Britain in 1783, wishing "the Thirteen Stars . . . of Confederate America, prove a luminous Constellation, enlightening the bewildered, and directing the footsteps of the oppressed of the world to the shrine of liberty."[36] With the ratification of the federal Constitution several years later, the appeal to cosmic harmony became even more explicit, as contemporaries saw their "fed'ral states politically join'd . . . as splendid stars" and orbiting "in perfect concord." Such political concord manifested "wisdom, justice, harmony and love," thus performing "a concert heaven itself might hear." The musical reference alluded to the ancient and widely recognized concept of the "music of the spheres," which regarded the perfect proportions in the movements of celestial bodies as a form of flawless heavenly music.[37] The images of political astronomy thus enabled Americans from the republic's inception and for decades thereafter to conceive their republican governments as natural and thus fundamentally harmonious, while witnessing political strife as epiphenomenal. The founding generations, who aimed from the republic's inception, in the words of James Madison, to "preserv[e] the harmony of the system,"[38] needed political astronomy to reassure them but also to transpose theoretical and obstruse theoretical concepts such as nation, republic, and confederacy, into ideas that were accessible and tangible.

However, much of political astronomy's power as a metaphorical language derived from its ability to convey and express the exact opposite of harmony, namely, dystopic fears of anarchy and disfunction. Against the harmonious model of a "clockwork universe," alarmists could pose ominous images of meteors and planets flying off their tangents to express the horror of a political system on the verge of destruction. Advocates of American harmony thus understood well, and often warned of, a cosmic state of affairs in which political congruence was shattered. In such disharmonic pandemonium, political stars would be "overwhelmed with confusion" and could "sink into darkness."[39] Such anxieties would particularly emerge during recurring moments of threat to the Union, when the worst fears of discord, disorder, and conflict materialized. The fateful breakup of the Union during the secession crisis could thus easily be interpreted as the collapse of cosmic harmony, in which "stars of [the] political firmament [were] torn from their orbits, and plung[ed] madly about."[40] Hence, political astronomy enabled Americans of the young republic to express both their noble political ideals of harmony and cohesion, as well as their worst fears of dissolution during moments of crisis. In a young federation created to assuage strife among the republics of which it was composed but had its (un)healthy share of moments of crisis, the value of such a dynamic language was obvious.

As should by now be clear, political astronomy was a particularly flexible language that enriched political discussion throughout the first fourscore years of the republic. An array of astronomical metaphors generated new modes of thinking about the major issues that preoccupied the young republic, among them federalism, citizenship, statehood, and expansion. Such a political cosmology must have opened up contemporaries' capacity to think in a broad sense about space (terrestrial and astronomic) and how it should be controlled, about how the political universe was governed, and how a celestial republic ought to function. This conflation of earthly and heavenly rule came at a time in which the young United States needed all the intellectual resources it could muster to buttress and validate an experimental and untried political order.

Political astronomy thus enabled Americans to better negotiate the main variables of their national life in a metaphoric language that was widely understood, surprisingly common, and inherently legitimatizing. Consequently, this book is a study of how such a series of metaphors helped shape American politics and culture, and how political astronomy expanded Americans' horizon of expectations by providing a system of reference that filtered and clarified the political reality through established structures and ideas. Federalists and Jeffersonians, Whigs and

Democrats, Northerners and Southerners, Indians and perhaps even enslaved Americans, could see themselves and their respective ideologies in the metaphors that political astronomy made regular use of. Hence, one of political astronomy's powerful properties was that it was capacious and flexible, providing a big tent within which all sides of a given debate could express themselves: While supporters of strong national government could revert to the role of the sun in governing its planets, for example, states'-rights advocates imagined constellational configurations as the most sublime, and thus "true," of models.

While it was often helpful in mediating and legitimizing, and thus in ameliorating clashes and crises that the young republic repeatedly faced, political astronomy may have simultaneously posed limitations on meaningful public discourse and thus foreclosed productive ways of thought and modes of action. Political astronomy implied a strict Newtonian mechanistic order, as well as the universal natural and cosmic laws that underlay both the astronomical as well as the political worlds. Those underlying assumptions were necessary for the conflation of the astronomical and the political, yet they tended to totalize claims about the good through a cosmic-moral and mechanistic logic. Indeed, non-negotiable truths, such as Newtonian mechanics or the assumption of a transcendental celestial harmony, as they were projected onto the human world, posed fixed limits to a discussion. Such totalizing thus inevitably limited the intellectual resources available for Americans, and thus their ability to deal with disagreement. Placing the American Union on the foundations of a universal cosmological order thus came with a cost: The debates at the heart of American sectional discord became much harder to negotiate when both sides claimed a fixed cosmic order and natural mechanistic laws. Political astronomy may thus have made mediation between divergent political notions harder, and ultimately impossible. As political astronomy took part in shaping political culture, as this book aims to demonstrate, it is possible to imagine that it actually contributed to the entanglement between the North and the South.

Political astronomy may have thus constrained the republic's ability to properly function, posing limits on how the republic could deal with discord and differences, possibly ruling out other modes of thought and barring different courses of action. This is not to say, of course, that without political astronomy the Civil War could have been averted, or that a different set of metaphors could have solved the ideological and moral strife that slavery and its expansion created. However, one may indeed ask, If political astronomy had not contributed to the naturalization of the republic's moral economy, if it had not helped establish unyielding and dogmatic laws as the basis for political claims, might the American system have found ways to negotiate difference other than falling apart into two separate and warring Northern and Southern constellations?

Early Americans had recourse to several tactics in their attempts to legitimize, contextualize, and provide meaning to their political experiment in republican government, and *The Star-Spangled Republic* continues the trajectory of my earlier work in analyzing the roots of American nationhood and political imagination. Particularly in *American Zion* (2012) and *Rome Reborn on Western Shores* (2009), I examined the historical sources of political consciousness and national identity in the early United States. Those works focused on appeals to history, classical and biblical, as a mode of national self-reflection and contextualization of the deeds of the present in light of a mythic, glorious, and revered past. While the early modern republican world on both sides of the Atlantic equated custom and tradition with the good and acceptable, and thus put great value on the historical validation of national projects, the appeal to political astronomy was a distinctly American mode of reasoning. *The Star-Spangled Republic* thus steps out of history and into the visible, physical cosmos to demonstrate the ways in which the heavens enabled contemporaries to make sense of and legitimize their novel federal republic, and to contemplate their place and role in the rapidly changing political and physical universe of the nation's founding decades. As the historian Joyce Chaplin reminds us, "the overwhelming majority of American history has focused on relationships among human actors, leaving the natural world out of the picture or putting it, at best, in the background."[41] While history and cosmos were part of the same project of understanding the United States and its place in the world, they were in some respects diametrically opposite. History provided models and examples on a human time scale in which forces of dramatic change reigned, whereas political astronomy presented seemingly timeless and eternal truths. Only

Introduction

an apocalyptic event, that is, the end of history, could halt the raucous world of historical change and compete with the promise of cosmic and everlasting harmony. Cosmos and history served the aim of making sense of the purpose of and securing the existence of the United States. They lend themselves, however, to different sets of interpretive schemes and predictions regarding the nature and future of the American Union.

The heavens' place in the life and mind of past societies, eighteenth- and nineteenth-century America included, was very different from its place in modern culture. Chapter 1, "The American Universe: The Conditioning of Political Astronomers," contextualizes astronomy in the world of late eighteenth- and nineteenth-century Americans and points out the ways in which they came to grips with and internalized the changing conceptions of the cosmos. The chapter sketches in broad strokes the main characteristics of the most comprehensive cosmological worldviews, as well as noting how they were acquired and disseminated. By no means an exhaustive survey, it focuses on key moments, ideas, and transformations in the development of these cosmologies, some of which were distinctly American. The chapter follows both the development of formal and scientific astronomy in the colonial and then early national world, and the popularization of the cosmologies that sprang out of that astronomy.

Such an examination is pertinent to the study of political astronomy since many Americans of the founding generations were versed both in the history of astronomy and in the cutting edge of the discipline in their day, while others remained deeply influenced by, or even developed their own vernacular ideas and idioms. This first chapter thus acquaints readers with aspects of the world that preindustrial Americans inhabited and the notions that underlay the application of astronomy and cosmic ideas to their thinking about politics. This chapter will explore notions ranging from that of a harmonic and immensely huge universe that harbored an infinite number of stars, to the meaning of the North Star as a symbol of freedom for fleeing slaves. In short, it will provide the foundation for understanding the celestial imagination and political astronomy in the early United States at the center of the book.

One of the fundamental models of political astronomy was that of the solar system as a group of physical objects that were governed and controlled by a central and sovereign powerful body. Chapter 2, "From the Sun King to Republican Solar Systems: Planetary Politics from the Revolution to the Civil War," explores this model by following the many Americans who republicanized monarchical astronomical views and made those views vital to understandings of the federal republic well into the nineteenth century. Old Regime political cultures made use of extraordinary anthropomorphic readings of the sun, which by the late seventeenth century had supplanted the earth in contemporaries' minds as the center of the solar system. In such understandings, the sun constituted the center of a planetary "system," which attracted, repelled, and presumably controlled lesser bodies. Such images easily lent themselves to majestic readings: The sun was king, and kings were, well, suns. Thus, a luminous and dominant heavenly body became the monarchical pivot around which revolved other lesser planets, representing in the political imagination the various parts of the nation.

Accordingly, by striving for the celestial harmony that the British imperial constitution never achieved, the federal Constitution spawned a mode of analyzing political power, particularly federalism, as an interaction among heavenly bodies. In the decades following the creation of the republic, politicians and commentators continued to interpret the relationship between the American states and the national government in terms of interaction among bodies orbiting around and gravitating toward each other. During the decades leading to secession and the Civil War, these astro-mechanistic visualizations enabled contemporaries to deliberate and clash over the stark differences in their understanding of the American Union, in order to better to gauge the stakes and possibilities that lay ahead. Was the Constitution a federal sun that bound the states together and constricted their ability to stray, as Northerners argued? Or were the states autonomous, willingly orbiting around the sun but properly drawing on their own respective spheres, as Southerners repeatedly asserted? This chapter unveils the great significance of the solar system in contemporaries' efforts to tackle the most acute questions of the budding American political tradition, a significance that still echoes as modern-day jurists, political scientists, and pundits discuss constitutional and common law "orbits," and branches of government's "spheres of influence."

Chapter 3, "The American Constellation: Political Firmaments, Stars, and Flags," shifts from a planetary to a stellar perspective, starting from the antimonarchism and republicanism of the American Revolution, which shattered the traditional political understanding based on the imagery of a single, central solar power. The Revolution gave rise to a wholly new astro-political mode of communicating the national order, in which the American states were viewed as stars, not planets. In such understanding (which would not replace but coexist with the planetary idiom, discussed in chapter 2), no kingly star, or single sun, overshadowed and dominated the others; together the American state-stars constituted a novel political system in which a plurality of individual stars held together, comprising a republican-like constellation more perfect than its discrete parts.

In place of the Old Regime view of the king as the sun around which the political realm and nation revolved, in the 1770s an alternative and revolutionary political cosmology emerged and was soon enshrined in the new American nation's formal symbols: a diffuse constellation of uniform floating stars devoid of a solar center, embodying egalitarian and republican values. From the republic's founding, through the expansion and the consequent addition of state-stars to the "new American constellation," the temporary collapse during the Civil War, and beyond, this constellational image provided—and still provides—a distinct vocabulary to articulate and express Americans' shifting attitudes toward, and understanding of, their confederated nation.

The "new American constellation," the image of the American federation as a fraternity of stars, still manifested on countless American flagpoles and numerous other material artifacts, has been strangely overlooked and has yet to be understood in its proper context. Throughout the nineteenth century it was sufficiently powerful to induce a majority of the new states that joined the Union after 1788 to adopt banners embellished with star-related symbols. Yet even more striking (and unnoticed) is the fact that the United States provided celestial inspiration not only to the American states that joined the expanding Union but also to numerous nations and states that established their independence during the age of nationalism. Scores of new countries took their cue from the American cosmological idiom and adorned their national flags with shining stars. The examples of polities as diverse as the European Union and the Cook Islands, with their Continental-like ring of stars, are particularly remarkable. The United States' political astronomy has thus not only shaped Americans' understanding of their nation; it has also had a powerful global effect on the ways in which numerous communities around the world imagine themselves and their relation to the world around them. The state-as-star and consequent image of the American constellation is remarkable unsung evidence of America's early wielding of soft power.

In the epilogue, "The American Star," I note that, until the emergence of the early modern image of the European sun king, it was rare, perhaps unprecedented, to treat living people in terms of stars. The sun king, standing at the center of the political nation, embodied the early modern state. But acting with what Ernst Kantorowicz famously called his "second body," the early modern king was also a private person, an individual possessing stellar qualities. Hence, two distinct traditions branched out from the image of the solar monarch: Whereas one, which earlier chapters explore, represented impersonal political bodies (usually states) and institutions (often the Constitution) in celestial terms, another described individual humans in terms of celestial bodies.

Men as stars, planets, or the sun, figures whose genealogy was linked to the culture of monarchical adulation, were potentially too offensive for a republic. However, even in the United States' staunch republican culture, Americans relentlessly referred to their leaders in solar terms. In particular, George Washington, a republican king if there ever was one, was understood as a sun "moving in his own orbit, imparting light to his most distant satellites." If at first it was more common to refer to "constellations of luminaries," as the nineteenth century progressed an individualistic culture of celebrity evolved, and references to constellational groups of celebrated people gave way more often to the adulation of discrete individual "stars." In a world that came to romantically appreciate the unique talent and genius of individuals, it was artists, and in particular theatrical performers, who have eventually replaced politicians as those primarily associated with stars.

Stardom eventually became a pervasive social phenomenon, ironically in tandem with the advent of mass urban centers and the consequent contaminating light pollution and thus loss of unmediated experience of the heavenly stars for most of modern humanity. Now the "star" became an expression devoid of its former contextual richness and profound meaning. The human star, which emerged out of a rich and centuries-old political astronomical discourse, became, by the first decades of the twentieth century, a hollow cliché. That might explain the fact that, while scholars have produced a rich literature about the phenomenon of stardom, the term itself has completely escaped their attention. The more pervasive and trivial the symbol of the star became—think of hotel or Amazon.com ranking systems of stars—the more detached it became from the actual heavenly bodies. The image of the modern star originated in sixteenth-century European courts, took a sharp republican turn in the American Revolution, and returned full circle to its regal origins with celebrity stars revered as modern-day monarchs. Hence, political astronomy still echoes loudly in present-day America. We need only recognize the deep impact that the stars made on our predecessors, and how their pale artificial imitations persist in the imagination of the American republic.

Looking back at Edwin Church's painting reminds us that arguably the most prominent American visual symbol was a natural object to which twenty-first-century humans have far less access than their predecessors. While American stars are represented as five-pointed geometrical objects, they stand for cosmic physical and three-dimensional entities. Regardless of their prominence in the national and visual culture of the United States, we have yet to understand why the founders chose stars as the symbol for their newly created states, what those stars meant to them and to following generations, and to what effect the symbol was used. Generations of Americans made sense of the terrestrial world and confronted the problems it placed at their feet through looking up to the skies and putting to use the models the heavens provided them. As they further studied and better understood the cosmos, the framing of the American world in celestial terms provided a sublime representation—and thus a powerful explanation—of a political entity, the United States of America, whose existence, like all human institutions, is owed to the power of collective imagination. *The Star-Spangled Republic* thus places for the first time American stars in their proper contexts—and orbits—and retrieves a rich, fascinating, and overlooked dialogue and set of questions about the cosmos and the United States, a discussion that still echoes and reverberates in twenty-first-century America.

When metaphors become empty clichés, they are simultaneously hardly noticed as figures of speech and put more frequently to use. As we shall see, by the mid-nineteenth century political astronomy had created a pool of potent images that would eventually lose their figurative attributes. From the Constitution as prescribing the orbits within which government branches must move, to the American flag and other national symbols studded with stars, and the social status of stardom, all are pervasive images that owe their existence to a broad and rich political astronomy that emerged in the early United States as an attempt to make sense of and impose order on the world. They still permeate modern America.

1

The American Universe

THE CONDITIONING OF POLITICAL ASTRONOMERS

IN *Memoirs of the Life of David Rittenhouse,* early America's most renowned astronomer attested to the significance of astronomy in the life of late eighteenth- and nineteenth-century Americans:

> The disposition of man to direct his eyes frequently upwards, and the faculty to do so, arising from his erect figure and the position and structure of the organs of his vision, furnish no feeble argument in proving, that this temporary lord of his fellow-beings on this globe has nobler destinies, infinitely beyond them; being enabled and permitted by the Author of his being, even while in this circumscribed state of his existence, to survey those myriads of worlds which occupy the immensity of space.[1]

They further indicate the tremendous transformations that had but only recently altered contemporary views regarding the nature of the universe. The movement from a geocentric to a heliocentric solar system, as well as the recognition that space was immense and harbored an enormous number of stars, was at the core of the new cosmologies that had emerged by the second half of the eighteenth century in Europe, and so also among their overseas colonists. The following pages chart the main characteristics of early Americans' broadest worldviews, as well as the means by which those worldviews were acquired, disseminated, and consumed. This chapter demonstrates the extent to which contemporaries engaged with astronomical information, and the different modes and intellectual filters through which they made sense of the universe. Political astronomy, the analysis of politics on a cosmic scale, depended at the very least on a token recognition of how the cosmos operated. This chapter delineates the ways in which numerous Americans of the founding generations of the United States were versed in the astronomy of their own age, but even more were conversant in popularized and politicized versions of contemporary cosmologies.

We shall thus encounter a cosmos inherited and inhabited by preindustrial Americans, and the notions by which citizens of the young United States projected astronomy into their political thought. Yet by the late eighteenth century more and more informally educated Americans of all sorts had to reckon with modern astronomical ideas and incorporate them into their cosmologies. As the nineteenth century progressed it became harder to uphold traditional views of the universe, and by the later midcentury the burden "lay squarely with those who preferred an intimate God and heaven."[2] The chapter first outlines the modes of production and dissemination of formal astronomy and astronomical knowledge and then goes on to outline the different attributes and meanings that wide swaths of early American society attached to the night skies. From enslaved people who saw the North Star as a beacon of freedom, to authors who popularized the notion of the universe in terms of fabulous clockwork, and to the numerous almanac readers who recognized its immense proportions and still saw the universe as a source of order and harmony, all conditioned and facilitated projections of the cosmos onto the American political order. What follows, in short, is the foundation and backbone of the cosmology and hence celestial imagination of the revolutionary era and the early republic that is at the center of this book.

The temporal rhythms of preindustrial societies were radically different from those that pace the world that we moderns learn to accept as given. Regulated to a much higher degree by natural forces, humans operated according to strict diurnal cycles until not so long ago.[3] The sun's unwavering travel through the firmament marked the passage of days and the changing seasons, and its setting meant for the most part that the day's activity had concluded. With electric light becoming commercially viable only after 1850 and universally used only decades later, the hearth, the oil lamp, and the candle remained the only sources of artificial light until deep into the nineteenth century. Early Americans, together with the rest of humanity, thus experienced nighttime as a natural force, and had little or no way to escape the constraints of darkness. With artificial light a scarcity, humanity was left to occupy a world devoid of the "light pollution" stemming from the halo of artificial electric aura associated with concentrations of modern human populations.[4] In such a state, contemporaries could rely to a surprising degree on the heavens for illumination, mostly of course on the moon when possible, but in its absence, they came to appreciate the many grades and shades of darkness dictated by different meteorological phenomena. Particularly when the "parish lantern" of the moon's light was unavailable, the light of the stars was a trustworthy source.[5] In a darker night, stars were brighter and more copious, to a degree that during cloudless nights they could even cast shadows. Such a darker world highlighted the moving arch of the moon, the seemingly erratic movement of the planets, and the sweep of the stars. Although contemporaries regularly experienced pristine and uncorrupted night skies, they did not lose the sense of its beauty and sublimity. Thus, an early nineteenth-century author from Georgia, typical of his day in his combination of scientific diction and sense of wonder, described for his readers the "interspace ... of jetty blackness, from which the fixed stars of all magnitudes sparkled with the brilliance attending the combustion of phosphorous in oxygen gas."[6]

This darker, star-ridden world inevitably primed its occupants to develop a close knowledge of and relationship with the sky—exponentially closer than that of later generations. The sun's position, for example, marked an approximation of the passing hours of a day in a world with few mechanical clocks, and also signaled the season. It was the early modern nights, however, when starry skies manifested their full glory, that differed so radically from those of later ages. Electricity was still scarce as late as 1889, when Vincent van Gogh painted his hypnotic masterpiece *Starry Night,* in which the stars (and moon) blaze and radiate so brightly. Other than in metropolitan areas, most of the terrestrial world (includ-

FIGURE 4. *The Starry Night,* Vincent van Gogh, Saint Rémy, June 1889. Oil on canvas, 29 × 36¼ in. (The Museum of Modern Art, New York; digital image © The Museum of Modern Art/Licensed by SCALA/Art Resource, NY)

ing Van Gogh's Provence) went dark after sunset. "The evening was still & tranquil & the sky perfectly serene, enriched with millions of stars shining in perfect beauty," mused an English traveler in the year that the Constitutional Convention assembled in Philadelphia.[7] Today, when the heavens are saturated and polluted by electric light and the night skies reveal few, if any stars, Van Gogh's nightscape seems foreign to the vast majority of humanity. Early modern night skies manifested another phenomenon that we are largely deprived of today, the hazy band of white light we call the Milky Way (a name bestowed by the Romans, *via lactea*) that divides the canopy of the visible stars. Nowadays, only above distant deserts is the night sky revealed in its full starry glory.

Inhabitants of the still-dark preindustrial world, who routinely experienced star-filled nights, developed a knowledge of the night sky that today is reserved for astronomers and serious devotees. Surely, few colonial Americans and citizens of the early United States engaged in formal scientific and mathematical astronomy. Yet a widespread, if not universal, familiarity with the night sky enabled even a poor late eighteenth-century Massachusetts farmer, "who never saw a watch, [to] tell the time to a fraction, by the rising and setting of the moon, and some particular stars." Enslaved people, who were often forced to maintain a nocturnal social life, used traditional techniques to tell time by the moon and stars so they could return safely before dawn.[8] Contemporaries also navigated on the ground and in the open sea based on the position of stars, predicted meteorological phenomena, and practiced rudimentary astrology all through their familiarity with the stars. In short, their lives were interlaced with the night's firmament, which meant that they were much more versed with the skies, stars, and constellations (the human construction of star groupings). The constant manifestation of starry nights, on the one hand, and the lack of indoor distractions after dark, on the other, made the night skies an important and central foundation for those who lived before industrialization.

The sky also functioned, of course, as the traditional location of heaven and the seat of God, and while "the heavens" were inaccessible physically, they held spiritual import for an untold number of believers. The heavens thus uniquely and powerfully mattered to contemporaries for reasons both transcendental (the skies were a place of immense preternatural import) and mundane (the night skies of a preindustrial society were a source of knowledge and, well, spectacular).[9] These factors explain contemporaries' intimate familiarity with the night sky, which in turn helps to account for the pervasiveness of celestial political idioms and metaphors in the early United States: Since metaphors present the unfamiliar through the familiar, what could make more sense than reaching for the stars when framing a rapidly changing ideological and political landscape?

Early American Astronomy, Scientific and Vernacular

Although this book is not a study in the history of science, the political discourses and modes of thought it uncovers and analyzes depended on the broad diffusion of scientific knowledge. The history of science has been reshaped over the past decades, turning from a discipline of great men and big ideas pertaining to a limited scope of established disciplines, into a more egalitarian and inclusive study that is as interested in the sociology of knowledge as in momentous breakthroughs in the laboratory or astronomical observatory. Traditionally, science in the colonial era through the Revolution and early republic was deemed unsystematic, inconsequential, and, for the most part, derivative. Colonial and early American science was long seen as the occupation of gentlemen hobbyists, its history focusing on colorful but episodic incidents (that often included thunderstorms and kites).[10]

This once consensual view has been shaken in past decades, however, as the transformation of the identity of the actors conducting scientific endeavors has been dramatic: While the long-standing consensus has been that the important story of knowledge in early America involved upper-class Euro-Americans, current historiography tends to expand and democratize "science" and what constituted a scientific project. The actors studied by historians of science now range from technicians laboring for the "great minds" and hence making science possible, to indigenous informants, skilled enslaved workers, Euro-American laypersons, merchants, apothecaries, and alchemists.[11] That shift has also brought gender-related issues to the fore, underscoring the women who practiced science in various aspects but also the fact that the study of science ("natural history" in particular) was infused with sexuality and gender.[12] While the focus on current issues, such as the environmental crisis, has brought to the fore an interest in ecological matters, the celestial realm appears to remain a stepchild of this collective historiographic endeavor.[13] The few historians who have focused on early American astronomy, which provides a backdrop for the history of a cluster of ideas that stand at the center of this book (that is, "political astronomy"), have tended to conclude that the study of celestial objects and phenomena was underdeveloped and, therefore, irrelevant to the history of science in the United States (and to the history of astronomy, for that matter).[14]

This rather bleak view seems to have changed, however. Historians have noted in the past that while North American science would maintain a backwater scientific position for centuries, the overall interest in astronomy was more intense and pronounced than in any nonagricultural science.[15] Sky watching in early America was, in the words of a recent assessment, "extraordinarily popular."[16] During the first decades after Harvard's founding in 1636, Henry Dunster, the institution's first president, still taught pre-Copernican and geocentric astronomy. Students learned under Dunster's tutelage of Aristotelian crystalline spheres that explained retrograde movement, and "little of the universe that Dante did not know."[17] Samuel Eliot Morison thus concluded almost a century ago that Harvard was founded "too early for her first generation of students to be upset by astronomical theories with which their ancestors were unfamiliar."[18] By 1659, however, documented evidence demonstrates that Harvard students were formally learning Copernican astronomy.[19] By 1672 they were corroborating Copernican astronomy through a telescope that was gifted to the university by John Winthrop Jr.[20] Five decades later the college's library already catalogued works of the trailblazers of the new astronomy: Galileo, Kepler, Gassendi, Boulliau.[21]

Early eighteenth-century elite colonists had already begun to accumulate significant astronomical resources, and astronomy had become a common theme in American intellectual society. Upper-class Americans took part in an Enlightened culture of gentlemanly science and assembled private libraries that boasted books of astronomical giants such as Copernicus, Galileo, Brahe, Kepler, as well as several editions of Newton's *Principia*. By midcentury several colonial colleges had added resident astronomers to their faculty, and leading figures such as the presidents of Harvard and Yale (Ezra Stiles and Joseph Willard) regularly practiced stargazing. During the latter half of the century skillful practitioners, first and foremost David Rittenhouse, engaged in more advanced astronomy, thus helping to establish Philadelphia as the scientific capital of colonial America.[22]

Colonial interest in astronomy gained enough momentum to sustain and prosper into the nineteenth century. The historian Sarah Gronim concluded that by the 1760s and 1770s, wide circles of New Yorkers were familiar with the "natural philosophy" (that is, science) of their age.[23] There is no reason to believe that New York was unique in this respect. In maritime communities, where "people wandered around with sextants and talked about planets and comets," astronomy was particularly common as it became a mode of entertainment.[24] Gordon Fraser portrays how the United States embarked soon after Independence on a conscious if disjointed project to map, measure, predict, and exploit astronomical space to cultivate the young nation's prestige, promote and protect commerce, and project force. This amounted to what he describes as the United States' early attempt to become a "space power." Fraser compellingly describes how national politicians were keen on predicting astronomical events years in advance to demonstrate American scientific prowess (as in the case of Vice President John Adams), or making available calculations of future positions of the moon, planets, and stars in a variety of national publications to lubricate American commerce.[25]

Astronomical observatories provide an example of institutional and capital-intensive projects motivated by the desire to explore the heavens. In the first half of the nineteenth century the string of newly constructed observatories in America were built as "instruments for the personal exploration of the planets and the stars," and as such were "monuments of civic development." American amateur astronomers did not achieve great breakthroughs through these early observatories, and their value thus remained largely symbolic. They reflected nonetheless a deep interest in the heavens, as well as a reflection of the status of astronomy. While president John Quincy Adams's attempts to establish a national observatory failed, the rhetorical tone he set regarding astronomy at his First Annual Message to Congress (1825), and his proposed program to erect 130 "lighthouses of the skies," propelled commitment and deep popular interest in astronomy in America.[26]

While observatories had a limited practical effect during the opening decades of the nineteenth century, throughout the vast land it was printed texts (and later the spread of public schooling) that mediated between the young American nation's citizens and the universe. Invigorated by modern technologies such as telescopes and early photography, the information Americans gathered was disseminated through printed text, which would remain throughout the century "the most important means by which large numbers of people would understand the universe." Throughout the nineteenth century the universe's structure, its history, and its ultimate meaning were all mediated through and disseminated by, printed texts, "the primary technology of [early] space power" in America.[27]

The unique American print culture, which played a larger role in the local culture than it did in many other contemporary societies, supported the broad circulation of astronomical knowledge in early America. Literacy rates were remarkably high, and a literate populace together with the ubiquity of cheap print facilitated the dissemination of natural knowledge in British North America and later in the early United States. American newspapers and local journals regularly and frequently published observations and speculations about nature, while countless reports observed, often quite casually, the dimensions of space, discoveries of astronomers, or transits of meteors and planets. Meanwhile, the development of an effective mail delivery system helped distribute the production of a decentralized constellation of numerous small rural printers. These factors combined to enable a diversity of ways in which literate early Americans were well-equipped to express their thoughts about contemporary science, and consequently think through astronomical metaphors about their political worlds.[28]

The dynamics surrounding household almanacs, the most widely printed material of the eighteenth and nineteenth centuries (other than the Bible) and holding a wealth of astronomical information, unveils how astronomical knowledge was at work in early America.[29] The acceptance of heliocentrism is a case in point, and to understand it, the historian Sarah Gronim has studied the upper Hudson Valley as a test case for late British North American colonial society. Gronim investigated almanacs, which she deemed "the most important expression of beliefs in British colonial New York about the nature of the universe," for indications pertinent to heliocentrism's reception. She found that in the first almanacs published in New York in the 1690s the Ptolemaic worldview dominated, whereas almanacs from the 1720s and 1730s reveal extensive beliefs about cosmology but also attest to the debates that raged with regard to the accuracy of a sun-centered universe. By the middle third of the eighteenth century, Gronim reports a noticeable shift from a Ptolemaic to a Copernican universe, and after 1750 almanac makers rarely referred to the geocentric worldview.[30] "How much more natural is Copernicus's scheme!" declares James Ferguson in *Poor Richard's Almanac*, printed when the debate was already settled. "Ptolomy is compar'd to a whimsical cook, who, instead of turning his meat in roasting, should fix that, and contrive to have his whole fire, kitchen and all, whirling continually round it."³¹ The case for heliocentrism was part of a broader debate over the "New Science," which was often delivered through theological argumentation. Benjamin Franklin took that route, praising Isaac Newton for tracing "the boundless works of God," while prolific almanac publisher Nathaniel Ames asked, "Who before the great Sir Isaac Newton did behold the wisdom of the creator in that he has bestowed on matter such a property as that every particle thereof throughout the creation has a tendency towards every other particle[?]"³² After 1750 the New Science moved to center stage, but only after its advocates had assured the wider American public that it supported rather than challenged Protestant doctrine.

In light of their pervasiveness, it is worthwhile to contemplate the role of almanacs, "America's most affordable and widespread form of print," as they are deemed to have played a key role in shaping and expressing early American cosmology.³³ Although until recently almanacs as a genre have received less than their due attention, their importance for understanding late colonial culture has now become clear. Almanacs were exceptionally helpful in disseminating astronomical knowledge and promoting a shared understanding of the cosmos across the colonies and were thus fundamental in shaping the cosmology of colonial Americans and citizens of the early United States. Originally an English genre, the high-water mark of English almanacs has been recognized as the years between 1640 and 1700.³⁴ In early America they gained popularity later, demonstrated through Charles Evans's *American Bibliography*, a twelve-volume index that took thirty-one years to complete and lists more than 1,100 different almanacs published between 1639 and 1799.³⁵ That staggering number represents a popularity that led contemporaries to suppose that "no pamphlet nor book, not excepting the bible itself, is so thoroughly examined as these annual productions."³⁶ They were, by many measures, "the single most important print genre of the late eighteenth and early nineteenth centuries." Rural people, throughout the eighteenth and into the nineteenth century, depended on those commercial almanacs, which consisted of miscellanies of astronomical information, quips, fables and histories, medical advice, and weather predictions, for much of their scientific education.³⁷

As established at the start of this chapter, early moderns lived in preindustrial and agricultural societies, and thus were by definition more astronomically inclined. With diurnal rhythms holding greater significance in their lives, early Americans relied heavily on the trove of astronomical information stored in the ever-popular almanacs. Almanacs served first and foremost as "calendars surrounded by a variety of additional content," with much of that content pertaining to the astronomical.[38] They helped to keep track of the passing days and months and charted the timing of sunrise and sunset, the phases of the moon in monthly tables, and the location of constellations in the firmament through the seasons. The information they bestowed and the guidance they offered ranged from the elementary, such as the time of the sun's rising and setting, to the advanced and more complicated, such as the position of the moon in the constellational zodiac, or the relational alignment of the planets (called "aspects," which were critical for astrological calculations; see below). Almanacs, which characteristically included sections titled "A knowledge of the stars and their courses," such as William Ball's 1744 specimen, were significant sources for the astronomical literacy of early Americans.[39] Editors produced their prints with a clear market and sales orientation, and included in their almanacs poetry, predictions, important dates, proverbs, and maxims. A conservative estimate suggests that by 1800 there were enough almanacs being printed in the United States to place one in every household, which led to "truly mind-boggling sales figures." Even in the South, with its far less developed print culture, almanacs sold "in numbers that strain belief but are unquestionably accurate."[40] Mathematician and astronomer Benjamin Banneker, known as America's "first Black man of science," provides a case in point. Banneker published a series of popular almanacs in the closing years of the eighteenth century that demonstrated that American readers accepted that a Black astronomer had the knowledge and ability to describe the cosmos. Not intent on hiding his race, Banneker's woodcut portrait appeared on the title page of his almanacs, resulting in many commentators fixating on his Blackness. Banneker's readers transcended racial bias in their thirst to know more about the physical universe.[41]

A peripheral locality such as the island of Nantucket underscores the centrality of astronomical knowledge to middling Americans. Astronomy consisted in Nantucket of much more than a practical study for the inhabitants of a maritime community, as it also served as a pastime for locals, who "wandered around with sextants and talked about planets and comets." William Mitchell, a schoolteacher, amateur astronomer, and father of ten including the century's most famous female astronomer, Maria Mitchell, spent every cloudless night observing the skies. His daughter Phebe recalled that "to the children, accustomed to seeing such observations going on, the most important study in the world seemed to be astronomy. One by one, as they became old enough, they were drafted into the service of counting seconds by the chronometer during the observations." Maria Mitchell, who would gain worldwide fame after discovering a comet in 1847 (duly named "Miss Mitchell's Comet"), recalled that when she was young, "after a few weeks of cloudy skies . . . I saw the stars in the evening of the tenth and met them like old friends from whom I had long been parted. They had been absent from my eyes three weeks. I swept round for comets about an hour, and then I amused myself with noticing the varieties of color. . . . The tints of the different stars are so delicate in their variety and the grouping has all the infinity of a Kaleidoscope, infinitely extended." Maria's fascination with the night skies would lead to a remarkable scientific career, but it also points toward a more general contemporary interest in astronomy. Maria's father would satiate that widespread interest with regular public lectures on astronomy, which were, according to Mitchell's biographer, particularly popular. A review of one of William's talks for the *Nantucket Inquirer* noted the speaker's "plain and perspicuous style," going on to praise his "lucid explanations, illustrated by diagrams &c. prove that his mind has often traveled far and wide over those astral regions which form the spangled canopy of evening."[42]

Yet to fully comprehend just how robust and widespread astronomical knowledge was, one must turn to the lower ranks of American society and racial hierarchy. Even grade-level Native students with minimal formal education received at least some astronomical instruction, as evidenced by a report on a Native school in Kentucky that listed, first and foremost, its students' astronomical knowledge.[43] In the early nineteenth century, Native American students from the "Choctaw, Creek, Chickasaw," and other tribes were reportedly "well grounded in astronomy," while Native newspapers published didactic astronomical articles similar to those that were found in mainstream prints.[44] For example, a column titled "Astronomy" digested the current state of astronomical knowledge, and "The Immensity of the Universe" described the "thousands of millions of stars in the heavens" and tried to help readers to "imagine" the size of the universe.[45] Native newspapers also reported sporadically on astronomical discoveries, such as that "the planet Saturn has three rings, instead of only two, hitherto believed," and dedicated columns to astronomical phenomena such meteors and meteoric stones.[46]

Much of Native astronomical knowledge was of course vernacular and passed on orally, and was often generated outside of institutional or formal spaces. As one nineteenth-century commentator remarked, the Natives "know the stars, and they understand the heavens." Remarkably the episode this commentator described provides a unique chance to witness how astronomical knowledge directly translated into the language of political astronomy: When a group of Pawnees first observed the American flag in 1819, "they saw the blue, representing the blue skies of the heavens, and they saw the stars upon the blue, which they knew were from the heavens." Across American society vernacular astronomical knowledge constituted the basis for conversations in the metaphorical language of political astronomy.[47]

Similar was African Americans' conditioning in vernacular astronomy, in a process scholars have recently termed "fugitive science." Fugitive science was a mode of committing to knowledge in the construction of paths toward, and imagination of, Black freedom. The literary historian Britt Russert has particularly found how the speculative space of an "out of doors" Black involvement in astronomy in the first half of the nineteenth century "produced alternative knowledges in the quest for and name of freedom." There are strong indications that at least some of that subversive knowledge may have been preserved and inherited from Africa, and scholars have specifically identified such transmission in the case of the aforementioned William Banneker. Banneker, America's premier Black astronomer, apparently received knowledge that originated in Africa through older family members.[48] This fugitive science, with astronomy as its backbone, underscores how even American society's most downtrodden population could engage in, negotiate, and transform the boundaries of canonical knowledge into a new science of freedom.

The American Universe

African Americans in metropolitan eras such as New York, however, would not have relied only on unorthodox modes of knowledge transmission and production, as astronomy was central to and an integral part of the curriculum in New York City schools. As opposed to subjects such as the classical languages that were reserved for the education of the elites, scientific disciplines were part and parcel of schooling across race and gender lines.[49] The African Free School, for example, founded by members of the New York Manumission Society, educated children of the enslaved and freed people of color and offered practical and skill-oriented education. The Free School thus offered tutoring in skills that would serve future sailors in the merchant fleet. Modern navigation included the lunar-distance method to find one's longitude without mechanical devices, hence treating the firmament, in the words of the historian Tamara Plakins Thornton, as "a source of data" contemporaries could "rely on and manipulate" for useful knowledge.[50] Accounts such as that of a Black ship's cook that astonished contemporaries with his sophisticated mathematically derived astronomical calculations may have been apocryphal but are still telling. While claims about universal astronomical knowledge may have been exaggerations, such education was surely "an ongoing reality for black men, particularly in New York," who were instructed to "consider the universal forces that moved moons, planets, and stars."[51] Beyond education in practical astronomy, however, free Blacks in the North were also informed that their enslaved brethren were making sense of their predicament through vernacular forms of astronomical observation. Hence, the poetry of George Moses Horton, an enslaved man from North Carolina whose astronomy-laden poetry was repeatedly published in the *Freedom's Journal*, attested to the role of celestial images and visions in African American cosmology as well as to the modes of that imagery's distribution.

The *Freedom Journal*, a popular African American New York–based newspaper, was edited by Samuel Cornish and John Russwurm, who did not set out to communicate information about the cosmos when they began publishing the newspaper. Established in 1827 and superseded in 1829 by *The Rights of All* (1829–30), the *Journal* revealed an ongoing engagement with the universe as a site for meaning making and presented, in the words of a modern student, an emancipatory cosmology, a "total system for understanding the relation between human politics and the cosmos," a complete "theory of the universe." In short, the *Freedom Journal* presented a serious engagement with Afro-Americans in astronomical imagination, which reached a readership that was much more diverse than formerly believed both in its geographical spread as well as in its demography. As in the case of other contemporary prints, widespread practices such as copy sharing and public readings resulted in multiple readers for each available copy convinced scholars that the *Journal* succeeded in engaging isolated readers, including in slaveholding states. As a testament to their effectiveness and reach, white Southerners were alarmed by Black newspapers and warned of the danger they posed.[52]

Nevertheless, it is hard to gauge the extent to which Black Americans participated in the political astronomy that this book traces. Only after 1850 does one find a consistent participation in the cosmic metaphoric language, apparent in Black publications (or those that targeted Black audiences) such as the *National Era*.[53] Before midcentury it is hard to come by evidence of direct and active involvement of African Americans in political astronomy. Even with the dearth of such evidence, however, it is important to consider the astronomical knowledge available to African Americans, if only to speculate on their potential ability to discourse on and thus participate in political astronomy. It is thus worth underscoring how even uneducated and enslaved Americans, who were denied the possibility to engage with astronomy through institutional venues such as *Freedom's Journal*, could still employ pervasive forms of vernacular astronomy.

Nat Turner, for example, was famously a revolutionary and a prophet, but he was also a stargazer who developed a cosmology for understanding the relation between the celestial and the political. Turner watched the skies closely for years and shared his premonitions and visions after an eclipse of the sun in February 1831, providing a stark example of a homegrown interpretive system that tied the celestial and the political.[54] The folk artist Harriet Powers (1837–1910) provides another example of vernacular astronomy by stitching representations of celestial events onto her captivating quilts. Untrained artists such as Powers demonstrated how Black communities could share and preserve for decades cosmological information they deemed meaningful. Powers's *Pictorial*

FIGURE 5. *Meteoric Shower of Nov. 13, 1833*, Adolf Vollmy, 1833. Several representations of the Leonid meteor shower convey the striking event and its effect on contemporaries. (From *Bible Reading for the Home Circle*, ed. O. Corliss, 1888; Library of Congress)

Quilt (1898), for example, depicted events that became part of oral tradition and occurred before her birth, such as the Dark Day of May 19, 1780, and the Leonid meteor shower of 1833.[55]

The Leonid shower of November 12, 1833, remembered as "the day the stars fell," is a case in point. Occurring every thirty-three years and caused by the passage of the earth through the meteoroid stream of particles left from the passages of a comet, the Leonid shower of 1833 was likely the most spectacular occurrence in recorded history (modern estimates suggest that there may have been up to 150,000 meteors visible per hour that year). The quilter Harriet Powers said of the event that "the people were frightened and thought that the end had come. God's hand staid the stars. The varmints rushed out of their beds."[56] Other enslaved Americans such as Jane Clark, whose account was only recently

FIGURE 6. The "Dark Day," first row, second panel, and the Leonid shower, second row, third panel, from pictorial quilt, Harriet Powers, 1895–98. Cotton plain weave, pieced, appliquéd, embroidered, and quilted. 68⅞ × 105 in. (Museum of Fine Arts, Boston; bequest of Maxim Karolik; photograph © 2025 Museum of Fine Arts, Boston)

recovered, vividly remembered the meteor showers for years. "It was on one of these early morning excursions" that she witnessed "the 'stars fall,'" Clark recounted. "The children were on their way to the spring. They were not old enough to be alarmed by the unusual sight but ran along trying to catch the stars as they fell."[57] Harriet Tubman, too, had a recollection of the shower, as did Frederick Douglass, who wrote of the 1833 shower in his *My Bondage and My Freedom*. Douglass recalled "that strange phenomenon when the heavens seemed about to part with their starry train. I witnessed this gorgeous spectacle, and was awe-struck. The air seemed filled with bright descending messengers from the sky. It was about daybreak when I saw this sublime scene. I was not without the suggestion, at the moment, that it might be the harbinger of the coming of the Son of Man; and in my then state of mind I was prepared to hail Him as my friend and deliverer."[58] Naturally not only enslaved Blacks but also lower-class whites, such as the young Abraham Lincoln, were impressed by the 1833 shower. Decades later Lincoln recalled:

The American Universe

> When I was a young man in Illinois I boarded for a time with a Deacon of the Presbyterian church. One night I was roused from my sleep by a rap at the door, & I heard the Deacon's voice exclaiming 'Arise, Abraham, the day of judgment has come!' I sprang from my bed & rushed to the window, and saw the stars falling in great showers! But looking back of them in the heavens I saw all the grand old constellations with which I was so well acquainted, fixed and true in their places.[59]

Contemporaries witnessed and noted the striking meteor shower as far west as Arkansas.[60]

The Conditioning of Political Astronomers

As we shall see in the following chapters, governance and cosmos intertwined in the early United States to create a unique and robust American brand of astro-politics. Astronomy remained a constant presence in American schooling: From books intended for young students to the curriculum of colleges, it was a staple of eighteenth- and nineteenth-century education. Broad swaths of American society were thus formally schooled in astronomy, as well as informally trained through media such as almanacs and newspapers. This was a necessary condition for political astronomy to become the wide-ranging project that it did after the founding of the United States.[61]

One noticeable aspect of astronomical instructional tracts was that they could easily slip from neutral descriptions of the universe, a scientific mode to which modern readers are accustomed, to a moral and theological language that would become alien to modern scientific discourse. Educators and commentators, for example, time and again praised astronomy and explained its importance as demonstrating the greatness of God and creation.[62] Indeed, that astronomy was perceived as the "greatest of sciences" owed much to the fact that it seemed to patently demonstrate God's greatness and omnipotence.

While one can hardly miss the theological motivations behind numerous contemporary astronomical texts, we have yet to notice an additional tendency they had, namely to portray the cosmos itself in a language that derived from human political bonds. Thus, in tandem with discoursing on political concepts such as republicanism and federalism through astronomical parameters (that is, the political astronomy at the center of this book), educational material conditioned Americans for discussing political astronomy through what may be called *astronomical politics,* or political astronomy in reverse.

Astronomical politics, as opposed to political astronomy, described the interaction between cosmic bodies through the repeated use of anthropomorphism, portraying the relationship between celestial bodies in human political terms. Such astronomical politics was evident in the characteristic explanation that, while the earth and other planets did "*govern* their secondary planets," simultaneously they were "*governed* by the sun," whereas satellites were typically depicted as "inferior" and "subject" to the control of their primary planet.[63] In making use of a language that alluded to hierarchical relationships of domination and control to describe vast astronomical physical objects, contemporaries imagined planetary liaisons that were political, needless to say, only in the eyes of their human beholders. Yet depicting planets through categories of governance and subordination described a solar system that would condition contemporaries in turn for contemplating human politics in astronomical terms.

Female education is particularly useful for understanding this form of astronomical politics. Even anecdotal evidence underscores the fact that, for educated American women in the first half of the nineteenth century, astronomy was a "favorite" area of study, in which they were "greatly absorbed."[64] Astronomy was a constant presence in the high school and college curricula of "young ladies," such as at the "Young Ladies' High School" in Rhode Island, which boasted astronomy as one of the few subjects it promised to teach.[65] Astronomy was also central in the syllabi of academies such as the Warren Ladies' Seminary.[66] In the Warren Seminary's curriculum not only was a semester-long course in astronomy mandatory, but students could expand their astronomical studies through advanced elective astronomical courses.[67] Further, girls' boarding schools as well as juvenile magazines (specifically intended for both sexes) proudly boasted astronomy in their catalogues.[68] Additionally, "ladies" and "young ladies" were actively encouraged to participate in series of astronomical public lectures, specifically through discounts in their price of admittance for females.[69] Astronomy books especially "intended for the education of young ladies" further underscore astronomy's central role in women's education. The predisposition to discuss astronomical relations in human political terms was evident in schoolbooks in general, and particularly in those intended and used for female instruction.

The astronomy books that specifically targeted female students demonstrate the pervasiveness and efficacy of "astronomical politics." The abovementioned Warren Ladies' Seminary made use, for example, of John Vose's *Compendium of Astronomy* as the textbook for its mandatory astronomical course. This two-hundred-page treatise purposely simplified and illustrated astronomical concepts, as it aimed for the instruction of female students in "common schools, as well as higher seminaries." The way in which Vose described the sun is particularly instructive, as the author portrayed it in terms that were traditionally preserved for monarchs, and in republican America for descriptions of the federal government.[70] Describing the sun's "grandeur," Vose depicted the way in which it "diffuse[d] its rays to an immense distance," thus giving "life and motion to unnumerable objects." In a language reminiscent of the way in which contemporaries commonly portrayed powerful political figures and institutions, the objects under the sun's dominion were "subject to his control." In a similar language of subjugation and control the *Compendium* repeatedly described the planets in human political terms as the sun's "attendants" that as such were "governed" by the solar star.[71]

Vose was joined by many others in conditioning young Americans, specifically young women, to think about the sun in political terms of governance. Elijah Burritt's *The Geography of the Heavens, and Class Book of Astronomy* also described the sun as a "vast globe" that "govern[ed] the [planets'] motions."[72] Another textbook aimed specifically at the education of females, Bartlett's *Young Ladies' Astronomy*, described the sun as a star to which the planets "all owe constant dependence."[73] Like Vose and Burritt, Bartlett anthropomorphized the sun as a dominating body that willfully and powerfully subjugated its obeying inferiors. It is thus perhaps not surprising that writers in women's journals such as the *Ladies' Garland* described the sun as holding a "circled throne," while poets referred to the solar star as a "regent."[74] Other classroom manuscripts followed suit, describing the sun in politically loaded terms as if it controlled an "empire" and held a "retinue of planets."[75] Geography books such as Guthrie's *A New System of Modern Geography,* which typically opened with a section on astronomy, time and again described the "planets, moons, and comets" of the solar system as "belonging" to the sun, while general science books described the planets as "entirely subject" to the sun's "superior influence."[76] Newspaper columns on astronomical subjects further described the sun as "rul[ing] an empire" of all objects "under [its] dominion," or as "carrying along with him all his attendant planets."[77]

Tellingly, the language in which the sun was commonly described, in tracts for general consumption but particularly in texts specifically aimed at women, was itself conspicuously gendered: The sun was repeatedly pronounced as male, whereas other bodies in the solar system were described as subservient females.[78] The moon, for example, was over and again framed as the female "spouse of the sun," and hence "his ... slave."[79] Yet the sun was not merely a male but, as such, a controlling patriarchal figure: a "great parent" to which the planets "yield[ed] to the paternal power of the sun which would draw them to himself."[80] The family itself had, of course, been seen since the days of Aristotle as the basic political unit of society, and in a male-dominated world patriarchy itself was blatantly political, with the patriarch perceived as the petty monarch of his family, the basic societal unit. In such descriptions, then, the sun was both a powerful male and dominating patriarch, descriptions that were the backbone of contemporary understandings of human politics.

Astronomical tracts, particularly those intended for young females but certainly not exclusively such texts, thus conditioned contemporaries to think about the cosmos politically. Although the relationships between the sun, primary and secondary planets, and satellites were strictly physical, they were time and again described as hierarchical, and in terms of domination and subordination, center and periphery, importance and insignificance. Those relations were, in short, understood through human politics. A two-way process was at play, which simultaneously fed off and further entrenched the political astronomy contemporaries constantly employed. The description of the universe in human terms thus conditioned Americans to understand politics in astronomical terms. Educated women, who were educated to understand starry and planetary relations in human political terms (such as the sun exercising *sovereignty* and *governing* planets throughout its cosmic *dominion*) would become more adept political astronomers. Not only women but also other astronomically educated and marginalized Americans would demonstrate similar metaphorical thinking. American Principles, an author for the *Cherokee Phoenix* wrote how hierarchy, "like the gravitation," at once "support[ed] and control[led] the ... political system."[81] Astronomical education in the early United States not only expanded Americans' knowledge about the universe but also conditioned and produced political astronomers. To explain planetary interaction, republican Americans reverted to the power relations that characterized monarchical relations. The same type of interaction also characterized the ways in which they made sense of their own federal republic, as we shall see in chapter 2.

American Cosmologies
The North Star

The abovementioned Leonid meteor shower was a remarkable and one-of-a-kind event that elicited numerous accounts across the continent from the broadest swaths of American society: Afro-Americans, Natives, and plain common folk left accounts of the fantastic event.[82] Yet Americans, free and enslaved, were preoccupied with the stars and regularly observed the sky regardless of extraordinary events, as in the darker world of preindustrial America sky watching was rather routine. While star watching was common among the general population, it was particularly practiced among the enslaved, who took the North Star as their guide on their way to freedom. The North Star, also known as Polaris, is a star in the constellation Ursa Minor that appears to remain in a fixed northern position, which made it a valuable navigational tool for many (Northern Hemisphere) cultures. The evidence that slaves took the North Star as a guide to orient themselves and navigate while they were on the move is abundant. Charles Ball's early slave narrative *Slavery in the United States* (1837) already exhibits a most attentive consideration of the North Star as a guiding device for the fugitive slave's movement.[83] In his 1847 *Narrative,* the freed slave Andrew Jackson confronted the matter directly: "There is scarcely one, who does not understand the position of the 'north star,' although that is about the extent of their knowledge of Astronomy." Demonstrating this point, antislavery activists often told the story of a slave who, badly injured by bloodhound attacks, arrived in New York in 1840 after a horrid journey from the South. With barely any English and knowing little of geography or politics, the man managed to escape the South by finding and following the North Star. In the Black abolitionist Martin Delany's novel *Blake; or the Huts of America* (1859), the protagonist Henry Blake offers a group of fugitives detailed instruction on mapping the constellations in order to locate the North Star, "the slave's great Guide to Freedom."[84]

While the North Star functioned as a handy navigational tool, it as importantly became a central fixture in the Afro-American imagination and a principal symbol of freedom for enslaved people. In narratives written by freed slaves themselves, such as the works by Henry Bibb and William Wells Brown, as well as those written with the assistance of white abolitionists, such as Sarah Hopkins Bradford's biography of Harriet Tubman, the North Star towered as a beacon of freedom and hope.[85] Often referred to as the Guiding Star or the Freedom Star, it became a stock topos in contemporary poems, memoirs, and slave narratives. The North Star in both the Black and abolitionist imagination, while guiding runaway slaves toward safety in the North, also represented freedom and escape from bondage. Its role in the abolitionist imagination was famously politicized through the title of Frederick Douglass's first newspaper, the *North Star,* a name that forged a salient link between Black resistance and Polaris. Polaris also played a role in Douglass's fiction, as the protagonist in his 1852 novella *The Heroic Slave* takes courage from the escape of a fellow slave, assuring himself that "The North Star will not be less kind to me than him."[86]

The image of the North Star was in such use also among white abolitionists that the literary historian Jared Hickman described a "North-Star Cult" in antislavery literature.[87] John Pierpont's work *Anti-Slavery Poems* (1843) was a centerpiece in that cult. In his poem "The Fugitive Slave's Apostrophe to the North Star," Pierpont describes a runaway who repeatedly pleads to the northern guiding star for assistance, direction, and courage on his journey to freedom. In the following poem, "Slaveholder's Address to the North Star," Polaris functions as the slaver's antagonist upon which

> every black, star-gazing nigger
> . . . .
> . . . gazes at thee, till the lazy
> And thankless rascal is half crazy.

While serving as an emblem of freedom for the slave, in the slaveholder's poetic imagination the North Star is transformed into an "abolition star."[88]

While the North Star was traditionally associated in the Euro-Christian imagination with Jesus, it was effectively relocated in the young United States to the realms of imagination of political Blackness. The star became more than a practical element of a "fugitive science," as it became a significant component of the Black and abolitionist political and astronomical imagination. The North Star pointed toward the location of a promised freedom and reminded enslaved runaways of their ultimate goal. It became, in the words of Jared Hickman, an "object of devotion for African Americans in an experimental metaphysics of becoming free."[89] Political astronomy in the early United States thus manifested different shades that appealed to the various groups composing a conflicted society.

Astrology

As African Americans injected political and liberational meaning into a single, fixed, and northern star, even wider swaths of American society were constantly searching for clues and divinations in the firmament. The new ideas about the nature of the cosmos that developed during the seventeenth and eighteenth centuries diffused among growing echelons of Europeans and the inhabitants of their colonies, in a process that would shatter and vanquish the millennia-old Aristotelian and Ptolemaic worldviews.[90] Yet it would be a crude mistake to think that even at relatively late stages of this complex transformation all knowledge of, or interest in, the heavens was derived solely through what we would today call "science." Astrology, the pseudoscience of revealing meanings in planetary motions, taught that the heavens were infused with order and significance and maintained a firm grip on contemporaries long after the scientific revolution.[91] Like other branches of early modern natural philosophy, astrology was a thorough and systematic effort to explain occurrences in the natural world, and offered to many a convincing explanation of how the universe functioned.[92] As such, astrology was not competing with other grand explanatory schemes like science and religion: in one form or another, astrology stood in close relationship with mathematical astronomy throughout the Middle Ages and beyond, and its promoters in Britain and particularly in the colonies attempted to reinforce core Protestant tenets by purporting to reveal God's ways in the cosmos.[93] For many, astrology remained a viable and legitimate system by which to make sense of the universe well into the nineteenth century and beyond.[94]

Astrology was based on the belief that the planets, as they moved in and out of positions of proximity to each other and in relationships to the twelve sections of the sky associated with the zodiac, systematically and thus predictably influenced the natural world. Assuming that the planets' placement was related to and could affect terrestrial undertakings had a philosophical foundation: If celestial movements were known to relate to oceanic phenomena such as tides, it was not prima facie absurd to think that they could similarly influence bodies and minds, and thus human action. As the prolific Massachusetts publisher Nathaniel Ames reminded readers of his 1738 almanac, astrology was "built on the effects and influences of the heavenly bodies on our earthly bodies . . . [and thus] has a rational and philosophical foundation."[95] Astrology resided side by side and in harmony with astronomy for a long time, with the borders between the two disciplines often vague and amorphous. So close were the two fields that the Latin terms *astronomia* and *astrologia* were often used interchangeably.[96] Practitioners of both understood them as empirical in nature, with astronomy studying the motions of the heavenly bodies mathematically, and astrology focusing on how the heavenly bodies influenced earthly happenings.

Whatever one may think of the value of a pursuit that later would be deemed eclectic and uncritical, if not all-out fraudulent, we must remember the high value that generation upon generation of humans have placed in astrology.[97] The dissemination of astrological knowledge through numerous handbooks, first and foremost almanacs, in which astrology served as the foundation on which those annual publications were constructed, attest to its continued sway in the age of Enlightenment.[98] Year after year, American almanacs introduced methods to reveal celestial meanings and were the most important source of astrological information in the colonies. Readers bought almanacs expecting to find more than an annual calendar and entertaining essays: Astrological calculations in almanacs guided readers through their daily tasks throughout a given year, from agricultural management to personal health. Beyond such functional aspects, the astrology found in almanacs offered readers a clear and comprehensive explanation of how the universe operated and advice on how to conduct their lives. As already noted, it would be wrong to assume that religion was in direct conflict with astrology, which has today gained the reputation of an occult practice. Eighteenth-century astrology was not generally considered a peripheral or subversive practice. On the contrary, for many decades American almanacs were awash with reminders that astrology would produce awareness of and admiration for the Creator, and by promoting astrology the almanacs supposedly illuminated the way in which God acted in the universe. Almanac makers thus saw their trade as a complement to orthodox Protestantism, and by the eighteenth century, astrology had been thoroughly synthesized with Protestantism and natural philosophy.[99]

A significant unintended effect of almanac astrology was that it further acquainted contemporaries with the cosmos and the visible celestial bodies that inhabited it, from the fixed stars to the planets to rarer occurrences such as comets and solar and lunar eclipses. Astrology was thus decisive in informing and familiarizing early Americans with the universe, and in perpetuating the habits of contemplating the cosmos and its relation to and correlation with their lives. Particularly by making contemporaries comfortable with thinking about causality between the heavens and humans, astrology helped lay the groundwork for Americans to think of their terrestrial politics in celestial terms. The belief in stellar and planetary influence on human life smoothed, and perhaps even enabled altogether, metaphorical thought about the cosmos and politics.

The Clockwork Universe

As the era's most complex and fascinating mechanism, the mechanical clock served as arguably the most prevalent metaphor for human societies and the state.[100] While engines might have potentially rivaled mechanical clocks in commanding the imagination of the era, even the novel steam engine did not come close to rivaling the ingenuity and prestige of the mechanical clock, ensuring that the clock's veneration was unprecedented in contemporary society.[101] Mechanical clocks sufficiently accurate to suit the needs of modern urban society (that is, erring no more than a few seconds over several months) were the product of the so-called British "horological revolution" of the century between 1660 and 1760. The resulting veneration ensured that in the seventeenth and eighteenth centuries the clock metaphor became "strikingly frequent, more frequent, probably, than any other." The metaphor coincided with the Newtonian cosmology, both in its timing and features, and both underscored the qualities of regularity, order, and harmony in different aspects of human life. The most consequential clock-related metaphor was doubtless the idea of a "clockwork universe," the comparison of the cosmos to a huge clock.[102]

A central characteristic of the scientific revolution (however defined), as well as its corollary Newtonianism, was the commitment of its participants to thinking "mechanically," which is to say, interpreting the world through the model of a machine.[103] The discoveries that paved the way to imagining the universe as a perfectly predictable machine were breakthroughs in astronomical understanding, which included the abovementioned paradigm-shifting heliocentrism and Newton's laws of motion and gravitation. The publication of these new ideas, which shattered old worldviews and solved old riddles, were followed by a period in which they settled down and were absorbed by growing audiences, eventually giving rise to new consensual cosmologies.[104]

Newton's ideas fed into the established worldview, in which the physical universe was seen as a great machine, a *machina mundi*. This universal "machine," once set in motion, performed the work for which it was called into existence by virtue of its construction. In its eighteenth-century incarnation, this metaphor pictured the universe as a self-regulating mechanism, which was most commonly illustrated by the pervasive figurative choice of a clock. As George Cheyne, a physician and disciple of Newton, put it, "The best Image or Idea we could frame of the System of the Universe was, as of a noble and immense Machin [*sic*] . . . whose Springs are an immaterial Principle (if I may so call that of Gravitation), which animates the whole and all its Parts." The so-called "clockwork universe" thus made figurative use of the age's most intricate and wondrously precise instrument to both explain and admire the complexity of the cosmos. The seemingly supernatural harmony and orderliness associated with the mechanical clock invited comparisons with the world itself, and consequently with God as a divine clockmaker. In this accurate, predictable, and punctual figuration, the cosmos was no longer subject to whimsical influences.[105]

Despite a harsh dispute between G. W. Leibnitz and Newton and his disciples regarding the freedom God had in a clockwork universe, the Newtonian view left God with a governing role over a magnificently complex universe.[106] Whatever the exact role of the Creator in operating (or observing) His mechanical universe, it was the self-imposed task of eighteenth-century intermediaries to relay this clockwork view of a fantastically synchronized universe to their contemporaries. James Hervey, an English clergyman who wrote prodigiously about the cosmos and whose *Meditations and Contemplations* (1750) was reprinted in Philadelphia, discussed extensively "the grand machine of the universe." This grand machine, he explained, consisted of a "multitude of globes . . . [holding] amazing magnitudes . . . perpetually running their rounds." Hervey was struck that "none mistake their way, or wander from the goal, though they pass through trackless and unbounded fields: none fly off from their orbits . . . none press in upon their centre . . . none interfere with each other." Rather, "all their rotations proceed in eternal harmony," and in doing so, and as expected from a superior clockwork, "keeping such time, and observing such laws, as are most exquisitely adapted to the perfection of the whole."[107]

By the late colonial period, North Americans were actively promoting this view of a "grand Machine of the Universe."[108] But it was the authors of a cluster of popular late eighteenth-century encyclopedic natural histories and geographies who were the most ardent promoters of the view of a mechanically precise universe, "which, though inexpressibly magnificent, [is] yet regular beyond the power of invention." The force of gravity, which Newton had discovered more than a century earlier, clarified why bodies were attracted to the center of the earth. But it also explained how, while each star had its own gravity, all bodies attracted each other by dint of their respective masses; that was the reason that the planets, the earth among them, held to their orbits. Novel material objects, among them terrestrial and celestial globes, allowed the educated elite to imagine the cosmos in greater detail.[109] But the most sophisticated and impressive aids to envisioning the planetary movements were the several intricate orreries that eighteenth-century American colleges purchased, which visibly and mechanically displayed to large provincial audiences the magnificent orbital motions of the planets and their satellites.[110]

It was the self-imposed task of revolutionary-era American intermediaries, such as the agricultural writer and natural philosopher Charles Vancouver, to relay to his compatriots this clockwork view of a fantastically synchronized universe. In the *General Compendium* (1785), Vancouver praised gravity and its normal opposing force ("a progressive force ... which each planet received when it was impelled forward") as preserving "the harmony of our planetary system." He marveled how the planets "perform their constant circuits at different distances" from the sun, each taking up its exact prescribed time "to complete its revolutions and proportioned to the greatness of the circle which it is to describe."[111] Indeed, heavenly bodies have "been found to perform their circuits with great exactness and strict regularity," attesting to the sublime reliability of the "nature of attraction, and the laws of circular motion," which took "place universally in all material substances." The title of New England natural scientist Nehemia Strong's treatise, *Astronomy Improved: The Harmonious Regularity Observable in the Mechanism or Movements of the Planetary System* (1784), left little doubt of this astronomer's clocklike regular and mechanistic cosmology.[112] Others, such as an anonymous author for an item published soon after in the *American Recorder,* similarly admired the magnificence and predictability of the "regular and unvarying" laws that dictate the movement of the planets.[113] Such portrayals reflected and helped to instill the Enlightenment-era idea of a mechanical universe in the minds of reading Americans in the early United States. As we will see in later chapters, in various ways this mechanical cosmology seeped into the representation and imagination of the novel American republican and federal political system.

The clockwork view of the universe was, at least initially, restricted to explaining and representing the solar system. The idea was publicly paraded and further entrenched through orreries, which, as noted, were intricate and striking devices that displayed mechanically the orbital motions of the planets and their satellites. Regardless of reports of ancient predecessors, and the fact that the most famous clocks of the late Middle Ages were primarily astronomical automata, the orrery was a modern marvel.[114] The orreries publicly displayed in late eighteenth-century America (as mentioned above, independently by several colleges) were, fittingly, built by watchmakers, who made use of their expertise with springs and cogwheels to mechanically represent the cosmic movements. The orreries became widely popular as viewers flocked to see these marvels that manifested the precise and predictable movements of the sun, the planets, and their known satellites, enabling viewers to realize and imagine the orbital celestial motions they so delightfully displayed.[115] The abovementioned David Rittenhouse, the premier American astronomer of late eighteenth-century America, was also a gifted watchmaker who constructed an orrery that was the most exact and precise of his day. Contemporaries flocked to see that orrery, which made its creator "a cultural hero to the educated men of the Revolution."[116]

As the nineteenth century progressed, simplified orreries became more widespread and common, reaching broad and new audiences through the efforts of the lyceum movement. That educational movement, founded by Josiah Holbrook (1788–1854) in 1816, aimed to develop common schooling for children and adult education. For that purpose, Holbrook established the Holbrook School Apparatus Manufacturing Company, which produced cheap devices to illustrate the sciences in educational establishments. One of the hallmark creations of the company was the "astronomical orrery," a device that was also known as a "planeterium."[117] Holbrook unfolded his educational vision in 1830, offering "to furnish common school apparatus," including "a simple orrery to represent the comparative size, distance and motions of the planets, with their

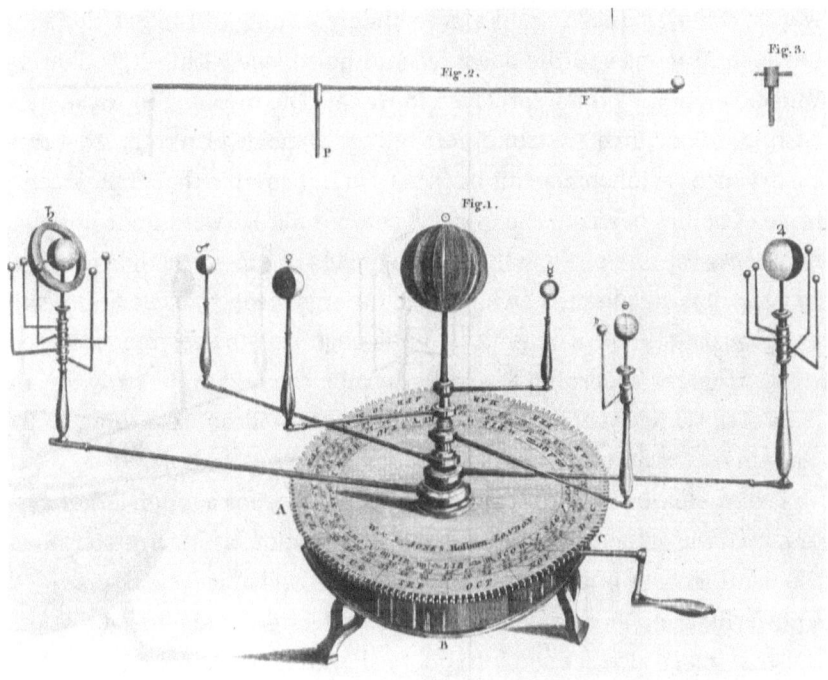

FIGURE 7. An orrery, or planetarium, George Adams, 1799 (London: W. & S. Jones, Holborn). (Library of Congress, LC-USZ62–110391)

several moons." Indeed, the "Planeterium, or Orrery," which represented "the size, relative positions, and annual revolutions of the Planets," was supposed to fill the need of teachers for "some instrument adapted to the capacity of common schools, which might divest this science [astronomy] of the mystery ... hanging over it." Students, as Holbrook appreciated, would derive from orreries a better understanding of the universe as well as "great intellectual pleasure."[118] The astronomical imagination of untold Americans would thus expand through the dispersion of numerous cheap orreries, enabling generations of citizens to appreciate the magnificence of the universe but also to participate in the political speech that derived its vocabulary from the cosmos.

Orreries, as mechanical presentations of heliocentrism, ascribed by definition a recognition of the miniature proportions and noncentral place of the earth vis-à-vis the rest of the planetary system. In other words, orreries encouraged a new understanding of the relationship between humans and the cosmos, and their place within it.[119] Charles Vancouver, among others, relayed in writing the meaning of these new cosmic proportions. "Astronomers tell us," Vancouver wrote, "that this earth which we inhabit, forms but a very minute part in that great assemblage of bodies of which the world is composed." He went on to attach a number to the size of earth that was "a million of times less than the Sun, by which it is enlightened," while even the large planets "exceed the earth one thousand times in magnitude."[120] Recognizing the cosmic "enlarged view of things," according to another writer, seemed to "destroy the effects of prejudice" and "inspire the properest of ideas" regarding man's place in nature and the character of the universe as a whole.[121]

The clock thus became a significant metaphor for a much larger system than the state or any other human institution, as it came to reflect the natural order of the universe itself. The mechanical clock provided a powerful metaphor by which this age understood the entire creation. But that image also seeped into political understandings in revolutionary America and later in the early republic. John Adams made the most famous of the American chrono-analogies when he described the United States declaring independence as "thirteen clocks [that] had been made to strike together—a perfection of mechanism." By the late eighteenth century, clock-related ideas of society and government in the early United States were embedded in the political imagination to the extent that the titles of two of the most important American political journals of the time reflected the fascination with them: Robert Treat Paine's Federalist *Federal Orrery*, and Philip Freneau's Jeffersonian *Time-Piece*. Drawing upon the figures of the orrery and the timepiece, parties on both sides of the political divide thus attempted during the 1790s and beyond to align their ideas and ideals with the mechanistic nature of the clock.[122] Decades later, Americans would still describe the universe as "majestically" operating "with more regularity and precision than [a] . . . machine."[123] That the clock was associated both with the universe and with the mechanics of American politics was not coincidental, as the United States and its unique brand of politics would be conceived as a cosmic state that was legitimized and justified through the fact that it was embedded in and correlated with the universe.

A Stable Universe?

Eighteenth-century astronomy was predominantly Newtonian and as such was inclined to depict a fundamentally stable, clockwork solar system, with the "fixed stars" mostly viewed as unmoving reference points in the sky against which the motions of the solar system could be charted. Newtonian physics could not, however, solve complex problems such as compound interactions between the planets and the sun, while observational astronomy posed problems (such as Jupiter's apparently shrinking and Saturn's expanding orbits) for the view of a stable solar system. Such problems with understanding the solar system as a clocklike and perfectly regulated mechanism were compounded by the destabilizing views that the solar system was at the center of neither the universe nor even of the milky way, and that the universe as a whole was not inherently stable. By the 1830s even American classroom textbooks concluded that "an advancement of the solar system, in absolute space, is now considered certain." The once stable and harmonic universe was expanding, moving, and changing.[124] But it was the discovery of new planets and satellites, and their incorporation into the way in which the solar system was imagined, even in tracts intended for young audiences, which forever shook the once immobile and sterile view of a fixed cosmos.[125] In particular, the discovery of Uranus in 1783, news of which quickly spread to and across the young United States, reshaped the way in which the cosmos was perceived. The new planet was initially named Georgius Sidiu in honor of the British monarch and alternatively Herschel after its famed English discoverer. The battle for the new planet's proper name raged for decades after its discovery, further spreading the sense of a universe that had lost its stability.[126] Yet as early as 1785, two years after Uranus's discovery, Thomas Jefferson had already conveyed from Paris the dynamic and changing nature of the cosmos. Writing to an acquaintance in Philadelphia, Jefferson wrote, "the number of double stars discovered by [the astronomer] Herschel amounts now to upwards of 900, being twice the number which he gave in the Philosophical Transactions."[127] The view of a perpetually stable clockwork universe was in retreat as a more dynamic and perhaps even chaotic cosmic view emerged.

The debate on the stability and immutability of the universe was conclusively infused into Anglophone circles through Nathaniel Bowditch's translation and commentary of Pierre-Simon Laplace's groundbreaking work on mathematical astronomy, *Mécanique celeste,* which was completed by 1818. Following the cracks that had appeared in the view of a clockwork universe, Laplace's theory of stability reassured American readers regarding the harmony and permanence of the universe, and thus by implication of the republic. Commentators from Harvard professors to journalistic essayists marveled at Laplace, "the Newton of France," and the Laplacian "order and perpetuity of the whole [solar] system," rendering "all disorder or confusion impossible."[128] Conscious attempts to construct a stable cosmos were evident even before the translation of Laplace in English permeated literati circles. "We would reckon him an imperfect mechanic," theologically argued a Virginian commentator, "who so ordered his clock-work that in its progression one part . . . should dash against another, and so ruin the compound fabric."[129] Against such hopes for a stable cosmos, and the fear of a chaotic one, we should understand the palpable relief of contemporaries like the young Abraham Lincoln during the 1833 Leonid meteor shower, who found the "grand old constellations . . . fixed and true in their places" in contrast to the panic welling up in the witnesses of the numerous meteors showering down.

The advance of computational and observational astronomy, however, continually challenged contemporaries' strivings for cosmic stability. Popular commentators could assume, for example, that the universe originated in "a central and primary chaos" and that over the eons stars and suns "have utterly vanished, and the spots which they occupied in the heavens have become blanks." The grim conclusion of such speculations was inescapable: "What has thus befallen other systems [w]ill assuredly befall our own."[130] The contrast of Laplacian visions of cosmic order would stabilize and thus comfort, yet would not be enough to quell fears of a universe rife with chaos and unpredictability.

The ideas of a cosmic clockwork and Laplacian order were therefore attempts to impart celestial stability on the cosmos, but they were also employed metaphorically in human affairs. The language of political astronomy would thus habitually function as an attempt to alleviate the anxiety of social and political Aristotelian *stasis*. Resolutions of an antislavery convention in Illinois reveal this dynamic. The participants resolved that they did not believe that "the Union of these United States" was "in the slightest manner endangered by the agitation" of the proslavery South. To demonstrate how unshakable the Union was, the resolution continued: "The planets of the solar system are in about as great danger of dissolving their union" with the sun.[131] Likening the solar system to a political union among the sun and the planets was intended to endow the American Union with the solar system's stability. This choice of metaphor was less than perfect, however, as by the mid-nineteenth century cosmic stability was by no means a settled matter. Indeed, in a mere decade the Union itself would be torn apart by sectional discord. In the coming chapters we shall come to see how the poles of cosmic stability and chaos, still under scientific and popular debate, repeatedly played out through the language of American political astronomy.

Deep Space, Infinite Stars

While contemporaries could glimpse an image of the harmonic orderliness and supreme regularity of the universe through the mechanical displays of orreries, there was an aspect of the universe that was even harder to fathom, namely the shocking discovery of its apparently infinite size. In the wake of seventeenth-century empirical discoveries and the development of computational astronomy, the notion of an ordered, stationary, and compact cosmos of "fixed stars" gave way to that of an effectively infinite universe. What Alexander Koyré more than half a century ago called the "deep revolution" in the human mind was fundamentally characterized by "the destruction of the cosmos and the geometrization of space," that is, by the shift from a tidy, harmonious, closed cosmos to the infinite, mathematical, rapidly expanding, and for all practical purposes inconceivably large universe.[132]

In the mid-eighteenth century, astronomers were above all concerned with the solar system and with charting and cataloguing empirical astronomical observations. The ultimate goal of such astronomy was to predict and explain the planetary motions, and the moving but unchanging canopy of stars constituted a mere backdrop for these observations and calculations. The distant and immobile stars were not interesting in themselves within such a framework. After 1750, however, interest in the stellar realm, nebulae, and galaxies gradually increased, and the historian of astronomy Michael Crowe has noted the transformation in astronomy by 1800 from a science of the solar system to one of universal proportions.[133]

Colonial Americans already appreciated by the mid-eighteenth century that the "Sun, with all its attendant Planets and Comets, is but a very small part" of the universe, whose size was "immense and inconceivable."[134] By the age of the Revolution the American reading public was aware that the earth, once thought the center of a relatively compact cosmos, was minuscule in relation to the magnitude of other celestial bodies and inconceivably tiny in relation to space.[135] The realization of the universe's size reinforced the already profound appreciation of its orderliness. It became clear to American popularizers of science that astounding mechanical precision did not stop at the confines of the solar system, as in the farther reaches of space "countless Multitudes of Globes ... [and] Multiplicity of mighty Spheres, must be perpetually running their Rounds, in the upper Regions! Yet, none mistake their Way, or wander from the Goal. ... None fly off from their Orbits ... none press in upon their Centre, with too near an Approach." The universe, it became clear, was "prodigiously vast; immensely various; and yet more than mathematically exact."[136] Indeed, it appeared so expansive that it seemed as if there was no "way of comprehending what and how vast that frame truly is."[137] The correlating notion of the universe was dazzling: an enormous system of systems, in which all the stars in the skies "be suns, with planets revolving round them like those in our system, and these again revolving round one common centre, a system of systems."[138]

To achieve such radical changes in the astral imagination, those who watched the stars in a post-Copernican world did not, like their predecessors, see points of light in the firmament but rather extremely distant suns that turned the universe into a multifocal space in which myriad heliocentrisms were possible.[139] Stellar astronomy, which had previously consisted of the mere charting of the fixed positions of stars, came to understand its subject of study as more than mere scattered illuminations on the firmament: Stars had to be thought of as great radiant bodies inhabiting a three-dimensional and enormously large space.[140] What resulted was an image of the universe that recently has been dubbed "elegant": Countless suns with their entourage of lesser satellites pervaded a cosmos that was infinite for all practical purposes, consisting of manifold harmonious systems of orbiting stars.[141]

By the eighteenth century, natural philosophers and their popularizers were regularly describing a cosmology in which the universe was copiously larger than hitherto imagined. This expansive view was not confined to the solar system but rather took on an exponentially larger scope. It was based on new astronomical observations and calculations that dwarfed previous beliefs regarding the universe's proportions. As dramatic as the recognition of the minuteness of the earth in relation to the solar system and its planetary members was the emergence of the view of what would later be called "deep space." The universe, it was becoming evident, was incredibly, almost incomprehensibly, vast and was populated by countless galaxies and stars, with each harboring its own gallery of satellites. In the words of an early American writer, the distances in space were "unlimited."[142]

In political terms, this new vision of a vast universe inevitably dethroned the sun from its previously privileged and overbearing position, which was often expressed in political terms as "governance" of the solar system. By the end of the eighteenth century, it would make little sense to view the sun as a monarchical universal ruler. Even though contemporaries still described the sun in political terms of command and domination, it would be much more in line with current astronomical knowledge to see the sun as an equal among numerous equal, if not superior, stars. As large as was the sun in comparison to the earth, in relation to the cosmos as a whole it was minuscule, and as such was deposed from its previously unique and favored position. This newly destabilized and reoriented cosmology had, among other things, political ramifications. It now seemed unfounded to view a human "sun king" as the center of a political-cosmic solar system, for the sun itself was just one among myriad stars, located in a small corner of a vast universe. For political revolutionaries such as the American founders, this new vision was not deemed a threat. Rather, it served as proof that the cosmos did not manifest or legitimize solar monarchism but rather reflected stellar republicanism. Monarchism, in this view, was appropriate neither to the natural nor to the human order. If anything, republicanism was reflected in the "equality" among numerous stars spread across a boundless universe. The core idea of republicanism seemed embedded in the fabric of the universe and was thus the most "natural" of political orders.¹⁴³

This tantalizing and reorienting view of an incomprehensibly vast universe was steadily spreading beyond a select group of gentlemen-scientists. These novel astronomical understandings were disseminated to wide audiences through effective intermediaries of popular knowledge in America. In this vein, a popular manual for young American men pointed to "innumerable ... glorious Bodies, which now are altogether invisible to us," but are known to exist in the "boundless space of the Universe."¹⁴⁴ Jedidiah Morse, the "father of American geography," propagated and elaborated this view. Morse was a well-known name in reading households in the early United States through the numerous editions of his geographical compilations. These textbooks suggest how and the extent to which the view of a seemingly infinitely large universe was disseminated in the closing decades of the eighteenth century in America.¹⁴⁵ Only in a late edition of *The American Geography* (1789) did Morse first acknowledge the extraordinary size of the universe. Turning to relativity to demonstrate the vastness of space, he pointed out that "our sun viewed from a fixed star, would appear no bigger than a star does to us." In other words, the sun was overawing only from a (relatively) short distance. From afar it was merely one star among many. From Saturn, the astronomer Rittenhouse reminded the members of the Continental Congress in 1775 in a famed lecture, "the Sun will put on something of a starlike appearance."¹⁴⁶ This increasingly accepted view must have been disorienting, for it underscored the minuteness, if not the insignificance, of earth and the solar system to which it belonged.

To underline stellar remoteness, and thus attempt to express the size of the universe, Morse pointed out that the fixed stars were "at least 100,000 times father from us, than we are from the sun." How could one come to terms with such a vast distance? To provide an idea of the meaning of such inconceivable expanses, Morse explained that a sound "would not reach us from Sirius, or the dog-star, which is nearer to this earth than any of the fixed stars, in 40,000 years. A cannon ball flying at the rate of 480 miles an hour, would not reach us in 700,000 years." Even light, whose speed of travel seems instantaneous, would take as long as a sailboat's intercontinental voyage. To delineate to his readers the relative smallness of earth ("a speck in the works of God") in comparison with the entire universe, Morse quoted Joseph Addison, noting that even the entirety of the solar system was "so exceedingly little" that were it "utterly extinguished and annihilated," it would not be missed "more than a grain of sand." In his final work on geography, Morse conceded that "the distance between stars was too great for the power of human beings to conceive; the understanding is bewildered and lost in the contemplation."[147] The universe, the astronomer David Rittenhouse saw, was characterized by the "prodigiously great . . . distance of the fixed stars" and the "immeasurable journey" of light from those distant bodies.[148]

Relativity was once again a useful tool to make sense of these immeasurable distances: "an observer," one author explained, "placed near any fixed star, would consider it alone as a real sun, and the rest only as so many shining points" (including the earth's sun as well, naturally).[149] By the end of the century, the new generous estimations of the size of the universe had seeped into books aimed at young readers, a sign that it was in the final stages of becoming consensual knowledge. *The American Preceptor*, a booklet providing "lessons for reading and speaking," dared its young readers to "contemplate those wild fields of ether, that reach in height as far as from Saturn to the fixed stars, and run abroad almost to an infinitude, our imagination finds its capacity filled with so immense a prospect, and puts itself upon the stretch to comprehend it."[150] A few years later, *A Short Introduction to Geography and Astronomy*, "designed particularly for the young masters and misses of New England," expanded in the form of a catechism on stars' "immense distances from the sun . . . computed to be at least 32,000,000,000,000 miles of distance from the earth."[151] As space had become too large for the human mind to grasp, these hard-to-imagine orders of physical magnitude altered perspectives on human jealousies and fighting, which in cosmic perspective seem petty and trivial. In the words of Rittenhouse, it "flatters no fashionable princely vice, or national depravity."[152]

The fixed stars' incredible distance from one another was striking, but that was not the only tantalizing feature of these distant world systems. By the Revolution, American popularizers of the idea of the new expansive universe were pointing out that the "number of suns or fixed stars, are continually increasing, according to the goodness of Telescopes, they are innumerable."[153] As time went by, estimations became more specific. Early in his publishing career, Morse still held a quite modest view of the number of stars. Specifically, in 1784 Morse claimed that "there are about three thousand fixed Stars, two thousand only of which are visible to the naked eye." As opposed to the larger and brighter appearance of the planets, the stars were "supposed by astronomers, to be suns to other systems."[154] Five years later the popular geographer's view had changed dramatically. The stars, he now believed, were "doubtless" (not "supposed," as only five years ago) illuminating suns, and as such were thought to consist of self-contained solar systems, with their own accompanying sets of planets. Hence, there were "as many systems as there are fixed stars," and the universe thus formed "one immense system of systems."[155] Beyond the complexity of this model of the universe, it was the unfathomable number of stars (each, we remember, constituting a system within itself) that elevated it into the dizzying stratosphere of incomprehensibility.

As late as 1789, Morse still estimated the number of stars in the few thousands. In the coming years, however, he and other observers and popularizers of updated astronomical knowledge had taken a striking step to a very different worldview. By 1796, Morse admitted in his latest edition of the *American Universal Geography* that the "whole number of stars may be justly considered as ... of no limitation."[156] Further, "as the telescope approximates perfection," he was convinced that we would become acquainted with formerly unknown stars and that their known numbers would continue to grow. In the regions of the Milky Way alone the visible stars were already "innumerable." David Rittenhouse went further, claiming that the number of stars even only within the confined planes of the Milky Way was in the "millions," indicating how astonishingly enormous and immeasurable was this "system of worlds beyond worlds."[157] The unnamed compiler of *The Instructor: or, American Young Man's Best Companion,* summed up the contemporary view of an outsized universe, reiterating that the stars were "innumerable," and that they inhabited the "boundless space of the universe."[158] A text intended for an even younger audience concluded in even more dazzling fashion: "Consider the fixed stars as so many vast oceans of flame, which are each of them attended with a different set of planets, and still discover new firmaments and new lights which are sunk farther in those unfathomable depth of ether, so as not to be seen by the largest of our telescopes, we are lost in such a labyrinth of suns and worlds, and confounded with the immensity and magnificence of nature."[159]

By the opening of the nineteenth century it had become consensual to speculate that, with the continuing perfection of telescopes and measuring instruments, "no limit can be set to [stars'] number or distances."[160] By the third decade of the century such notions were common even in the peripheries of American society, where Native American newspapers, such as the *Cherokee Phoenix,* often discussed the "thousand millions of stars in the heavens" and the millions more "in the unknown depths of space and placed for ever beyond our ken."[161]

The shift to a universe hosting countless suns with their entourage of lesser satellites pervading a cosmos that was enormously, inconceivably large, and one that astonishingly abided by fixed and mathematical laws of nature, was being steadily incorporated into the popular cosmology by the late eighteenth century. More and more American citizens of the early nineteenth century came to imagine, appreciate, and debate the awesome aesthetics of "deep space," a realm of unimaginable expanse and seemingly infinite magnitudes that hosted a limitless number of stars and planets.[162]

Cosmic, Musical, and Political Harmony

Yale College mathematician-astronomer Nehemia Strong published in 1784 a series of lectures he had delivered under the title *Astronomy Improved: Or, A New Theory of the Harmonious Regularity Observable in the Mechanism or Movements of the Planetary System.* Within that somewhat cumbersome title, it is the phrase "harmonious regularity," an attribute that Strong observed in "the mechanism or movement of the planetary system," that catches the eye. We have already examined the mechanical nature of the clockwork view of the universe, which Strong's title acknowledges. It is the perceived harmonious aspect of the cosmos to which we now turn our attention.

Humans have long recognized cosmic harmony, a pleasing consistency and congruous order, as the underlying principle of the universe. If nature was indeed fundamentally harmonious, it was essentially orderly and thus benign, as generation upon generation actively wished it was. The most discernable patterns in nature, and thus perceptibly harmonious, were celestial, from the diurnal movement of the firmament to the longer monthly and annual cycles. While harmony itself was a concept strongly associated with music, the nexus of harmony-music-astronomy was an ancient one, dating back at least to the sixth century BCE. Tradition attributes to Pythagoras of Samos the relating of music and astronomy by way of an analogy between sonic intervals and the revolutions of the planets.[163] Originally linking musical harmony to ordered numerical relationships, Pythagoras and his successors went on to weave heaven and earth, and then God and man, and society and the individual through the language of music. Pythagoreans supposed that, like a string that produces a musical pitch according to its length, the planets similarly emitted a corresponding note in their travel through their respective Ptolemaic crystalline spheres. The movements of the system came together in a polyphonic cosmic harmony, which existed in nature as part of a master plan (and would become for Christians God's plan). This theory, which has come to be called *musica mundi,* or the music of the spheres, was part of a grand-scale outlook that ever since antiquity linked the harmonic motions of the planets to an all-encompassing cosmic harmony. That congruent order pervaded all of creation, including humans, and was accessible for them to discover. For millennia this grand harmony was conceived as no mere metaphorical flourish but as a real, defining, and inseparable characteristic of the universe.[164]

Pythagoras thus initiated a harmonic tradition that persisted for millennia, as pillars of Western philosophy during antiquity and the Middle Ages such as Plato and Boethius further developed the notions of cosmic harmony. The Great Chain of Being, the medieval idea of universal hierarchical order that extended from God, to the spheres, and down to the lowest forms on earth, was a powerful expression and proponent of the belief in an ordered and harmonic universe.[165] Yet the emergence of the heliocentric worldview in the sixteenth century tested the harmonic tradition, which had developed within and was "anchored firmly to the geocentric Ptolemaic cosmos."[166] The frustration with the uncertainty that the New Science brought about, which seemed to endanger the entire harmonic structure of the cosmos, was famously summarized by the English metaphysical poet John Donne, who bemoaned, "Tis all in pieces, all coherence gone."[167] While Nicolaus Copernicus, the modern originator of heliocentrism, was invested in arguing for the congruity of heliocentrism and the language of cosmic harmony, it was Johannes Kepler who took on the project of salvaging that noble idea. Although Kepler is best remembered for his laws of planetary motion, the historian Aviva Rothman points out that Kepler "devoted his life to the cause of harmony. . . . [H]is ultimate goal was both to reveal the harmony in nature and to work toward a worldly harmony that might follow from it."[168] In *The Harmony of the World* (1619), the astronomer studied the distances of the planets on the basis of the harmonies they orchestrate by their orbits. Kepler's explorations of harmony in its various manifestations—from the musical to the astro-cosmological—should be understood in the context of the war that began in Europe three years before the publication of *The Harmony of the World* and would ravage the continent's communities for another twenty-seven. Nevertheless, Kepler's cry for the restoration of prewar civility was firmly grounded in, and responsive to, the Pythagorean harmonic tradition.

While the celestial planetary system presented a striking and immaculate manifestation of harmony, Kepler and others pointed out that it extended to humans and their social institutions. Harmony transcended the musical and mathematical and pervaded the moral and political, as it linked the congruous ordering of the universe with the lives of the humans that inhabited it. The social realm participated in the cosmic harmony, and everything true about humanity had to reflect that broad, all-pervading agreement and coherence. Like the planets moving in their unvarying orbits, the patterns and institutions that humans formed were thus expected to be consistent and pleasing.[169] Even human bodies were considered healthy only when the four humors were balanced in harmony. No wonder, then, that as the human body was associated with the polity through the predominant metaphor of the "body politic," the state itself fell under the classification of harmony: The harmonious state was good, and the good state was in harmony. Hence, as harmony underlay both ordered music and the ideal ordering of the state, music and politics continued to proceed united side by side, with well-governed societies and states understood to be "in tune" or "well-tempered."[170]

The harmonic tradition not only survived the intellectual challenges caused by the tectonic and paradigmatic changes of early modernity, but it flourished. By the eighteenth century, harmonic concepts were so pervasive that "symmetrical organization, parallel techniques, perfect proportions, and unity were all commonplace, [and] were found in everyday life, in every academic discipline and creative pursuit." The baroque movement followed by the Masonic tide in the eighteenth century further drove this Enlightenment-era harmonic resurgence, particularly in the field of music.[171] American colonists for their part accepted the universe as purposefully ordered, with harmony as an attribute not only of music but also of the natural world and the political order. Hence, Mercy Otis Warren, the famed Patriot author and poet, observed lyrically, "The musick of the spheres resounds / . . . through a galaxy of light / By Newton's eye unseen, / Beyond the telescopic view."[172] Correspondingly, American schoolchildren were cued to become filled "with a pleasing astonishment, to see so many worlds hanging one above another, and sliding round their axles in such an amazing pomp and solemnity."[173]

The Enlightened late eighteenth-century American universe was, in the words of Gordon Wood, one of "laws, measurements, predictions, and constancies or regularities of behavior," in which harmony was a central characteristic.[174] As in any harmonious structure, *political* harmony created order out of chaos and promised resolution over discord. As the American political world was shaken by revolution, the traditional cosmos itself was on the cusp of change. Coinciding with the creation of the republic, new ideas about the composition and structure of the cosmos gained new prominence among widening circles of laypeople.[175] Like planets moving in their regular orbits, Americans expected human events to form discernible configurations that would manifest the overarching harmony ingrained in the world. Harmony in revolutionary America and the early republic became not only a description of the ultimate nature of the world but also fundamental for understanding the republic itself.[176] The rest of this book will reveal how the interconnectedness of the universe and its celestial bodies with the novel political configurations that Americans founded would repeatedly manifest itself during the first centuries of the republic's existence.

Conclusion

Political astronomy depended on the wide dissemination and popularization of what has been recently called "natural knowledge" that humans develop about their living and inanimate surroundings.[177] Hence, the emergence of political astronomy in America during the late eighteenth century and its decades-long flourishing thereafter corresponded with, and depended on, the by then widely acknowledged Newtonian understanding of the universe. This unique mode of understanding, analyzing, and discoursing about the political realm was thus enabled by the massive popularity of almanacs and newspapers and the rise of a new genre of natural histories, which digested and democratized astronomical knowledge for a lay public.[178] Astronomical knowledge held a prominent place in those ubiquitous tracts in various forms, perhaps not surprisingly in a preindustrial world devoid of light pollution in which, every night, starry skies manifested their full glory. In that early American world, citizens of the young republic seem to have been ever fascinated and enamored with astronomy, "the first and greatest of sciences . . . the most useful to mankind."[179]

The mutual influence and stimulation of astronomy and politics in early American life was evident in a series of lectures on science presented at the Portland Academy in Maine, a state that was dubbed, in the promotional material for the lectures, as the "Eastern Star" of the American republic. The open lectures focused on "descriptive astronomy," and "particularly of the asteroids and superior planets," as well as on the planet Herschel (Uranus), "with the comets and fixed stars." The public interest in modern astronomy in the early republic, underscored by these lectures delivered on the periphery of the American academic world, is telling. Even more telling is the fact that the lectures' sponsor believed that they would promote a political and national cause, namely the "increasing brilliancy on our political constellation." By the nation's jubilee year, the diffusion and democratization of astronomical knowledge went hand in hand with the pervasiveness of political astronomy in the United States.[180]

Throughout the decades following the creation of the republic, many

Americans continually expressed their appreciation of, and demonstrated their acquaintance with, a magnificently regulated heliocentric solar system. The most politically and socially marginal among them looked up to the North Star for guidance, geographical and moral; they sought to bestow human hierarchies and meaning on the interaction of the planets; they looked at the universe and understood it as a massive chronometer; they learned through various and mostly informal channels that the sun and its accompanying planets were dwarfed by an incomprehensibly expansive universe that held a stunning number of stars and embodied perfect harmony. Equipped with this vernacular knowledge, a broad swath of American society could readily apply its cosmic imagination to more earthly matters. We now turn to the pervasive modes of rhetoric and thought through which early American citizens, ranging the whole gamut from nationalists to states'-rights advocates, elevated and clarified their political universe and congealed their attachment to their novel Union, while at the same time providing it with a sense of cosmic justification and inevitability.

2

From the Sun King to Republican Solar Systems

PLANETARY POLITICS FROM THE REVOLUTION TO THE CIVIL WAR

On April 1, 1860, B. F. Lemen penned a letter to former House Representative (and soon to be presidential candidate) Abraham Lincoln. Lemen included an elaborate and imaginative commentary on the state of the American Union on the verge of civil war. Writing from Colorado, "the large Observatory in the Rocky Mountains," and unleashing a barrage of astro-political images, he expressed his hope that "the labored calculations of the political astronomers of the South" would fail, and that "the great Southern Comet will not Strike, our American Earth and dash it into fragments." As the Republican Party geared up for a national convention that would elect a presidential candidate, Lemen depicted the South as an asteroid bearing a "Fiery appearance [with] nothing more, than a thin and exceedingly light vapor, or gasseous matter." As opposed to the unruly and threatening Southern comet, the Northern "Star Spangled Atmosphere" was "well regulated in its revolutions . . . [and] its universal laws are too well Founded to be over thrown, or blown away by mear gass, or boddies containing no heavier matter than puffs." Lemen further elaborated on the political astronomy of the Union: "Our Political world has the Propelling forces, or George Washington power,—which drives onward, amid the meteoric stones and gaseous vapors of wandering Stars—It also has the impelling and repelling Thomas Jefferson, Republican forces—which holds its own matter, and at the Same time, repells

Extreme, and obnoctious execrations, or, all extraneous substances. It also has a gravitating or adhesive influence, which is the magnetic blood of the Fathers of the First revolution. That power binds the whole Super Structure toward one Common center."[1]

Lemen's painstaking elaboration of American politics as a planetary system adhering and responsive to republican mechanical forces may seem frivolous to twenty-first-century readers. But in analyzing the American federal confederacy in planetary terms, as an astro-political structure that reflects the dynamics of the solar system, Lemen was making use of a common trope that his compatriots had been relying on heavily for over fourscore years. Politicians and commentators repeatedly interpreted the relationship between the American states and the national government in terms of interaction among bodies orbiting around and gravitating toward each other. During these decades, competing astronomical traditions highlighted, on the one hand, cosmic order and stability while, on the other, pointed out that the universe was rife with chaos. During the years leading to secession and Civil War, these competing understandings enabled contemporaries to deliberate and clash over the stark differences in their understanding of the American Union, its character and purpose.

Representing the Union of American states as a solar system made a powerful metaphor, which enabled contemporaries to concretize abstract political notions and structures, and to examine their views of the novel American political system. The metaphor mixed the familiar structure of the solar system with abstract political notions, such as federalism, enabling contemporaries to communicate, discover, and invest meaning in their republic. It enabled them to see their novel polity as rooted in and reflecting nature, and thus as embodying political truths despite its lack of historical precedence, while never losing track of the astronomical model that, in the words of an early nineteenth-century observer, was the "perfect, great, and magnificent" creation of "the Divinity [that] upholds and governs the immense extent of his works, and preserves order, beauty and harmony, throughout the stupendous fabric of the Universe."[2] Like the solar system, many hoped, the republic would be immune to the chaos and instability inflicted upon the early United States. This is not to say that there was agreement as to the exact relation of the United States and the solar system, and what were the exact lessons that the astronomical model bestowed on the political. Nevertheless, throughout the decades following the Revolution and preceding the Civil War the elaboration of astronomical metaphors enabled Americans to deliberate and clash over the ultimate meaning of the unique and experimental aspects of the United States and its accompanying political theory and culture.

This widespread interpretation of the political world, particularly but not solely of federalism, in terms of interaction among planets orbiting around and gravitating toward or repelling each other demonstrates a major and overlooked mode of making sense of and understanding abstract American political ideas, such as the federal confederacy. Articulating the American states as a harmonious and natural formation of planets revolving around a common center was a discursive convention that substantiated the legitimacy of the United States, explained its political structure, and helped negotiate anxieties as to its chances of survival. Indeed, we cannot properly understand early American politics, federalism, and constitutionalism unless we realize the extent to which contemporaries made sense of their world in astronomical terms. As the cosmos was further studied and better understood, the framing of the American world as a solar system provided a sublime representation—and thus a powerful explanation—of a political entity whose existence, like all human institutions, was grounded on the power of collective imagination.

The discussion of the United States in solar terms that continued for decades after the Revolution bore the unmistakable hallmarks of Enlightenment and Newtonian language. Yet, as we saw in the first chapter, this mode of thought had originated centuries earlier. While humans across cultures and civilizations have personified and deified the sun since the dawn of history, the European Renaissance seems to have marked a new phase in equating rulers with the sun.[3] Albrecht Dürer's monumental early sixteenth-century woodcut of Maximilian I's (1459–1519) chariot is characteristic in positioning the sun shining above the emperor with a Latin inscription, *Quod in Coelis sol, hoc in Terra Caesar Est* (What the sun is in the sky, Caesar is on earth), thus identifying the Holy Roman Emperor with the sun.

FIGURE 8. *The Triumphal Chariot of Maximilian I*, Albrecht Dürer, 1522. (The Metropolitan Museum of Art, New York; gift of Junius Spencer Morgan, 1919)

Dürer's impressive depiction is the more remarkable when we appreciate that it was created in a geocentric world in which the sun was merely a planet revolving around the earth. In the following decades, as Europeans steadily converted to a heliocentrism in which the sun was more justifiably interpreted and hence imagined as reigning supreme, the image of the monarch as the sun would gain momentum. The dawning of the notion that the planets were orbiting a solar center that attracted, repelled, and presumably controlled the other lesser bodies brought about an outbreak of majestic readings of the sun.

Spawned by Copernicus's *De revolutionibus,* heliocentrism's eclipse of the geocentric worldview represents one of the most decisive paradigm shifts in human thought. Copernicus's monumental treatise generated a political reading of the new planetary relationship. In a fashion that nineteenth-century Americans would happily adopt, which I termed in the previous chapter astronomical politics, the Renaissance-era Polish polymath asserted, "The sun is not inappropriately called by some people the lantern of the universe, its mind by others, and its ruler by still others.... [I]ndeed, as though seated on a royal throne, the sun governs the family of planets revolving around it."[4] This anthropomorphic reference to the sun as ruler, monarch, governor and patriarch, and to the planets as its subjects (or "family") in a single sentence is striking. This sixteenth-century allusion anticipated how people would politicize physical and cosmic relations in the coming centuries, doing so in ways that reflected the rapidly transforming societies and institutions of a restive world.

While it took time for the counterintuitive Copernican revolution to be universally acknowledged and absorbed, by the eighteenth century, as we saw in chapter 1, the once far-fetched idea that at the center of what was now deemed the *solar* system, if not the universe, stood the sun and not the earth was gaining ground fast. Serendipitously, the widening recognition of heliocentrism corresponded with the rise of political absolutism, the ideology of the monarch's absolute power, a convergence that facilitated a most potent image of the king-as-sun. By the eighteenth century, monarchical absolutism, an ideology that also fueled attempts at "state building," a project that aimed at creating more potent states with an elaborate apparatus, prevailed in much of western Europe.[5] Early modern politics and political thought facilitated such tectonic changes and developments in the organization of society and governance that new modes of explaining and understanding political entities were soon demanded. Polities, for example, were now universally represented as "bodies politic," in which monarchs typically functioned as the head, while the other organs stood for discrete governmental branches and social classes.[6] Yet in light of the consolidation of a new type of regime and new ideologies of governance, namely the European nation-state and absolutism, early moderns also increasingly used the powerful cosmic idiom that represented and equated rulers of state with luminous astronomical bodies.

Eager to participate in the millennia-old identification of the sun as a superior body and the attribution to it of human qualities, early modern Europeans repeatedly depicted strong monarchs, who were now understood as the embodiment of their respective states, as celestial bodies, particularly the sun. While humans in the past had seen the sun as divine, seldom, if ever before, had living rulers been depicted as the sun.[7] Indeed, early modern kings from Philip IV of Spain (adoringly called by his subjects "the planet king" after the sun) to the English Henry VIII and Louis XIV of France were presented as majestic, aloof, and powerful suns. Reigning through a revamped doctrine of divine right, kings were seen, like luminous stars, as inherent to the cosmic order. The most recognized specimen of such usage is, of course, the image of Louis XIV (1638–1715), universally known as the "Sun King," an epitaph explained in Louis's royal memoirs by the fact that the sun was "the most noble" of the heavenly bodies.[8] During Louis's reign, the German jurist and political philosopher Samuel Pufendorf (1632–1694) provided a fascinating image of the Copernican sun king. Kings, according to Pufendorf, like the sun, were a dazzling phenomenon that belonged to the world of nature. Spending their lives in courts as rulers of nations, kings were ever "exposed to the publick view, [with] every eye ... upon" them. With their image and their behavior the focus of intense public scrutiny, kings were "curiously watch'd" at all times and could thus "no more be hid than the Sun in the Firmament." Like "the Sun in the midst of the Firmament," the king "pierce[d], enlighten[ed], and warm[ed] all round him with the influence of his Beams." Like the Copernican sun, the king was the focal point of his system, positioned to gather enormous and constant attention from all that surrounded him and in turn to grace them with his presence and to pass on his sustaining powers.[9]

While early modern Europeans (as also their colonial scions, as we shall see) were conventional in attributing a human face to stars, they were unique in systematically describing living humans in terms of solar qualities. William Shakespeare, for example, who operated in a by now

FIGURE 9. Louis XIV, the young "Sun King," depicted in a ballet in which he performed as the sun. (Bibliothèque Nationale de France)

largely Copernican Elizabethan world, made his dazzled Romeo utter unforgettably, "Juliet is the Sun." Juliet was, of course nothing like a massive and distant gaseous inferno. Yet Juliet was like the sun: she irresistibly attracted her suitor and was the center of his universe, and she radiated heat and light that nourished Romeo's inner being. Shakespeare's famous four words teach us much, perhaps everything about what Juliet meant to Romeo. They also instruct us about the most common concept of the sun king. Depicting kings (and Juliet) as what they were not (the sun) told contemporaries exactly what they were.

Louis XIV of France is the most recognizable instance of a sun king, an image he consciously cultivated from his youth. Yet Louis was only one among a string of European sovereigns who promoted a solar image. Strong monarchs, who throughout early modernity were understood to be the embodiment of their respective states (Louis XIV's *l'état c'est moi* being the bluntest manifestation of this notion), were thus conveniently depicted as suns.[10] Across the continent, European kings were presented as majestic, aloof, and powerful suns. Reigning through a revamped doctrine of divine right, kings cultivated their image as glowing suns inherent to the cosmo-political order.

Englishmen were actively deploying comparable astronomical—if not always solar—language as early as the sixteenth century. To take another Shakespearean example, the playwright represented Henry V, a medieval English king, as "[t]his star of England" (Henry V, epilogue). Elizabeth I (1533–1603), widely recognized as Astraea, the "star-maiden" daughter of Zeus, was remarkably rendered on the frontispiece of John Case's *Sphaera civitatis* (The spheres of the government [1588]), a commentary on Aristotle's *Politics*. The representation shows the Virgin Queen presiding majestically over the spheres of a (still) Ptolemaic universe, each sphere hosting and representing Elizabeth's moral and political virtues.[11] Like a harmonious planetary system, the monarchical political structure would remain harmonious as long as established hierarchies, or "spheres," were maintained. With a solid tradition of representations of English monarchs through celestial qualities, it comes as no surprise that decades before Louis XIV became identified as the Sun King, the image was already familiar in Britain. It was lavished, for example, on James VI on his progress southward from Scotland in 1603 to become James I of England, in succession to Elizabeth, acting out the role of "the new sun after the old one's death."[12]

Old Regime political cultures mobilized anthropomorphic readings of the sun, which by the late seventeenth century was surpassing the earth in contemporaries' minds as the center of the solar system, if not the universe. The sun, a central, massive, radiating body constituting the center and fulcrum of a planetary "system," attracted, repelled, and presumably controlled other lesser bodies. Such understandings easily lent themselves to majestic readings, in which a luminous and dominant planet became the monarchical pivot around which many other planets, representing in the political imagination the various parts of a nation, revolved. The solar image positioned the king, according to the historian James Daly, as the source of human comfort, the body politic's *primum*

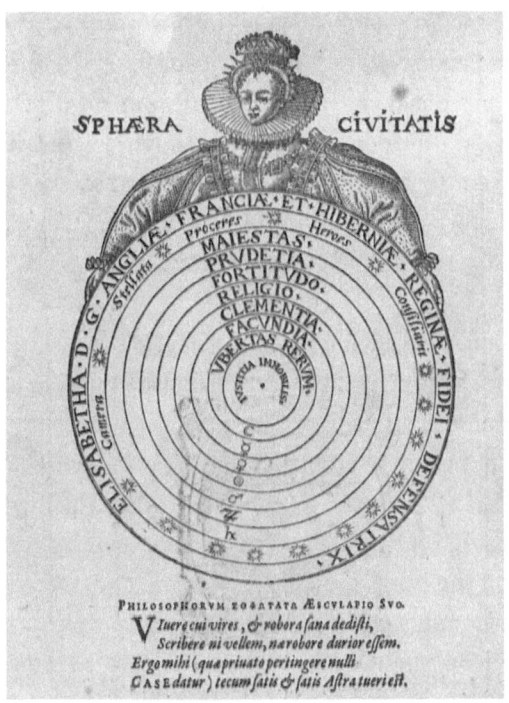

FIGURE 10. The title page of John Case's *Sphaera civitatis*, 1588.

mobile; all other authorities were inferior orbs, while "there was a high premium on each political or social entity minding its own business and respecting the rights of the others." Here was yet another benefit of the celestial imagery: Like a harmonious planetary system, the monarchical political structure would remain harmonious as long as established hierarchies, or "spheres," were maintained. Centuries later, revolutionary Americans would resort to comparable reasoning, albeit with a marked republican accent.[13]

Isaac Newton's laws of physics, of gravity as a universal force in particular, were steadily disseminated after their conception in the *annus mirabilis* of 1666. Gravity as a universal inverse-square force was revolutionary, not for answering why an apple should fall from a tree on the head of a natural philosopher but specifically for explaining the wondrous mathematically predictable orbits of the planets. The force of gravity clarified why bodies were attracted to the center of the earth. But it also explained how, while each star had its own gravity, all bodies attracted each other with respect to their masses; that was why the planets, the earth among them, held to their orbits. In Newton's own words, he "deduced that the forces which keep the planets in their orbs must [be] reciprocally as the squares of their distances from the centers about which they revolve."[14] Newton's ideas diffused far and deep in tandem with the progress of the eighteenth century, and with "the transformation ... complete in northern and western Europe," mechanically based science "had left the hands of its first crusaders and visionaries and gone into the everyday language."[15]

With the sun acting as a common balancing center for the solar system, the metaphor of sun kings gained further vigor: Planetary monarchs were not seen merely as the fiery center of a solar political system but as holding a complex order in harmony and balance.[16] Hence, after the displacement of the Stuarts in the "Glorious Revolution" (1688), the new monarchs were commemorated on medals and coins representing on one side their profiles and on the other a radiating, central sun. By the second half of the eighteenth century, the attribution of solar properties to the Hanoverian monarchs, who came to rule Britain after 1714, became routine.

Even on the periphery of Western civilization, American colonials commonly addressed the sun in kingly terms, such as "Day's Monarch," while others referred to its "royal pomp." Some concluded that the sun was a "glitt'ring monarch," and, even more impressively, "a sovereign ... accompanied with [its] planetary Equipage."[17] Decades later, at the turn of the eighteenth-century United States, the sun could still be described in terms of power politics: "the dread sovereign of a thousand orb ... who keeps each planet in its proper place." In the early nineteenth century, poets still mused how the sun shined "with undiminish'd flame, And rule[d] diurnal skies."[18] As early Americans looked to the skies and identified human attributes in a celestial body, their expressions were in line with a tradition as old as recorded history. But it was specific to an age that witnessed repeated claims by kings to absolute monarchical power that the sun was seen as a supreme monarch.

Much of English as well as colonial North Americans' metaphorical use of the sun to describe their monarchs rested on the solar qualities of dominance, heat, and light. These properties were repeatedly associated with the sun, with monarchs imagined as dominating and central while

FIGURE 11. Both sides of a medal depicting the profile of William III (1689–1702) and an image of the sun under the motto "I shall not deviate." (Private collection)

blazing and glittering as they distributed their sunny qualities among their earthly subjects. These Copernican aspects of the image of the sun king ("Copernican" due to their representation of a massive body dominating a system, whether planetary or political, through its sheer size and location), emphasized the monarch's centrality, potency, and indeed indispensability. These Copernican attributes of the sun king would never disappear. Yet by the eighteenth century, a novel Newtonian layer of meaning was added to this already powerful image. Newtonian language induced a new array of monarchical images that consisted of predictable orbits prescribed by the king and harmonic spherical movement of the different elements of the body politic.

The celestial image of the Hanoverian kings, who came to rule Britain after 1714, reflected the novel scientific notions of the eighteenth century. Specifically, the image responded to the post-Newtonian view of the universe as a perfectly predictable machine, the "clockwork universe" discussed in chapter 1. The British king could now be seen as situated at the center of a Newtonian universe, a political sun that had no need to coerce his planetary subjects, who were rather swayed by the power of his monarchical gravitational force.[19] Newtonianism came into play between the metaphorical and the concrete: Were humans attracted to each other according to the same laws that attracted celestial bodies to each other? Did colonies revolve around the mother country as a satellite spun around its primary planet? Or, rather, was this mode of thought merely a useful analogy? While the answer may have changed from author to speaker to

From the Sun King to Republican Solar Systems

audience, by the second half of the eighteenth century this Newtonian mode of analysis was becoming ever more popular and colloquial.

The popular celestial images of English kings did much to articulate the constricted nature of constitutional monarchy: even solar kings were held to universal laws that checked their actions and balanced the harmony of the political universe. It was Lord Bolingbroke in the first half of the eighteenth century who explained this view in the most detailed way, declaring that the monarch "can move no longer in another orbit from his people, and, like some superior planet, attract, repel, influence, and direct their motions by his own. He and they are parts of the same system, intimately joined and co-operating together, acting and acted upon."[20] Hence, while Newtonianism seemed to ensure kingly harmony and predictability in the political system, it was also helpful in undermining the figure of an omnipotent sun ruler.[21]

By the mid-eighteenth century. the New Science had seeped into everyday discourse. With the intuitive belief in the immobility of the earth eroding, and the counterintuitive belief in its circling of the sun quickly gaining ground, journalists, learned societies, coffeehouse-goers, and public lecturers all spoke differently about the physical world that they inhabited.[22] While the application of the Newtonian cosmos to politics was an important aspect of the eighteenth-century planetary discourse, the heliocentric Copernican foundation (the sun as central, massive, and dominant) of that language remained significant. The inherent tensions between a heliocentric image of the sun ruler as the quintessence of his system and a constricted Newtonian sun king would characterize Enlightenment-era descriptions of and appeals to British monarchs. The Copernican and Newtonian qualities of the planetary political world could, however, complement each other, as the monarch was represented as a radiating, nourishing, and life-giving ruler (hence underscoring his heliocentric or Copernican qualities), who presided over a harmonious and mechanical (and thus Newtonian) system, which he balanced. Even after the loss of the Continental colonies, the monarch could still be seen in England as a "glittering orb" around which aspirants "ambitiously revolve . . . [as they] gravitate to royalty." Ambitious contenders for royal patronage, as commentators on the upper echelons of the British court noted, "as all the minuter luminaries [who] gravitate to the sun in our solar system," wished to "feel their colors brighter ... when a ray of favor falls upon them."[23]

Perhaps because Americans resided on the periphery of the British solar system, and were thus not exposed to the human presence of the king, they accepted this image eagerly. In a study of monarchism in colonial America, the historian Brendan McConville has identified and contextualized the specific solar imagery that the Hanoverian monarchs elicited with increasing frequency early in George II's (1727–1760) reign. That language was particularly popular in British North America among colonials who were, ironically, much warmer toward their distant monarchs and lacked the English indifference to the German-born Hanoverians who had never visited America. From early in the Hanoverian reign, Americans, although rarely referring to their sovereigns directly as "sun kings," repeatedly addressed their distant British monarchs in indisputably solar and celestial terms. Early in the eighteenth century a Bostonian cleric declared that royal rulers were "lights that are set on High" who "must approve themselves fixed in their Orb & move like the Sun, who as a Gyant runs his race & nothing can turn him aside."[24] The Georges were deemed "shining sovereigns" spreading their "superior rays," and described as "glittering princes" crowned with "celestial bright" gliding "thro' shining worlds" to govern "Britannia's ruling court."[25] The solar image also implied, however, that as with all good things, too much sun was harmful; as a mid-eighteenth-century Briton, most likely thinking of Louis XIV, the French Sun King, pointed out: "the human eye, is not more incapable of enduring the dazzling Lustre of the Sun, than the Heart of Man, the bewitching Charms of despotic Sovereignty."[26] Such language reflected back to the sun, which could now be understood in anthropomorphic and overtly political terms as a "sovereign ... accompanied with [its] planetary Equipage." Colonial Americans, like their European counterparts, were to such an extent habituated to use the sun to describe and identify kingship, that that dominant star itself was now seen through a political heliocentric prism as a "glitt'ring monarch."[27] So powerful was that image that even decades after the rejection of monarchy and the creation of an American republic, Americans could still describe the sun in ostensibly monarchical terms, moving "in his diurnal course, in all the pride of light ... the dread sovereign of a thousand orbs."[28]

By the second half of the eighteenth century, the solar identification of the British king had become a commonplace in the North American colonies. Reflecting on his upbringing in the 1750s and 1760s, Benjamin Rush reminisced how he had "been taught to consider [kings] nearly as essential to political order as the Sun is to the order of our Solar system."[29] Victories in the French and Indian War after 1759 and the death of George II in 1760 elicited a particularly meaningful flurry of analogies of the British king to the sun. The string of British victories in Canada evoked analogies between "Sol [who] the glorious Sight displays, / With rising Beams with setting Rays," and the British monarch, who "the conquering Scepter sways." Upon his death, George II was portrayed in Newtonian terms as a shining "star ... [moving] in his own sphere."[30] The wartime accession of George III (1760) could thus be described as the crowning of a shining star: "all the Skies tempestuous Clouds deform, / With brighter Radiance cron'd, the God of Day, / Clears the thick Storm, and chases night away." George III was, in short, "Britannia's Sun, [who] thro' the Gloom, appears" to lighten British "Hearts, and dissipate[] our Fears."[31] The second and third British Hanoverian kings were widely seen by their American subjects as "Georgian Sun[s] ... The happiest Light that e'er on *Britain* shone." But if these monarchs were widely perceived in their American colonies as "Georgian Suns," they were not perceived as sun kings on the model of their absolutist French rivals. As opposed to their English counterparts, the popish suns across the Channel were deemed coercive and encroaching, not able to draw and hold their subjects through their benevolence like the Hanoverians.[32]

Even after Parliament passed the Townshend Acts in 1767 and the struggle between Westminster and the colonies was raging, American prints continued to depict "a Monarch glowing with youth," who is "like the ray of morning which shoots forth to dispel ... night."[33] As late as 1769, with imperial tensions running high, a New Yorker used the solar image prescriptively, pointing out that a "monarch, like the sun, should shine on all." In their North American colonies the English kings stood, as McConville observed, like benevolent suns at the center of the British universe: Protestant, restrained, rational, and liberty-loving. American colonists, McConville concluded, believed that Britons across the empire were drawn to their kings' orbit through "love and affection, the human form of Newton's gravity."[34]

After 1776 the metaphor of the sun king would be completely revolutionized, with the Copernican view applying not to the British king but rather to America itself, rising "like the meridian sun, which shines ... brilliant & glorious."[35] With political and constitutional power shifting away from the Crown toward elective institutions throughout the British Empire, "crowned heads and privileged orders" would be seen after the Revolution and in a thoroughly republican United States as "passing clouds in our [republican] political firmament," that could "only exist in the sunshine of royalty."[36] A brave new republican world, which would carry over but reorient the heliocentric and Newtonian attributes of the king and his Old Regime entourage, was about to emerge.

The tense years leading to Independence witnessed attempts to rearrange and rationalize the empire, and some Englishmen, such as, for example, the anonymous author of a published letter to Dr. Tucker in London, were willing to propose that the colonies be represented in the House of Commons. Presumably, such a move would have made each colony a de facto "little empire within itself, subject to its own laws, and obedient to its own regulations." The letter's author described these proposed mini-empires in a now familiar image: "a smaller system in the construction of the universe, that whilst it seems only to regard its own center, is actuated by that common principle that sustains the whole, which whilst it regulates all the motions peculiar to that system, at the same time makes us subservient to a higher scheme and bends it about one common centre, where Great Britain is placed with power and dignity to controul the whole." Just as planets controlled their compact system of moons and were controlled by larger systems, thus would colonies maintain an autonomy that would be curbed by a looming British sun.[37]

No one grappled more with the unraveling of the British North American Empire through the solar metaphor than former Massachusetts Governor Thomas Pownall (1722–1805). Pownall's descriptions of the empire as a planetary system reflected the changing times, but his adjustments of the metaphor to explain the newly forming balance of power demonstrated a political imagination remarkably flexible. In 1764, a year before the opening of the contest between the metropole and the colonies that would lead to Independence, Pownall described the British Empire as a celestial system in which colonies orbited in their "proper sphere," receiving their "political motion" from "the first mover (the government of Great Britain)." In this representation, the British government has replaced the king as the system's center, reflecting the change in the contemporary British balance of power between Parliament and king. It was now an impersonal administration that was, like the sun, "the center of attraction, to which these colonies ... must tend."[38] A decade later, as the colonies were asserting their will in opposition to their British lords, Pownall asserted (in 1774, the same year in which the aforementioned letter to Dr. Tucker was published), "the center of power, instead of remaining fixed as it now is in Great Britain, will, as the magnitude of the power and the interest of the Colonies increases, be drawn out from the island." This effect of the drawing out of power from the British Isles reflected the fact that in politics, as well as in demographic and economic principles as the case of the British Empire seemed to prove, operated "the same laws of nature, analogous in all cases, by which the center of gravity in the solar system, now near the surface of the sun, would, by an encrease of the quantity of matter in the planets, be drawn out beyond the surface." Pownall continued to describe America's growing influence in explicitly astronomical terms, of a planet's swelling mass: The "center of gravity in the [British] solar system, now near the surface of the [English] sun, would, by an encrease ... the quantity of matter in the [American] planets."[39] In the years leading to the Revolution, American Patriots would become adept at mobilizing celestial imagery in their political rhetoric.

Only a few years later, with the former colonies now an independent Union of states, Pownall described the young United States in similar planetary terms: a "new system of power, moving round its own proper centre ... founded in nature ... growing, by accelerated motions into a great and powerful empire." Once more the image was unambiguously planetary: The American Congress was "a new primary planet, which, taking its course in its own orbit, must have an effect upon the orbit of every other planet, and shift the common centre of gravity of the whole system of the European world."[40] After the long and bloody War of Independence that resulted in separation from the mother country, commentators in America continued to frame the British Empire in similar terms: "his Britannick Majesty," an observer in New York complained, intended "to plant Lunar colonies [in Port Roseway, Canada] with the American Loyalists . . . expect[ing] to live and view all the planets, with their satellites; under the British dominion."[41]

While Britain could still be represented as a solar system in which the king was the sun, the republican political revolution that swept America entailed an intellectual transformation. When that transformation was complete, Americans would no longer read the skies as a realm of hierarchical subservience to a solar monarch; they would read the cosmos as manifesting starry republican egalitarianism. With a rich planetary discourse pervading the public sphere, American revolutionaries even before Independence began to adopt the images of a solar system for explaining the transformations that their political structure was undergoing. Revolution itself was, of course, an astronomical concept originally derived from the cycles of the heavenly bodies. It was Copernicus's model of the circular movements of celestial bodies, according to Reinhart Koselleck, that "opened the way for the concept of revolution which entered politics." The adaptation and confluence of the celestial and the human, of astronomy and politics, in late eighteenth-century America rested on the idea that while human societies, like the numerous stars in space, fluxed in "seeming wildness," both were "governed and directed" by laws, physical or human.[42]

As Americans were debating independence in the early months of 1776, a cautious author in the *Connecticut Courant* warned his compatriots of the dangers of premature separation from the British Empire. Unlike the harmony that a Newtonian universe promised, "the colonies would be like so many balls in the air," he warned, "without any earthly power over them, or bond of union to connect them, or any solid foundation underneath, to support and uphold them." The American colonies were not ordinary "balls" but rather "planets in their natural orbits" that must adhere to "articles of confederation, a political sun that answered the same purpose in the political, as the centripetal force in the solar system."[43] Here is an early expression of a mode of analyzing American politics that would become common in the decades to come: the metaphor of the American (yet-to-be) states as planets that interacted both with each other and their common, sunlike, constitutional center. No harmonious existence awaited the American confederation—still thought of as a loosely knit league of independent polities—should it not act "naturally" before securing an "earthly power" to "support and uphold" the parts that composed it. If they waited patiently, however, this commentator in the *Courant* believed that the situation would change. Articles of confederation "formed and solemnly ratified and confirmed by all the colonies, as the bond of their union and basis of their government," would create a different, harmonious political cosmos. Such articles would "answer the same purpose in the political, as the centripetal force in the solar system," the commentator argued. Like the centripetal force that "preserve[d] the planets in their natural orbits and prevent[ed] their flying off in excentric courses," so would timely and thoughtful articles of confederation bind the colonies and cause them to coalesce. Balance, order, and stability presented as the ideal of this cosmic idiom, while chaos and confusion were the dangers it helped to define. In this particular case, constitutions would act as a physical power in revolutionary America to hold the state-planets together, as the laws of nature of Newton and the laws of republics of Machiavelli would seamlessly regulate the worlds of physical and political bodies.

Thomas Paine, arguably more responsible than anyone else for steering the American public toward Independence, concluded the imperial phase of the planetary image with these famous words: "In no instance hath nature made the satellite larger than its primary planet, and as England and America . . . reverses the common order of nature, it is evident they belong to different systems."[44] The sun and common celestial center, Paine starkly pointed out, could no longer be located in England; rather, a new dawn was rising on a new American planetary system.

That the planetary metaphor would evolve from its early modern royal and Copernican origins to serve a modern federal and republican world of meaning may seem obvious in retrospect, but it was in no sense inevitable. Yet after 1776 many citizens of the young Union of American states adopted the view of their new political universe as a solar system. Consequently, Americans debated, explained, and made sense of their polity through planetary images that primed their opinions and beliefs regarding the "naturalness," and thus the legitimacy, of their republic. In the face of a range of changing issues and a dynamic set of contexts, the identification of similarities between the United States and a solar system maintained its basic facets, namely a controlling (if at times overbearing) center and the bodies over which it ruled (who would regularly seek their autonomy).

In a world less saturated by media than our own, banknotes and coins provided revolutionary Americans with an important opportunity to represent graphically their new political creation, the United States. Revolutionary money wore many shapes and forms, but one image that emerged in 1776 stood out in particular: Paper notes of fractional denominations bore the image of thirteen rings forming an endless chain (figs. 12 and 13), an image that would appear once more after the Revolution on a commemorative European medallion.[45] The spherical discs obviously stood for the thirteen newly created states, and the fact that they were linked together suggested the firmness of the newly forged Union. At the center stood a celestial image, a blazing solar depiction of the American Congress.[46] Similar textual representations became common as, in the following decades, public speakers habitually described the Union in terms of "a constellation of free states, with no public force, but public opinion,–moving by well-regulated law, each in its own proper orbit, around the brighter star in Washington"; with the federal republic "the sun in the centre, and . . . revolving planets on their errands."[47] Accordingly, generations of Americans drew their understanding of their political universe through the imagination of states, institutions, and parties, as planetary bodies participating in a system they thought of as "solar."

When a revolutionary commentator remarked in the fateful year of Independence that, although "the Sun might seem, to admiring mortals below [as] the grand monarch of the heavenly bodies," the skies in fact hosted "other suns and other worlds innumerable," it was evident that the political image of the solar system had crossed the republican Rubicon. If the skies manifested numerous republican solar systems, then the sun, and suns in general, should in fact "be considered as *Presidents*,

FIGURE 12. Continental one-third of a dollar. (Courtesy of the Colonial Williamsburg Foundation)

FIGURE 13. Contemporary commemorative medallion. (Courtesy of the Colonial Williamsburg Foundation)

not *Monarchs.*" These solar presidents presided through principles of "perfect equality," and "gravitat[ed] towards each other, with wonderful adjustment, mutually attracted and mutually repelled."[48] This idea that a republican solar system was benevolent and benign, not monarchically coercive, was expressed graphically during the revolutionary years, in the likes of the abovementioned paper money and other insignia. The

FIGURE 14. The Cowpens Flag, 1781. (Redrawn by Nat Case)

Cowpens Flag, to take another example, was one of several star-spangled patterns for the new American flag. Since the Flag Act that the Continental Congress passed in 1777 did not specify a particular star pattern for the thirteen stars, several competing designs emerged. The American flag would eventually convey a constellational, and thus nonplanetary, model of the American federation (see chapter 3). Within this process of the formation of the Star-Spangled Banner, the Cowpens Flag thus signifies a link in the transformation from a solar to a constellational model for the American flag. On the Cowpens Flag, which was famously carried during its namesake battle (1781) by the Third Maryland Regiment, twelve states were represented by stars revolving around a thirteenth central star. Tellingly, the central star (presumably standing for Maryland but potentially representing any state) was an indistinguishable five-point star similar to the rest of the constellation depicted. In the Cowpens design, while the central body was still distinct by virtue of its pivotal position, it was nevertheless an equal star among celestial peers, no longer a domineering sun.

Even before Independence, America was likened to a sun, "which shines more brilliant and glorious after it had been veiled in clouds."[49] Pre-Independence America was a Copernican sun, analyzed in terms of its centrality, not yet Newtonian, understood as a restraining mass through the power of gravity. The expanding astronomical knowledge almost immediately impacted the language of political astronomy. Hence, in the years following Independence the new American "system of power" could be seen like the recently discovered Uranus—"a new primary planet" that was "moving round its own proper centre." The nexus of kings, stars, and revolution was not lost on American commentators, who remarked sarcastically that "when George the IIId lost the United States, he was compensated by the discovery of the Georgian Sidus, by Herschel." Astronomical discovery would continue to echo in the rhetoric of Britons such as Edmund Burke, who saw "the appearance of a new state . . . in a new part of the globe . . . [that] has made as great a change in all the relations, and balances, and gravitation of power, as the appearance of a new planet would in the system of our solar world."[50]

The decades following the creation of the United States witnessed the proliferation of political astronomy in different occasions and contexts. For example, a Fourth of July toast printed in the *Richmond Enquirer* commended "the Statesmen and Soldiers of the Revolution: The Planets and Suns which wheeled unshaken through the firmament of Freedom."[51] However, the most common mode of describing the American Union by far was through depicting the American states as planets revolving around a federal sun. Such a presentation enabled and channeled the discussion toward the analysis of the Union in terms of attraction and repulsion, of gravitation and balance. While such language was almost by definition partisan, politicians, commentators, public speakers, and authors regardless of political persuasion would marvel throughout the first half of the nineteenth century at the "constellation of free states, with no public force . . . moving by well-regulated law, each in its own proper orbit, around the brighter star in Washington." This "glorious" federalism was analogous to the "beautiful display of infinite wisdom, that fixed the sun in the centre," with its "revolving planets" orbiting harmoniously. Americans would never lose track of the fact that the immense magnitude and breathtaking exactness of the astronomical model made one feel "an overpowering sense of the wisdom and glory of Jehova!"[52]

The allocation of power and autonomy within the federal structure, and the boundaries between the state-planets and the federal sun—arguably the most contentious political issue in pre–Civil War America—stood at the core of the Newtonian solar interpretation. Even before the Constitutional Convention of 1787, prominent citizens such as Noah Webster proposed a federalism of sorts, in which states would, "as bodies politic . . . [be] sovereign and independent [but] as members of a large community . . . mere subjects." To clarify his plan, Webster explained its resemblance to "the harmony of nature in the planetary system." Like the planets that "govern their secondary planets, and at the same time, are governed by the sun," the American states would be simultaneously governors and "mere subjects." Webster further suggested that a duality of sovereignty and subjecthood was endemic to the animal world, and thus an American political system that reflected such a hierarchy would create a harmonious and thus natural system, while its failure would generate chaos.[53] In the numerous subsequent discussions regarding the distribution of political power and sovereignty between the states and the federal government, spanning the decades that followed the creation of the American republic, such views assisted those engaged in this conversation to think through and express their views.

With the conception and inception of a more centralized Union in 1787, the image of the American states as planets and the Union as a solar system was now configured to make sense of and articulate the federal novelty. The Constitutional Convention was symbolically presided over by the retired General Washington, who sat throughout the proceedings on a massive armchair with a gilded half sun at its top. Upon the successful conclusion of the Convention, James Madison reported Benjamin Franklin as saying, "I have often looked at that behind the president without being able to tell whether it was rising or setting. But now I . . . know that it is a rising . . . sun."[54] Franklin's now famous remark, hinting that the United States was a sun rising to greatness, is particularly telling in context, as it came after prominent delegates repeatedly clashed during the sessions over the meaning of the solar image of the American Union: while John Dickinson, presenting the Anti-Federalist view, "compared the proposed National System to the Solar System, in which the States were the planets and ought to be left to move freely in their proper orbits," James Madison quipped that the proposed federation should "controul the centrifugal tendency of the States." While their political views clashed, both statesmen agreed on the validity of the "illustrations borrowed from the planetary system" (Madison), and more precisely on the similarity of the "proposed National System to the Solar System, in which the States were the planets" (Dickinson). They disagreed, however, over the balancing of the centrifugal and centripetal forces acting on the states; the question was how to keep them from "flying out of their proper orbits and destroy[ing] the order and harmony of the political system."[55] As John Adams put it,

America needed a constitution that would control "those attractions and repulsions, by which the balance of nature is preserved . . . [similar to the way] by which the heavenly bodies are continued in their orbits."[56] With these images galvanized during the drafting of the Constitution, public speakers communicated over the following decades the widely accepted notion that "the constitution is the sun of the political system, around which all legislative, executive, and judicial bodies must revolve."[57]

The solar-political image was not rigid, however, and the Constitution was not by any stretch the only institution or object that could serve in this trope as a system-controlling sun. The federal Union itself was regularly described as a system of planets, each with an allotted degree of autonomy ("orbit"), which interacted with other sister planets (by "attracting" and "repelling"), keeping the system intact ("in balanced and harmonious equilibrium") as long as each held to its proper designated conduct ("sphere"). Antebellum commentators believed that the Union acted as a political sun, pointing out that, just as there was a "point within the sun's disk, where if the eye could be placed it would see the planetary world revolving above a common centre, with the most perfect order and harmony," so a similar idea presented itself in the United States, where "the several states mov[ed] on quietly in their orbits."[58] Such images suggested, either implicitly or explicitly, that the Union itself functioned as a sun for the republic. Apparently, it became most useful for contemporaries to understand the distant federal government as a sublime and well-balanced construct, acting as a central sun that preserved and sustained the political firmament. By creating a system in which states moved in their "own proper orbit, around the brighter star in Washington," the creators of the harmonious American system of government may indeed seemed to have acted, in the words of Thomas Jefferson, as "demigods."[59]

Solar understandings of the United States were particularly useful for a federation plagued from the start by faction and threats of disunion.[60] To picture the novel Union of states as harmonious suggested not only that the Union functioned properly but also that it was "natural" and thus fundamentally true. The nexus of harmony, political truth, and legitimacy explains why the image of states as constituting "bright orbs" in a political firmament controlled by a "bright sun," revolving peacefully in a "prescribed course, attracting and attracted, giving and receiving light" would become so common, and thus presumably useful, in antebellum America.[61] Even on the verge of the dissolution of the Union in late 1860, a Virginian commentator attempted to explain his state's (still) neutral position in relation to the secession movement by articulating the image. Virginians, this author wrote, wished the Old Dominion to remain "an independent planet"; they wanted their state to "have an orbit of her own ... not to gravitate towards New York away from Alabama, nor towards Alabama away from New York. If any gravitation is to be done let it be done towards her, or let the existing attractions maintain the present orbits." In fact, the relation of the various states as late as the winter of 1860 seemed the best that could be devised, since if the system were to be disturbed, through coercion or secession, each state would "fly to no calculation can foresee. First one and then another of these orderly stars will 'shoot madly from its sphere.' Confusion will be general—the ruin common."[62]

Americans of the early republic tended to idealize their Union by describing the American states as "primary planets, co-ordinate and co-eternal—they will revolve ... for ever, under the influence of moral attraction, round the common centers of union and happiness." However, unable and unwilling to ignore the disharmony and conflict that characterized the period's politics, they elaborated tactics involving political astronomy to make sense out of those tensions. They could, for example, praise and embrace discord by claiming that "the voice of the American people" was "sometime like the thunder, sometimes the music of the spheres." Alluding to celestial phenomena that were either violent and menacing or that signaled the underlying harmony in the structure of the universe reassured people that the seemingly unruly and intractable republic's behavior was "natural" and thus good, or at least acceptable. Another, much more popular tactic was that which Senator (and later President) John Tyler of Virginia took to the Senate's floor in 1833. Within the context of South Carolina's threats of secession from the Union over the "tariff of abominations," Tyler lengthily described to his fellow senators "that beautiful [federal] system, which, if truly carried out, was calculated to render us the happiest and most powerful people on the face of the earth," and went on to compare it to the solar system: "It was

From the Sun King to Republican Solar Systems

the sun . . . the Federal Government . . . giving light, heat, and attraction to the planets revolving round it, in their proper orbits. No two could come in contact with each other; they rolled on in ceaseless splendour." This ideal portrayal came, however, with a stark warning. The perfect state could be preserved only conditionally, "*so long* as they preserved the course pointed out by the constitution."⁶³ Cosmo-political harmony came with a clear threat of anarchy.

Yet decades before the Union's ultimate test (and temporary dissolution) in the era of the Civil War, the image of the United States as solar system had been required to accommodate the addition of new planets to its cosmo-political structure, as new states were carved out of the Western territories and incorporated into the United States. Such an expansion had the potential to unbalance a congruous system, offsetting its center of gravity and thus ruining its delicate equilibrium. Contemporary astronomical discoveries proved, however, that expansion of the solar system itself was not outlandish: Contemporaries witnessed the discovery of Uranus in 1781, enlarging the number of planets to seven, and Neptune was sighted in 1846, making an eighth planet. Hence, as new states were incorporated into the Union, contemporaries effortlessly described them, too, as "luminous orbs," ascending to take their station and revolve "in that vacant part of space" (whether it be terrestrial or cosmic) in the West. The two trans-Appalachian states of Kentucky and Ohio, in particular, were seen as "producing, out of their bowels, a new world, with a complete planetary system and all its necessary appendages." Hovering around the American Union, which functioned as a "political sun," each new state seemed a new world unto itself, which brought forth its own satellites in the form of "a moon, and all its planetary system, complete." Although harmony and the permanency of the universe were not settled matters, such a political cosmology could accommodate the United States' growth through the prism of Herschel's popular theory of cosmic evolution. Like the early nineteenth-century cosmos, these new planetary structures would keep "moving with the most perfect regularity and good order, in their own proper sphere."⁶⁴ As the Union kept expanding, contemporaries made similar reflections about the correlations of their federal structure with the complex and magnificent planetary construct. Characteristically, with the admission of Michigan and Arkansas in 1836, toasts were raised to the "[n]ew planets in our political firmament—may the sun of Democracy continue to be surrounded by satellites of their order and brilliancy."⁶⁵

As should by now be clear, it was common from the creation of the United States to the Civil War era to view the Union, which often stood as a metonym for the American government or the United States itself, as a political sun. In the words of a pseudonymous Virginian author, "the Union like the sun" cherished and preserved "a whole planetary system."⁶⁶ No one expressed this notion better than the commentator who described the Union as the "sun in the centre," around which revolved the state "planets."⁶⁷ Others regularly referred to variants of "this Federal Sun," and "the sun of our Union," while some saw "the Government of the United States" as occupying "the same relation towards the States that the sun does towards the solar system; that is, the centre of gravitation."⁶⁸ Significantly, references occasionally evoked pre-Newtonian Copernican notions, especially when uttered in times of crisis. For a Tennessee senator who opposed secession in late 1860, the political sun's nourishing and life-giving gifts to the republic were imperative: "Our Federal Union is the sun in our political firmament, diffusing warmth, prosperity, and happiness from the Atlantic to the Pacific, and shedding light throughout the world."⁶⁹ The continuities and adaptability of such democratic and republican speech with a language that had evolved in an unequivocally monarchical culture are remarkable. The European sun king, the alpha and omega of the Old Regime, was reborn and refitted in America as a federal sun.

This well-developed planetary discourse was not monolithic, nor were its parameters entirely stable. For some it was the president who acted as the sun, while cabinet secretaries were destined, "like satellites, to illumine & aid their [presidential] primary Planet."⁷⁰ A more common view was that the Constitution functioned as the American sun. Even before Independence, a commentator wished for a constitution "which would answer the same purpose in the political, as the centripetal force in the solar system," and thus "preserve the planets in the their natural orbits and prevent their flying off in excentric courses."⁷¹ Similar rhetoric would resonate for decades, as with the congressman from North Carolina who pointed out in 1814 that "the constitution is the sun of the political system, around which all legislative, executive and judicial bodies must revolve."[72] When in 1833 a legislator from Pennsylvania characteristically named the Constitution "the sun . . . of our political firmament," he embellished the image, adding that the laws were the "moon" and the policies the "stars" of the Union.[73] Many would thus have agreed that a successful constitutional sun would enable the united states to revolve "like the solar spheres, harmoniously in their constitutional orbits."[74] Permanently lurking behind such wishful thoughts was the danger of a disharmonious cosmos of discord and strife, one that corresponded with the actual American political universe.

The planetary metaphor was a powerful heuristic instrument for exploring the political world, and as such extended beyond the image of the American states as planets revolving around a constitutional sun. The understanding of federalism itself as functioning as a sun was long-lasting. For many decades after the republic's creation, federalism still presented "the grandest and most sublime effort of the human genius on the subject of government," and was still analyzed in terms of "the Federal and State Governments in their respective proportions and divisions of powers moving harmoniously in their respective orbits . . . [in a] plan . . . most beautiful and well ordered."[75] Summoning the "sun of federalism" that sets "above the political horizon . . . to give ever lasting light to the United States" became a common way to talk about the American Union and its government.[76]

As soon as the federal Constitution was introduced to the states for ratification in late 1787, partisans elaborated on variants and alternatives to the Union-as-sun. The sun was not a fixed variable, as evidenced by a proponent who remarked that, while the Union functioned as "the sun, cherishing and preserving a whole planetary system," the suggested federal judiciary branch (as opposed to a state) would act as a "satellite waiting upon its proper planet."[77] Years later, a South Carolinian presented a scheme in which the judicial branch itself would function as a solar fulcrum: "Like the Sun, which by its superior powers, keeps the planets in their Orbits, the Federal Judiciary will be competent to keep the Legislature and Judiciary of their state in their proper sphere."[78] Whether the judiciary was seen as a satellite or a sun in its own right, contemporaries obviously explored schemes that went beyond the state-federal government solar paradigm.

That observers extended the planetary image in imaginative ways underscores its continuing appeal and usefulness. The clashes of the Jacksonian era provided additional opportunities to test the limits of the spheres of influence and of the orbiting American bodies politic. Collisions between the revolving planet-states could be avoided, according to a joint statement of the chairman and secretary of the Democratic-Republicans of Plymouth, New Hampshire, as long as state and federal governments were "confined to [their] orbit, and acted within [their] own sphere." However, collisions happened, and remedies, such as nullification, seemed worse than the transgression. If only "the action of the general government be confined to its own orbit, in accordance to the exalted sentiment of General Jackson," such collisions could be avoided.[79] During the Bank Wars, a Southern critic likened state banks to orbs, which should be "limited in [their] sphere, revolving in a confined circle." In such a view, what was "deficient in the moneyed system of America" was a "common centre, to which each State institution may gravitate, though revolving in its own appropriate orbit." Not to leave such an articulation ambiguous as to its astronomical source, this critic asserted that "we need a common [financial] sun, around which the minor satellites may revolve in all the harmony of the solar system."[80] When times got tough, even a federal bank could be a sun, proving that astral constriction and autonomy were relevant in realms beyond the narrowly defined "political."

In a remarkable speech, Virginian Speaker of the U.S. House of Representatives (and future U.S. Supreme Court Justice) Philip P. Barbour (1783–1841), further articulated the solar metaphor to expound on the working of the American system of government. Praising President Jackson for vetoing the Bank Charter, the Speaker, in a speech in Amherst Courthouse, expressed the hope that "each and every department, in our complex Constitutional System, shall move in its respective orbit, and thus each perform its allotted part towards the fulfillment of the great purpose of the creation of all—national strength cemented by national harmony." Barbour's orbital and spherical logic was grounded in a world of planetary motion, made clear by the Speaker's confident hope that the federal legislature take "its position in the political firmament, by the side of the Federal executive, [and] shall with that body, constitute a constellation, to which . . . we shall look to guide our course."[81] Once more, the impression of political movement around a solar center enabled contemporaries to concretize political abstraction through planetary images of interaction in a man-made firmament. It enabled them to place their faith in a system "holding so many lights [in its] political firmament" that, "should any particular one attempt to mislead by an undue brightness, it would be merged in the season by the sun of our Union."[82] It also provided a model of cosmic harmony for their acrimonious earthly politics to follow.

As we have learned from important studies of the Newtonian predisposition in the American political tradition, Newtonianism enabled contemporaries to articulate American politics in terms of machinelike accordance and predictability. Hence it was perfectly intelligible for John Adams to think of the Union as thirteen "clocks . . . made to strike together—a perfection of mechanism."[83] If the United States was, as it was repeatedly described for decades after its creation, "an additional planet . . . illuminat[ing] the political firmament," it would have been only natural to expect it "to be influenced by the same laws, and to be subject to the same accelerations," as other similar systems.[84] Accordingly, the widespread discussions of "orbits" and "spheres" with regard to the separation of powers within the federal structure was often conducted without explicit reference to the sun, or any other celestial body. By focusing solely on the mechanical aspects of such images and ignoring their inseparable affinity to astronomical observations, mental images, and frameworks, however, historians may have misinterpreted their origins, ignored their longevity, and thus misconstrued their ultimate meaning. Indeed, the tendency has been to treat such utterances in their own terms, as mere mechanical metaphors, while they should actually be understood in the wider context of political astronomy. In *The Federalist Papers,* no. 9, for example, Alexander Hamilton tackled objections to the proposed constitution arising from anxiety regarding the "enlargement of the Orbit within which such [constitutional] systems are to revolve either in respect to the dimensions of a single State, or to the consolidation of several smaller States into one great confederacy."[85] Again, in

The Federalist Papers, no. 15, Hamilton, now discussing the deficiencies of the existing confederation, raised the issue of an "eccentric tendency in the subordinate or inferior orbs, by the operation of which there will be a perpetual effort in each to fly off from the common centre." Others of a similar Federalist persuasion maintained the same ideas expressed in comparable language, believing that "unbalanced by a general government . . . *states [will be] flying from their orbits.*"[86] Similarly, Senator John Breckinridge of Virginia (1760–1806) argued, in a speech to the U.S. Senate on the independence of the judiciary, that the separate governmental department were "intended to revolve within the sphere of their own orbits; are responsible for their own motion only; and are not to direct or controul the course of the others."[87] These characteristic public statements, which analyzed the American political edifice in terms of spheres of influence, orbits, attraction and repulsion were part and parcel of the language of planetary movement, and should be understood as such and in tandem with the rich broader language of political astronomy. Such utterances not only point at the mechanistic nature of American politics but also indicate the wider discussion involving politics and celestial harmony, the naturalness of the American Union of states, and their implications regarding America's destiny.

These descriptions of political spheres and orbs that are most often read out of context were matched by mechanical language that was explicitly planetary. John Adams, for example, articulated a celestial logic as he pledged his defense of federalism: America, Adams pointed out, needed a constitution that would control "those attractions and repulsions, by which the balance of nature is preserved." Adams left little doubt regarding the nature of the images that propelled his political imagination, concluding that a constitution should act as a sun, curbing "the heavenly bodies . . . in their orbits, instead of rushing to the sun, or flying off in tangents among comets and fixed stars: impelled, or drawn by different forces in different directions, they are blessings to their own inhabitants and the neighbouring systems."[88] Orbital allusions and spherical movements were thus not abstract mechanical references and are better understood in an explicitly astronomical context that indicates their origin. These expressions evolved and were cultivated in the framework of an imaginative planetary idiom, and there is little doubt that contemporaries were well aware of that genealogy and that they perceived these images as such. Take, for example, the comment that "the constitution fixes limits to the legislative authority . . . and prescribes the orbit within which it must move." While such an observation might be read as an example of a strictly mechanical and abstract explanation of politics, this Whig author chose to articulate the astronomical imagination from which he derived his images: "Power in the people is like light in the sun, it is native, original, inherent, and unlimited by any thing human. . . . [P]ower in the government . . . is like light in the moon, for it is only borrowed, delegated, and limited by the expressed will and intention of the people."[89] The Copernican aspects of these reflections, particularly the sun's nourishing attributes, enabled this author to elaborate on the image of the Constitution as receiving its power from the sun ("the people"), and thus act by limiting and constraining the respective governmental branches. In a congressional speech on the Sedition Act of 1798, Representative John Dickerson further demonstrated the power of this solar analogical mode. Gazing at "the sun of our political firmament, through an attenuated atmosphere," the onlooker was "dazzled with its splendor—sees nothing but light and perfection." However, if one were to view it "through a more obscure and dense medium, he would see in this luminary certain dark spots indicative of decay." In light of the Adams administration's harmful acts of 1798, the First Amendment, once the Constitution's "most resplendent limb, is now obscured in dim eclipse, shorn of its beams, shedding around disastrous twilight."[90] Not content with abstract mechanics, these authors made explicit and elaborate astronomical references, demonstrating how rich these metaphors were and the extent to which that language enabled those who used it to reflect on and work out their ideas.

The planetary language was so pervasive and effective in describing American federalism that it seamlessly seeped into descriptions of non-American federalisms. When describing the Swiss cantons, each of which had its free constitution, it seemed to an American observer a "singular spectacle to see a score of factions of a nation, each moving in its own orbit, and desirous of being each for itself the centre of a universe, without any disposition to move around some common sphere, which should regulate their route, and prevent them from running against each other."[91]

Missing the fact that this was a description of a European federalism, readers might easily have concluded that this was a portrayal of their own political system. This spherical and orbital language may have been so effective because political power itself was described in solar terms: When in its original and pure form, that is "in the people," political power was "like the light of the sun . . . original and underived from anything human." Once delegated to government, however, power became "like light in the moon . . . borrowed, delegated and limited." The stellar attributes of power explained the need for a constitution that would fix limits to legislative authority and would "prescribe . . . the orbit within which it must move." Government, magistrates and even elected representatives should thus "answer to 'us, the people' . . . and consequently must be confined by, and act within the [prescribed] sphere."[92] Conceiving of power in planetary terms, the political universe was wholly a planetary one.

The language of planetary power continued to offer a handy and common mode of analyzing political authority throughout the era of the early republic and beyond. To take but one example, during the War of 1812 a writer in a New York newspaper pointed out that President James Madison ought to be obeyed "when acting within the sphere of his constitutional authority." However, the president could be countered by legislatures who "move in another orbit."[93] During that controversial conflict, prowar Democratic-Republicans regularly voiced their concerns that the Anglophile Federalists were attempting to carry the United States "out of its American sphere . . . and so near the orbit of England."[94] Those opposing the war pointed out that the "states of New-England . . . can never be satellites in any system: But like primary planets, they will revolve round *the sun of federalism.*" During times of conflict and danger to the Union, readers had to be reassured regarding its fate. Hence the commentator added that only "the Almighty hand which created" the universe, physical and political, could "dash them from their orbits forever."[95]

Comparable mechanical images of the proper working of government continued to proliferate in the decades following the War of 1812. "When governments confine themselves to public improvements and the establishment of justice," one proponent of small government argued, "they are in their proper sphere." However, he continued, "when they take out of the hands of individuals and society, the duties of charity and humanity, and the advancement of religion, trade and the arts and sciences, they wander from their orbit."[96] Others explored the particularities of a *federal* government. In a Senate speech delivered in 1833 by the Virginian William Rives, which echoed many of the themes we have already encountered, the senator elaborated on the way that the states were "sovereign within their several spheres, as the Union is in the sphere marked out to it, and that the harmony of the whole system is only to be preserved by each power revolving in its proper orbit."[97] Planetary spheres and orbits were evoked to characterize a balanced and harmonic system. Harmony could be preserved only if the passing bodies were to move *properly*, that is, without getting too close to a scorching sun, encroaching on their brotherly bodies or fleeing to too far a distance.[98]

In the unstable political circumstances of the early republic, the solar system, seen as an exemplar of an eternally predictable and self-correcting structure through the work of Laplace and others, provided a model for the order and regularity that were in increasingly short supply in the realm of American politics. The thought of an indefinite and self-correcting celestial mechanism was comforting in a time when many feared the impending disintegration of American society. Contemporaries may thus have wished that the American federal order, like Laplace's stable universe, would be "secured against natural decay," that "order and regularity [would be] preserved in the midst of so many disturbing causes, and anarchy and misrule eternally proscribed."[99] Hence, a year before sectional tensions first seriously rattled the integrity of the Union around the Missouri question, Thomas Jefferson wrote to Laplace's American expositor that "it was comfortable to believe that the system does not involve within itself the principles of its own destruction."[100] Jefferson may have been referring to the solar system, but, as we have already seen, by the end of the second decade of the nineteenth century the Union and the solar system were conflated to such an extent that their meanings may have been inseparable. Within months Jefferson would be talking about "holding the wolf by the ear," referring to the innate destructiveness of the institution of slavery.

Decades later, John C. Calhoun made clear that "to realize its perfection, we must view the General Government and those of the States as a whole, each in its proper sphere independent." Hence, "to preserve this sacred distribution as originally settled, by coercing each to move in its prescribed *orbit,* is the great and difficult problem." Calhoun further believed that although the federal government was "in reality, a government . . . within the *orbit* of its powers, it [was], nevertheless, a government emanating from a compact between sovereigns . . . [thus] having, beyond its proper sphere, no more power than if it did not exist."[101] Andrew Jackson expressed a similar sentiment in planetary lingo in his celebrated (or rather infamous) Veto Message, arguing that the government of the United States would not be "maintained or our Union preserved by invasions of the rights and powers of the several States. In thus attempting to make our General Government strong we make it weak. Its true strength consists in leaving individuals and States as much as possible to themselves—. . . not in binding the States more closely to the center, but leaving each to move unobstructed in its proper orbit."[102]

Regrettably, political suns were not always able to live up to their designated role and succeed in preserving harmony and equilibrium. In fact, while planetary language could depict an ideal of harmony and stability, with the question of cosmic stability itself under debate, political astronomy could effectively express anxious images of turmoil and even anarchy. A Vermont Whig could warn, for example, the election of a Whig president in 1840 notwithstanding, of "a bright star that has lately risen to its brilliant course" being "plucked forever from the political firmament by the hand of disunion."[103] In parallel to the orderly language of orbits and spheres of influence, which was a language of control and stability, there emerged a critical strain of commentary that unleashed a language of disorder and confusion. Particularly in moments of political instability, during which a chaotic political astronomy of state-planets dashing against each other and flying off their tangents would replace a stable and clockwork federal order.

For millennia, comets (or "blazing stars" or "tailed stars")—icy bodies that heat up and may leave impressive tails—together with meteors, the fiery disintegrations visible as they passed through the earth's atmosphere, were viewed as threatening, portentous phenomena. These and other celestial phenomena such as eclipses were viewed as marvels that disturbed the sense of harmony and order in the cosmos, inspiring awe and trepidation. Seen as celestial monstrosities and harbingers of destruction from tempests, earthquakes, wars, plagues, or famine, comets had been associated from ancient times with the downfall of nations and princes.[104] Such interpretations stemmed from a conception of comets as contrary to nature and prevailed from antiquity through the Renaissance.[105] Nevertheless, by the end of the seventeenth century, elites in England and Europe had begun to reject the traditional opinions regarding the nature of comets and no longer saw them as portents. Comets were thus in the process of being transformed from transcendent signs into heavenly bodies that obeyed the laws of Newtonian physics. Indeed, the great Newton himself set out to prove that they were members of the solar system.[106] But while educated contemporaries publicly scoffed at the traditional dread of comets, in the popular imagination they still functioned as heavenly messengers (or even causes) of dread and disaster.

American public writing demonstrates a continuing fascination with comets, which, like other heavenly phenomena, were vastly more visible than today due to the lack of light pollution.[107] Even on the verge of the nineteenth century, comets and meteors remained, in the words of a contemporary, "judged to be the forerunners of extraordinary events."[108] Although by the late eighteenth century much was understood regarding their nature, it was not easy to jettison centuries of fretful associations. A characteristic account of comets published during the revolutionary era presented an eclectic but rather characteristic description of their nature: While comets and meteors were said to adhere to Newtonian laws of motion, nevertheless these passing bodies were described in a premodern idiom as so "many hells to punish the damned."[109] These irate bodies were routinely deemed "dim and noxious" elements in the otherwise orderly outer space, whose "pale vapors interrupt darkness, but increase the gloom of night."[110] Contemporary commentators never abandoned such entrenched associations and continued to make use of comets and meteors to describe political disorder and danger.

Comets and meteors thus functioned during the years of contest with Britain in their traditional role as ominous marvels. Patriots, such as the famed polemicist Junius Americanus (Henry Lee), pointed out that "the whole people of America are virtually insecure," as they were taxed and

The Star-Spangled Republic

legislated without being represented. The danger of this dire situation "must hang over the Americans like a baneful meteor, perpetually threatening the destruction of their property."[111] Interestingly, in a rebuttal to Junius, Samuel Johnson elaborated on this age-old celestial language, claiming that although Junius himself should be "taken for a comet, that from its flaming hair shook pestilence and war," onlookers would soon discover that he was "only a meteor formed by the vapours of putrefying democracy . . . [which will] plunge its followers in a bog."[112]

While both sides of the imperial contest thus invoked meteors and comets, Patriots could view comets as a positive marvel, for example, when they described their republican experiment as "something celestial" to which "the states of America look up" admirably and ask in disbelief, "what strange meteor is that?" More commonly, however, Britain itself was the "blazing meteor" that Americans needed to "extinguish . . . for ever, in the boisterous element that surrounds her."[113] Loyalists, on the other hand, promised to "dash proud [John] Hancock from his meteor throne."[114] Consequently, Revolutionary-era writers commonly described a harmful political event or process as a rapid "meteor [that] darts through the air," hopefully dissipating as "it reached that Terra Firma of our Constitution." The language of comets and meteors could also be used for social critique, with American public virtue (or lack thereof) depicted as having "more of the properties of a meteor . . . than that of a bright luminary."[115]

During the Critical Period, as the government functioning under the Articles of Confederation drifted from city to city without a permanent capital, a Boston newspaper jeered, "The high and mighty and most gracious Sovereigns of the C[ongres]s, not being stars of the first magnitude, but rather partaking of the nature of inferior luminaries, or wandering comets, again appear in the wandering orb, assuming various directions and courses, sometimes regular and uniform, at other times, vain and retrograde."[116] Such language of chaos and disarray would regularly be employed during the crises that rocked the young republic, describing a hellish political firmament that was a grotesque mirror image of a harmonic and desirable clockwork universe. This language conjured a gravity-less and order-less existence, characterized by *wandering orbs,* drifting *inferior luminaries,* and, most ominously, *comets.*

John Adams was a supporter of a stronger connection between the states and commented from London, where he served as the United States ambassador to the Crown, on constitutional issues. During the Critical Period, Adams feared the ascendancy of an American political world that would lack a firm constitution and would therefore devolve into a deranged sky filled with comets, like "those angry assemblies in the Heavens, which so often overspread the city of Philadelphia . . . threatening to set the world on fire, merely because the powers within them are not sufficiently balanced." America must have, in his view, a constitution that would control "those attractions and repulsions, by which the balance of nature is preserved: or . . . those centripetal and centrifugal forces, by which the heavenly bodies are continued in their orbits, instead of rushing to the sun, or flying off in tangents among comets and fixed stars." Pro-order Federalists, such as Adams (and Alexander Hamilton, as Publius addressing the necessity of the "enlargement of the Orbit within which such [federal] systems are to revolve"), believed that the danger of state-planets surrendering to the centrifugal forces of disunion would end once a binding and comet-terminating constitution was instituted.[117] Americans who, like Adams, came to support the establishment of a stronger central government than that prescribed by the Articles of Confederation (and were dubbed, ironically, Federalists), also believed that "unbalanced by a general government, the human character would be humbled by the distressing but sublime idea of states *flying from their orbits*."[118] Yet pro-constitution Americans, such as one Mrs. Gardner from South Carolina, could also describe meteors favorably (and poetically): "The Patriotic plan unites each state / And forms a Constitution truly great / Aspiring genius! Panting after praise; / And like dazzling meteor, wonder raise."[119]

Americans continued throughout the early years of the republic to mobilize this traditional imagery of comets and meteors. Jeffersonian Republicans saw England as "a despicable meteor, which disappears before the Republican luminary,"[120] while arch Federalists and anti-expansionists, such as Fisher Ames, feared that the United States, after the Louisiana Purchase, "by adding an unmeasured world beyond that (Mississippi) river," was "rush[ing] like a comet into infinite space."[121]

Throughout the first half of the nineteenth century, meteors ("shooting stars") and comets continued to be called upon to describe wondrous "eccentric productions" of "singular" political events, such as the failed creation of the Jewish "city of refuge" of Ararat on Grand Island, New York.[122] At times, when state action seemed ill-begotten, comets were conjured to describe a dire situation. A New York statesman, defending his state from accusations of irresoluteness during Jackson's presidency, asserted that New York, had "never been found to be a political meteor, traversing the abstruse regions and metaphysical mazes of the political firmament."[123] "Shooting stars" were used not only to denote threatening events but also irregular, unforeseen, and unwelcome occurrences, such as when Senators John Calhoun and William Rives switched party affiliation. "A remarkable phenomenon occurred in the political Heavens," wrote a South Carolinian: "the blazing Whig star of South Carolina [Calhoun], and the brilliant Democratic star of Virginia [Rives], madly shooting from their spheres, passed each other and exchanged places in the political firmament."[124] Hence, if the most basic function of society was to create an orderly and functioning system that would instill stability into fluctuating human actions, the primary danger to that system was a "fearful rush" as a result of "the political world" being "struck by some cometary body passing too near its orbit."[125]

When sectional conflict ratcheted up, comet-related language followed, providing stark warnings in the political skies. As the political crisis of 1850 was brewing, Southerners were predicting that if a new compromise between the sections could not be achieved, it would bode, in the words of the future president of the Confederacy, Jefferson Davis, a "conjunction of [the] political firmament" that "would likely be destroyed by the attraction of the planets."[126] But even directly after the (retrospectively short-lived) Compromise of 1850 was achieved, a despondent Virginian could note that "we live to see the 'full orbed' comet of Disunionism shooting athwart our political firmament, disturbing the harmony of our system, and threatening to throw it into chaos."[127] A decade later, on the brink of war, Northerners described "the stars of our political firmament torn from their orbits, and plunging madly about, or tilting one against the other."[128] In the meantime, and mere weeks before their states seceded from the Union, Southerners still hoped that "the malign star of disunion [that has] cast its lurid glare over the political firmament" would not "jostle the government of the United States from its constitutional orbit."[129]

In early 1860, with the elections that would tear the republic apart mere months away, Northern politicians continued to extoll the virtues of America's political astronomy as benign and effective. In a congressional speech in February, Senator James Doolittle of Wisconsin lavished praise on the "two enduring and apparently opposing forces or tendencies . . . which move[] the planets in our system." While the centripetal force alone "would hurl them from their spheres, to wander at random through the universe, until destroyed by collisions, or bound by superior force to some other system," the centrifugal force countered this disastrous tendency. Translated into American politics, while one force "enlarge[d] the powers delegated to the General Government, which is called Federalism," the other "sturdily . . . maintain[ed] the reserved powers of the States, which is called Republicanism." Aspiring politicians, such as Doolittle, beseeched their peers that it was only from the two forces combined that the American "system . . . owed its true harmony, its real glory." Doolittle and his contemporaries understood that without preserving the balance of the forces, the American planetary system would rapidly self-destruct.[130] As the secession crisis unfolded, national politicians such as Doolittle wished to keep the Union intact. Others who concurred that their "confederation may be likened to the great system of the universe" attempted to provide answers on how to preserve their political cosmos. Even in the North, some believed that it was "only by the benign and gentle influence of attraction that the bright stars of our constellation can be kept in their orbits. Those [Republicans] who attempt to spur or bridle them will . . . fare like the rash fool who aspired to direct the chariots of the sun."[131] Most Northerners, however, would have agreed with those who warned their Southern brethren regarding the danger of the American "constellation [going] out in darkness" as its state-stars were "dragged from their orbit" by Southern demagogues, becoming consequently "wandering stars."[132] Whether one sided with gentle influence or rather believed in coercion as a strategy to hold the

Union together, with the Southern states seceding, citizens of the United States acknowledged that it might be "impossible to restore to their accustomed positions those stars which have shot madly from our political firmament."[133] Others cautioned that the "malign star of disunion" will cause the orderly American planets to "shoot madly from [their] sphere. Confusion will be general—the ruin common."[134]

What a far cry was this world of rushing comets from the orderly and idyllic astro-political world articulated throughout the decades following the Revolution, in which the "glorious constellation of co-equal sovereignties . . . high in the political firmament" was "so accurately balanced, so deftly poised, so firmly held together by the cohesive power of attraction." Without the sectional conflict and the ensuing war, "centuries might have come and gone and seen no change" in the American planetary system.[135] Indeed, a perfect balance that transcended and defied change and thus corruption and decay, the bogeyman of republics, was among the solar image's most desirable attributes. By midcentury, however, mounting anxiety can be discerned in solar readings of the republic. Americans surely desired "to see all the States moving around one common centre, in a harmony as beautiful as that of the solar system," and for the sake of that end "each State must keep within its own orbit." Yet in contrast to the apparently (if wrongly understood) unchanging celestial firmament, corruption was possible in terrestrial politics. That the states "may . . . shoot madly from [their] sphere" was becoming a more realistic possibility by the day.[136]

By the Civil War era, a familiar image—that of thirteen interlocked spheres revolving around a uniting sun—had resurfaced on a commercially printed envelope. Some fourscore years after the appearance of the original image that fortified an emerging nation against its imperial lord (fig. 15), this revived image was intended to help unify a house divided against itself. The planetary metaphor of unity and balance ensured through a common sun not only remained relevant but was supposed to strengthen Americans' belief in the durability of their republic in a time of existential crisis. Even in the Confederacy, founded on the principle of states'-rights, official proposals for a flag for the young slaveholding nation represented the central government itself by a "star larger than those individual representations of each of the member states."[137] Grassroot proposals for the Confederacy's flag campaigned even more bluntly for "a Flag of the Sun," which echoed the comparisons of early modern monarchs to sol, with the sun on the proposed flag described as spreading "light, heat, life, quickening energy, fertility, purity, love, joy, elevation, glory." But the main reason for choosing the sun as a vexillological symbol for the newfound Confederation was that it would act as a metonym for "the National Constitutional Government dispensing its blessings to all the States, and forming the centre and bond of unity between them, as the sun holds together, illuminates, warms, and cheers the solar system."[138] Central power and its cosmic representations had their allure even for a people who broke their national bonds on account of perceived encroachments on their states' autonomy.

For decades the image of a political solar system had primed Americans to understand, react, and, arguably, feel in specific ways toward their federal republic; the idea that the Union was analogous to a planetary system had acted as an organizing principle for making sense out of the United States. Attraction and repulsion, autonomy and restriction, healing warmth and scorching heat were physical attributes evoked to instill order in a novel political construct that otherwise might have meant little and would have been difficult to fathom. The language of planetary politics grounded the different levels of the federal structure in cosmic harmony and celestial movement. By analogizing orbiting planetary bodies to political bodies, contemporaries reinforced the "naturalness" of the unprecedented edifice of their national government, and thus helped to explain and legitimize it. That language was so effective that two decades after the Civil War ended it enabled Americans to express disbelief that, not so long ago, "a red war comet swung for four years along an orbit that cut the Northern and Southern stars into two groups." Luckily, however, "the attraction was too great for the [comet's] disturbing influence," and the North and South "were ... united never to part again." By the late nineteenth century, the American states once again "formed the most complete system in the universe."[139]

Glancing back at the image on the Civil War–era envelope (fig. 15), its overtly cosmic image manifests a stark difference from its revolutionary

FIGURE 15. "United Forever" envelope, ca. 1860. (Library of Congress, Liljenquist Family Collection of Civil War Photographs, LC-DIG-ppmsca-34706)

ancestor. The circle of interlocking discs is now enclosed by a spherical layer of stars that did not appear on the revolutionary original (see fig. 12), representing the many state-stars that had joined the republic since its creation (as well as a furled American flag and a bald eagle holding in its beak a banner with the imprint "pluribus"). The many stars revolving around the original image of interlocked discs demonstrated that the new states now clearly and visibly outnumbered the original thirteen. It also alluded to another powerful cosmic representation of the Union of American states. Indeed, the image of the United States as a "new constellation" of state-stars was as old as that of its representation as a solar system. Yet in the wake of the vast expansion of the federal government during the war and the North's conclusive victory, the planetary image became less relevant to the transformed American federacy. In the previous decades the antebellum federal government, often described as a "midget in a giant land," profited from asserting itself as a dominating sun vis-à-vis autonomy-seeking state-planets.

With the debate on power and autonomy decided on the battlefield of the Civil War, the solar metaphor, which had helped negotiate the relationship between the states and the federal government, became outdated. Planetary politics were rooted in early modern monarchy, emerged with the creation of the republic, and declined in late nineteenth-century United States when they lost their explanatory appeal. In the changed political landscape of post–Civil War America, states would not again seriously challenge the energized federal government. With the negotiation between the planetary periphery and the solar center decided for all practical purposes, the image of the federal sun set, and has yet to dawn again. High in the political firmament, however, still shone a constellation of American states, a configuration to which we will now turn.

3

The American Constellation

POLITICAL FIRMAMENTS, STARS, AND FLAGS

Turn to the political firmament, for the great constellation of
American States . . . it will burst forth with renovated brightness—
glittering and to glitter, until its full orbed lustre shall shine forth,
brightening the vision of the patriot and lighting up his soul.

—"Speech of Mr. Segar of Northhampton,"
Richmond Enquirer, March 17, 1838

IN A QUIRKY, full folio-long fictious dialogue published on the first day of 1882 in the *New York Herald,* three eccentric professors, Dalrymple, McCarty, and Hellstern, converse on a variety of topics, from ventriloquists to the New Year's festivities. Halfway through their rambling discussion, Professor McCarty, with "his cheeky voice and Yankee accent," points to the "galaxy of stars" on the American flag. "If you count them you will find that they number exactly thirty eight," the professor didactically notes. First, he directs his fellow New Yorkers' gaze toward "the great Empire Star on the east," then notes "the Golden [California] Star," and on to "the extreme west, the large [Virginia] Dominion Star to the south and the brightening [Texan] Lone Star away to the south and west." The professor then calls the attention of his audience to the way in which the American stars are "beautifully clustered and all are shining brightly," as they form "the most complete system in the universe." In 1882, he said, "it would never strike you to observe their mutual attraction that a red war comet almost disrupted the constellation twenty years ago." Luckily, after the disastrous Civil War, the Northern and Southern groups of stars were "now reunited never to part company again." As to the future of the American constellation, the professor opines happily that the drive to add new stars remains as potent as ever. Referring to the largely Mormon Utah territory, he notes "the Deseret asteroid that is as big as the Silver star" but could not yet become another star in the Union "because it practices polygamy." At this point professor Dalrymple quips nostalgically that he remembers fondly the olden days "when there were only thirteen" stars that comprised the American constellation.[1]

In the 1880s, more than a century after the creation of the American republic, discussing the federal nation in terms of a constellation of stars had become embedded in public and private speech. By this time, the image of the state-as-star, and the consequent image of a constellation of star-states, has arguably become the most salient symbol in American political language. Impressed on the Star-Spangled Banner and other iconic national emblems and countless lesser articles of Americana, the constellation of stars may also be the least explored and thus least understood of American national symbols. In previous chapters we have seen how political astronomy originated in the use of an early modern cosmology to present European monarchs as suns at the center of stately solar systems, and thus helped ground a revamped absolutist ideology that was based on the image of a single solar center of power. However, this Old World image of the sun king, which gained considerable traction in the North American British colonies, was republicanized and revolutionized after 1776. This recalibrated political astronomy became fundamental in shaping the ways in which American citizens made sense of and justified their novel federal republic, and the ways in which they understood their new country's destiny.

The current chapter follows the rise and evolution of the image of the state-as-star and consequent constellation of American stars, and the ways in which it functioned as a powerful tool to make sense of political identities during the formative years of the American founding and beyond. For decades this overlooked system of thought in American politics translated ideologies into starry projections upon the federal republic and was capable of generating contradictory understandings of the meaning of the United States. It thus offered a common ground for debating the most basic tenets of American political thought. While political astronomy, and in particular its constellational variant, remains a central foundation of the visual culture of twenty-first-century American politics, its roots are found in the halls of Renaissance princes and the courts of early modern monarchs. Without understanding its origins, development, and meaning during the revolutionary era and the early republic, we cannot fully understand the cognitive tools and interpretive frameworks that contemporaries put to work in making sense of their world. Constructing politics in cosmic terms encouraged them to contemplate and carefully articulate their interpretation of republicanism and federalism and enabled them to present their hopes and misgivings in a powerful language that impressed the political nation onto the most sublime aspects of the natural world.

Throughout the formative decades of the United States' political culture, stars and constellations provided images that made the novelties of American political life accessible and meaningful. Indeed, political astronomy was at its base a tool for critical thought that encouraged debate about and analysis of fundamental aspects of American life. While today the constellations and starry images are still omnipresent in our public spheres, they present to us a mere hollow shell of their former dense and meaningful selves. Hence, we cannot properly understand the evolution of central issues in American history, national sentiment, and the nation's culture and politics without reconstructing the mental devices through which late eighteenth- and nineteenth-century Americans themselves produced their concepts and ideals.

As American hearts and minds were converting to the idea of republican independence after the outbreak of hostilities in April 1775, revolutionaries began to question the image of the king-as-sun, which they had long subscribed to and countless European monarchists had cultivated for centuries. The political astronomy of Benjamin Rush and his Whig contemporaries, who as colonial subjects claimed to have "been taught to consider [kings] nearly as essential to political order as the Sun is to the order of our Solar system," was becoming irrelevant if not outright offensive.[2] Yet as Patriots severed their ties with the British Empire, they again looked to the skies for more than mere aesthetic gratification and navigational uses. Patriots refocused their view of the heavens, shifting their attention from the sun to the stellar constellations for justification and proof for their experiment in revolution and federalism. The brave new republican world that Americans were making thus fostered an evolution of the older, solar-oriented modes of political thought, which now branched out into a stellar political astronomy.

An oration delivered in Philadelphia in February 1775 by David Rittenhouse (1732–1796), scientist, surveyor, watchmaker, and member of the American Philosophical Society, displays the then state of astro-political revolutionary sensibilities. In his astronomical lecture, Rittenhouse extolled the "sublime geometry" of the American night skies, whose secrets Isaac Newton had reduced "to the most beautiful simplicity." By choosing to dedicate his celebratory oration to the members of the Continental Congress, Rittenhouse linked the political and celestial. Those congressmen, upon whom, in his words, "the future liberties, and consequently the virtue, improvement in science and happiness, of America are instructed," would reconvene in a few months to find themselves conducting a war and declaring independence. The relationship Rittenhouse wove between the members of Congress and scientific astronomy, between politics and the cosmos foretold what was to come: The Congress to which Rittenhouse dedicated his astronomical speech in 1775 would soon enshrine among the new United States' major national symbols the image of an American constellation of thirteen states, represented by thirteen stars.[3]

The following months, which eventually led to Independence, witnessed the emergence of a novel American astro-political discourse that correlated with and responded to the fast-moving and dramatic revolutionary developments. One of the manifestations of the view of the transforming political world was the symbolic grammar that presented each of the American states as a distinct star and, consequently, the United States as the "new American constellation." We have previously seen that the sun had customarily represented a king, with the system of planets surrounding the "king star" representing a whole political nation. However, the extent to which European sun kings were represented in solar terms in their "natural body," or rather in their capacity of personifying the body politic, was ambiguous.⁴ It was clearly from the second capacity that revolutionary Americans took their cue as they began taking stars as standing for nonhuman and discrete political societies, the soon-to-be-sovereign American states. We have seen in chapter 2 how theorists and practitioners continued throughout the revolutionary era and beyond to employ the solar image to analyze the relations of the states and the central federal government in a planetary language of attraction and repulsion, and of orbits and spheres of influence. Nevertheless, this planetary language, which was ostensibly borrowed and applied from the courts of European monarchs and was beneficial for analyzing constitutional mechanics, was at its root a language for analyzing power relations. As such, it was not suitable for understanding and communicating a crucial aspect of the American republican universe. A solar uni-centered universe was only partially equipped for representing a union, *the* Union, of distinct and autonomous polities of state-stars.⁵ But rather than altogether abandon the heavens as a source of creative political imagination, revolutionaries now discerned in their political firmaments a new, striking, and potent image: an American constellation of state-stars that communicated the republican nature of the harmonic relations among the system's self-governing federal components.

When, in January 1776, Thomas Paine published anonymously the earth-shattering pamphlet *Common Sense,* one of the most striking images he used to demonstrate the "unnatural" connection between Britain and America was astronomical: "In no instance hath nature made the satellite larger than its primary planet, and as England and America, with respect to each Other, reverses the common order of nature, it is evident they belong to different systems." A few months later, in April, when complete separation from the British Empire had become a viable option, one of Paine's supporters published an extraordinary piece in the *Pennsylvania Ledger.* Perhaps reacting to Paine's own astro-political language, this author allowed "the reigns of . . . imagination" to guide himself together with "the ingenious author of Common Sense" on a heavenly tour. Like Dante guided by Virgil and Beatrice through the depths of the Inferno to the heights of Paradise, this author soared—in his imagination—up to the sky together with Paine: "aloft into the wilds of fancy, the dull beaten tracks of monarchy, we left far behind us." In the skies, the two space travelers found no monarchical structure, as had countless humans before them. Rather, they discovered "a republic amidst the stars." An ingenious reading of the cosmo-political meaning of the universe followed. The Pennsylvanian conceded that, in a heliocentric world, "the Sun might seem, to admiring mortals below [as] the grand monarch of the heavenly bodies." Yet the universe contained not one, but countless "other suns and other worlds innumerable." The vastness of the universe, which comprised a practically infinite system of solar systems, a multiplicity of galaxies that formed a cosmic unity, in itself ridiculed the notion of the sun as absolute king of the universe, and hence monarchical claims in general, let alone those of "sun kings." Indeed, the many suns that populated space "might only be considered as *Presidents, not Monarchs*, of the vast system." Like Paine, who found the institution of monarchy unnatural, this cosmological reading found the institution of monarchy utterly unsubstantiated in nature. On the contrary, "the various constellations which enspangle the sky, [are] united upon the principles of perfect equality." Egalitarian and autonomous republics, not authoritarian monarchies, were the political bodies written in the skies. Republican equality was demonstrated through cosmic harmony: "gravitating towards each other, with wonderful adjustment, mutually attracted and mutually repelled," the celestial republics existed in peace within themselves and their neighbors. As opposed to monarchical governments, which were based on the attracting and repulsing powers of a massive center, the "republic amidst the stars" was one of Newtonian contentment, fraternity, and a peaceful and harmonic equilibrium.[6]

This Pennsylvanian author clearly and consciously made the crucial move from a sun-centered political astronomy to a starry republicanism, and from a celestial kingly hierarchy to astro-egalitarianism. Accordingly, the fundamental astronomical representations of the United States would not be associated with solar systems. Rather, the Union of American states would be mainly and habitually described henceforth as a constellation of stars. Constellations are of course the product of the human imagination, designating an area on the celestial sphere in which a group of visible stars forms a perceived outline or pattern. Often depicting objects, animals, or mythic personas, constellations have helped humans across cultures and eras to navigate the skies and find meaning in star formations (as seen from the vantage point of the onlooker). By the late eighteenth century, it had become obvious that constellations were not "really" out there but were the result of the seeming two-dimensionality of the firmament. Nevertheless, constellations remained highly effective and well-known mnemonic devices in a world much darker than ours. With the creation of the American republic, contemporaries began referring to the United States in the constellational terms with which they were so well acquainted from centuries of conditioning in stargazing and practical astronomy.

A mere week after Independence, a writer for the *Independent Ledger* requested from his readers that the newly created United States "be extolled ... to the stars, who support the honor of your ... new constellation, the thirteen stars." Those who chose not to support the new constellational republic, the writer wished would "sink into darkness."[7] The use of the term "new constellation," which was applied to the United States and would become a staple of political astronomy in the coming decades, was less revolutionary than it may appear at first glance. The known and trusted constellations of the Western tradition were catalogued by the second-century geographer Ptolemy, and functioned over the next two millennia as mnemonic devices, facilitating an intimate familiarization with the night skies and providing the cosmos with meaning for untold millions. Nevertheless, the eighteenth century saw a dramatic change in this stable picture of the firmament. A key figure of this Enlightenment-age makeover was the French astronomer Nicolas-Louis de Lacaille, who in 1750 led a scientific expedition to the Cape of Good Hope. One of the remarkable outcomes of Lacaille's astronomical observations of the Southern Hemisphere was a flurry of new constellations that the Frenchman organized and named and that were soon widely recognized and sanctioned. While Lacaille's constellations reflected new knowledge that derived from the age of exploration, their nomenclature expressed remarkable Enlightenment-age sensibilities. The forty-eight classical-age Ptolemaic constellations bore names that derived from Greek mythology, from Cassiopeia to Perseus and Hercules. The names Lacaille bestowed on the new Southern constellations were modern, reflecting an Enlightened intellect, and were rapidly and universally adopted: The French astronomer named thirteen of his fourteen newly configured constellations after modern scientific instruments, from the telescope to the microscope and octant. In other words, as opposed to the traditional archaic and mythical attitudes toward the skies, these constellations alluded to modern science and technology, and to the new knowledge that was achieved through them. The contrast suggested by the nomenclature of old and new constellations could not have been starker.[8]

Contemporaries were exposed to the new constellations through updated star maps and celestial globes that were published and widely distributed soon after Lacaille's return to Europe. Indeed, as the historian Tamara Plakins Thornton points out, American consumers favored terrestrial and celestial globes that featured new geographical and astronomical discoveries. In 1784, for example, a Philadelphia merchant advertised "a pair of nine-inch Globes," that is, a set of terrestrial and celestial globes "with all the latest discoveries," while another sold "12 and 18 inch globes" that included "the latest and most improved principles."[9] Astronomical class books of the early republic already integrated the new constellations, which became part and parcel of the "Geography of the Heavens," as did annually updated almanacs.[10] Hence, by the late eighteenth century, "new constellations" were not novel and surprising figures of speech but rather a distinct category that resonated among reading Americans. The new constellations demonstrate the remarkable feedback between scientific and political astronomy that were advancing hand in hand. The expanding knowledge of the night skies and the broadening of the celestial imagination carved out a new space for political astronomers, who now in turn found it intellectually and mentally easier to create their own Enlightenment-age "new American constellation."

The fact that the image of the United States as a constellation was already in use at the time of Independence is striking and demonstrates just how accessible and handy was political astronomy. In the following year, with the Continental Congress Flag Act of June 14, 1777, the already-circulating constellational image was formalized, gaining an everlasting authority and influence. The difference from the old image of the solar king was conspicuous, as one kingly sun was replaced by a group of stars.

No less striking was the fact that, while it was always clear exactly what the sun represented (whether it be a monarch or the Union), the stars were identical and interchangeable and represented an unidentifiable American state. While the sun represented a recognizable, distinct, and usually exceptional and unparalleled entity, the stars were a symbol of equality through virtual interchangeability.

This new constellational image introduced two revolutionary innovations to the prevailing political astronomy of the day. First, the celestial bodies in this figure were not the sun but rather distant indiscriminate suns, that is stars. This move from the relative confines of the proximate solar system to intergalactic space was the corollary of an inherent push for democratization. In this cosmic perspective, the once-mighty sun was seen as not even an equal among its peers but as a rather average, if nearby star. The new language of political constellations presented a provisional model to articulate the political world, one in which no overbearing body overshadowed the "political firmament," which presented a harmonic and egalitarian political cosmos. The very idea of the constellation model was thus contrary to the traditional and overbearing planetary language, as it promoted not hierarchy but equality among state-stars. The solar-planetary model (elaborated in chapter 2) and the constellational model were thus at odds: if states wished to maintain their "independence, and continue to occupy their place as a respectable constellation in the political firmament," they would need to beware, in the words of Virginia Congressman Philip Barbour, not to perform as "little twinkling stars" that "the meridian blaze of this Federal sun" would easily and completely eclipse.[11] Furthermore, and as already noted, the use of the image of the political constellation signified a shift from monarchs-as-stars to American states-as-stars.

This double movement, the turning away from the sun to the stars, and from a monarch to the state as the focus of this language, would define much of the American political astronomy thereafter. The American flag was central both in driving and in underscoring this transformation, and it held a long-standing role in solidifying the image of the American constellation in the national imagination. Considering its decisive function in enshrining and popularizing the image of the new constellation, it is imperative to better understand and contextualize the Star-Spangled Banner's creation, design, and symbolism.

A fateful resolution of the Naval Committee of the Continental Congress declared on June 14, 1777, that "the Flag of the thirteen United States, be Thirteen Stripes, alternate red and white; That the Union be Thirteen Stars, white in a Blue Field, representing a new Constellation." This laconic decree neither elaborated nor explained the meaning of the flag's use of stripes, nor of the colors red, white, and blue. It did not stipulate the shape or size of the stars, nor their order and layout. In fact, not until 1912, during the presidency of William Howard Taft, would the exact shape, order, and proportions of the flag be finally established. The authorization of the flag and its design in 1777 was, according to one authority, "a highly practical affair, without fanfare," hence we know nothing about the forces and motivations behind the creation of the Stars and Stripes.[12] However, since the United States was the first modern nation, the adoption of a new national flag was by definition an unprecedented move. Unlike its predecessors, the United States' flag did not represent a sovereign or a monarchic dynasty, nor was it centered around a heraldic coat of arms. Moreover, the Stars and Stripes was increasingly flown all over the place, much more so than older flags, the display of which was usually confined to military installations and ships. The American flag was a new breed of flag, a cloth that represented a people, a nation-state.

The American flag may have been unprecedented, but as we have just noted, its official order was concise to the extreme. To understand the sparse language of the Flag Act we must remind ourselves that early modern flags were not the effective vehicles for rallying national and patriotic passions that they have nowadays become, and that their symbolic meaning tended to be local and obscure. Flags served mostly as military standards for identification and as communication devices, and it was at sea that their use as large, colorful, and distinguishable objects of identification first became established practice (hence Congress's Naval Committee initiation of the Flag Act). In the colonies, Americans could glance at the British Union Jack flying over Crown property, such as official buildings and military installations. But while they could, they rarely would, as the North American British colonies were overwhelmingly rural, and most Americans spent their whole lives in the vicinity of their farms, with local centers of English power few and dispersed. Hence, the majority of colonial Americans rarely encountered flags, and many never have even observed a billowing British flag. Consequently, in the English imperial world, flags did not spontaneously inspire the average citizen's adoration. Even the American flag would become a universally revered and beloved icon of freedom and liberty only as the nineteenth century progressed, and it would gain this universal adoration as a direct consequence of the Civil War. In the paintings and drawings of the early republic it often appears as a decorative element, framing more favored national icons such as the Goddess of Liberty and George Washington. For a long while the Stars and Stripes would thus remain on the margins of the cultural and symbolic world of the new nation.

At the moment of imperial disintegration and the creation of the United States, the language of nationalism, including its visual lexicon, had yet to be born. That may explain the tardiness with which the new United States moved toward adopting a national flag, a concept that would mature only decades later. At a time in which the use of a national flag was still limited to a small number of buildings, installations, and ships, a Great Seal seemed to be a more pressing issue (more on that below). It took almost a full year for the Second Continental Congress to pass the Flag Act, which was, at least in retrospect, minimalist to a fault. The congressional resolution left many variables and their meanings, from the choice of colors, shapes, and proportions, unelaborated. We can only attempt to come to terms with those fateful choices, to deconstruct the motivations behind them, and reveal the ideas that drove them. It is a worthy endeavor as those variables were important in creating a pervasive and revered visual language that still saturates our lives centuries later.

With the surge of colonial resistance to strong-handed imperial measures in the 1760s, local and symbolic representations began to show up on colonial standards and flags. Among these were the snake (likely Benjamin Franklin's creation) and, more specifically, an indigenous rattlesnake, which symbolized vigilance and opposition; and the liberty pole and the pine tree, which were New England symbols of local self-reliance and moral rectitude. Meanwhile, liberty caps and the Goddess of Liberty also emerged as useful emblems for rallying support to the American

FIGURE 16. The Rebellious Stripes. (Redrawn by Nat Case)

cause, gaining traction in certain localities and times during the tumultuous revolutionary years. Among these new emblems was the Rebellious Stripes, a banner raised first by the Sons of Liberty in 1767, consisting of nine vertical alternate red and white stripes.[13]

The Rebellious Stripes may have set a precedent for American Patriots, but it was not the direct predecessor of the American flag. That role was preserved for the Continental Colors, the first generally accepted Continental flag, which was in use between 1775 and 1777. Also known as the Great Union and the Grand Union Flag, the Continental Colors had thirteen horizontal stripes of alternating red and white (as opposed to the Rebellious Stripes' vertical columns), supposedly representing the unity of the thirteen mainland colonies, with the crosses of St. George and St. Andrew adorning its canton (the upper inner quarter of the flag's field). The stripes manifested a degree of variation, as various flags displayed red and blues stripes, or red white and blue, and while thirteen stripes was the norm, their number could vary.[14] Some of the choices for the design of the Continental Colors are somewhat perplexing. Was the retention of the British Cross (which customarily represented the king of England and Scotland) an intentional gesture hinting at the possibility of reconciliation? Was it a "signal of submission," as George Washington surmised?[15] Whatever the reason behind the design, this temporary flag would never win the hearts and minds of the American rebels. Even as a banner for naval identification, for which it was predominantly used, it proved a poor choice as its design made it difficult to distinguish from the British flag. It did, however, bequeath to its much more successful successor the concept of a single national flag as well its thirteen horizontal alternating red and white stripes as a symbol of confederate unity.[16]

The Star-Spangled Republic

FIGURE 17. The Continental Colors. (Redrawn by Nat Case)

The anonymous designer(s) of the American flag and the author of the decree that gave birth to it may have felt that the use of red, white, and blue, as well as a canton and field, did not necessitate explanation because those elements were already in widespread use in late eighteenth-century flags and standards. Nevertheless, five years *after* the Flag Act, and in the context of elaborating on the design of the Great Seal, which bore similar colors, Congress bestowed meaning on this particular choice of colors: the white signified purity and innocence, the red vigor and valor, and the blue vigilance, perseverance, and justice. However, as the historian Arnaldo Testi points out, these correlations have the retrospective ring of ex post facto rationalizations as the colors may well have been adopted for more prosaic reasons: They were familiar from their use in other designs, and the fabrics and dyes were in common use. In other words, the colors of the British flag were adopted simply because they were readily available in the struggling wartime, preindustrial economy of the young American nation.[17] White purity, red valor, and blue vigilance may be noble connotations, but it was the immediate accessibility of the colors that prompted Americans to dye their flags with such recognizably English pigments.

The most striking feature of the flag was the thirteen white stars, which appeared beside the red and white horizontal stripes in a blue canton in the flag's upper-left corner. Each star ostensibly represented an autonomous state in the new confederacy, but the vague and sparse specifications of the Flag Act suggested that, theoretically, any possible arrangement of the stars was legitimate. Consequently, there were numerous variations in the early flags, from the first thirteen-star flags, and well into the nineteenth century. Even more than the inconsistencies in the sizes and layouts of the stripes, the canton, and the field in numerous early flags (not to mention the fabrics and pigments), the stars themselves varied to an extent that bewilders modern viewers used to the uniformity of the fifty-star flag. The colors of the stars varied, as early flags could boast red stars, such as in the Chester County Militia Color, carried at the revolutionary Battle of Brandywine. Stars' shapes varied as well, and stars with "any number" of points were used on early flags, some of which even demonstrated stars with different numbers of points on a single flag. Stars often came with six or seven points, as in the heraldic tradition, but could number up to eight. Many flags used the now-familiar five-point star, but that shape was in no sense universal or the norm.[18]

While stars' color and shape varied, those factors were rather incidental in terms of political astronomy. However, the arrangement of the stars on the flags, and sometimes their respective sizes, reflected ideas from the realm of political astronomy regarding the relationship between the states they represented and the American federation. Even more than with the other elements of the flags, a spectacular variety of arrangements of stars appeared and disappeared during the evolutionary stages of the American flag. The stars could be arranged in a full circle; sometimes in a circle of twelve with a central star; in horizontal rows, occasionally forming a square frame around the blue center; in an arch over the number seventy-six; and the many stars might even form the shape of one larger star. Early flags often arranged the thirteen stars in rows (usually between three and five), with popular figures consisting of rows of 3-2-3-2-3 and 4-5-4. However, eighteenth-century stars could also be arranged in rows of 4-4-5, 4-4-3-2, 4-3-5, and 5-4-3-2.[19] While the numerical distribution of the stars in rows did not inherently matter in terms of a meaningful political astronomy, the distances among them did. Many, probably most, flags boasted stars that were arranged in a "staggered" fashion, that is, set in an equidistant form (consequently causing some rows to be shorter and some to be longer horizontally, hence the different configuration of rows in different flags). A uniformly laid out field of stars, to which we are accustomed through the modern American flag, expressed the underlying idea of equality and harmony among state-stars.

In such a dispersion of flags, no star dominated another or expressed any particular quality. State-stars were equal and uniform, identical siblings in a constellational family who lost their unique personality when seen as part of the Union.

While staggered stars in many forms were popular, it was in no sense the exclusive design during the first decades of the republic. Stars could be dispersed in shapes such as an arc, such as in General Schuyler's Flag, or a rectangle, as in the Plan of Fort Harmar (sketch of both details below). As in the staggered arrangements, these patterns expressed a similar set of ideas regarding political congruency and equality. Circular arrangements were a special favorite of painters, designers, and flag makers, since the ring traditionally and expressly suggested unity and perpetuity. Called medallion patterns, the famed circular arrangement has come to be known as the Betsy Ross Flag, named after the Philadelphia seamstress whom myth credits with making the first American flag. With the expansion of the republic, as additional stars were added to the original thirteen, they continued to appear in various configurations of straight rows, arranged vertically, in columns, and in a square border.

Beyond the possible arrangement and alignment of the stars, historians have struggled to determine their exact origin, or even why the particular shape of a star was used in the first place. While studies have been dedicated to the history of most elements contained in the American flag, the origins of the stars, the most distinct shape imprinted on the flag, have remained obscure and typically less explored. Regardless of the prominent place of the symbol of the state-as-star and the consequent American constellation in the American political vocabulary, vexillologists and historians of the American flag seem at times to have accepted unsubstantiated conjectures regarding the origins of this idiom. While several authors have simply disregarded the question of the stars' source or meaning,[20] the leading assumption of those who have explored the question of the origins of the stars seems to be that their lineage descends either from the Masonic star-laden visual tradition or, alternatively, from the coat of arms of George Washington's family.[21] The crucial point, however, is that the use of the symbol of the American constellation and the state-as-star involved a remarkable intellectual reconfiguration, tightly linked to the emergence of American republicanism.

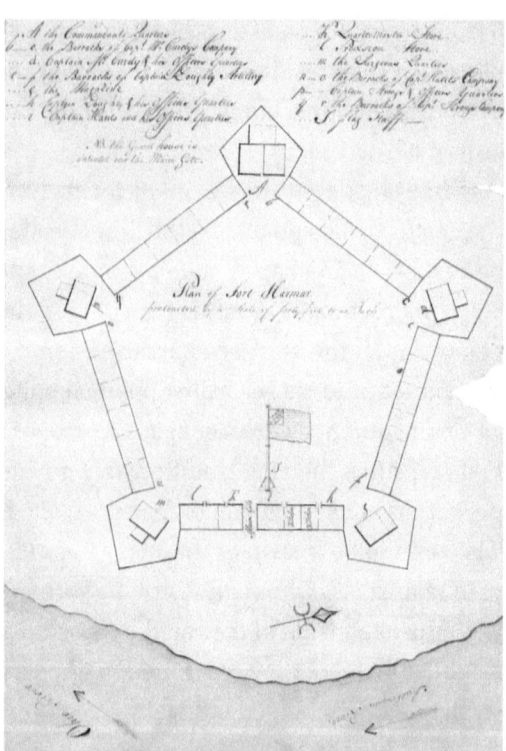

FIGURE 18. Plan of Fort Harmar with a sketch detail of flag showing thirteen stars arranged diagonally in rows of 4-5-4 (1786). Many idiosyncratic shapes appeared in the final years of the eighteenth century. (Courtesy of the William L. Clements Library Image Bank, University of Michigan)

Late eighteenth-century political readings of the heavens were already an established tradition, as we have seen in previous chapters, and even had a New World variant in the form of "patriotic astrology," which expressed colonial Spanish Americans' belief in the beneficial and soothing heavenly influences on South America. However, only in the early United States did a political astronomy that linked contemporary ideologies with the stars emerge. Hence, since the attempt to locate the origin (or originator) of the symbolic representation of the state-as-star is to chase a mirage, it is more fruitful to uncover the reasons for its adoptions and the meaning and significance of its visual language for contemporaries.[22]

Remaining silent on all elements of the flag other than the stars, the Flag Resolution elaborated only that the thirteen states formed "a new Constellation." This points to the remarkable originality of the new American flag, which implied that United States was written in the skies, a novel and unprecedented political constellation.[23] The symbol of state-

FIGURE 19. General Schuyler's Flag (canton detail). The thirteen stars of this flag (dated "after 1784") are arranged in an arc over an eagle with a shield. (Independence National Historical Park)

FIGURE 20. The Betsy Ross Flag. This well-known design was one among several competing layouts of the constellation of stars. The variation was possible due to the nonspecific language of the Flag Act (1777). (Redrawn by Nat Case)

as-star and the consequent image of the United States as a new constellation thus involved an intellectual reconfiguration tightly linked to the American republican Revolution and the emergence of nationhood in the United States: it was egalitarian, without a symbolic monarchical center to which to pay homage. Republican ideology found its primal visual representation in the image of the political constellation composed of state-stars. That familiar and fateful portrayal would instigate a rich and significant political astronomy that would accompany the United States throughout its history.

The republicanism and antimonarchism of the American Revolution shattered the traditional political understanding based on the imagery of a single solar power center. We have seen at length how European absolutist kings were viewed as suns, an outlook epitomized in the image of Louis XIV but prevalent across the continent, England included. In this view, kings were suns placed in the middle of a solar "system," the nation, which reigned harmoniously over revolving "planets" (traditionally understood as standing for either social orders, state apparatus, or magistrates). A crucial revolutionary move took place in America: From a monarchic sun the political universe was transformed into an egalitarian starry constellation, from a celestial kingly hierarchy to an astro-republican firmament. The Revolution (initially, we should remind ourselves, an astronomic term denoting the rotation of the heavens) gave rise to a wholly new mode of communicating the political-national order. Now, with the American states viewed as stars, no single sun, or kingly star, overshadowed and dominated others; together the American state-stars constituted a novel political system in which a plurality of individual stars held together, comprising a republican "constellation" that was more perfect than its discrete parts.

In place of the king as sun around which the political realm revolves, in the 1770s an alternative and revolutionary political cosmology emerged and was enshrined in the new nation's symbols: a diffuse constellation of uniform floating stars devoid of a solar center that embodied egalitarian and republican values. From the republic's founding, expansion, and the consequent addition of stars to the "new American constellation," through its temporary collapse during the Civil War, and beyond to our own day, this constellational image provided a distinct vocabulary to articulate and express Americans' shifting attitudes toward, and understanding of, their political Union.

This idea that a republican solar system was benevolent, benign, and not monarchically coercive was expressed graphically first and foremost on the flag but also on the likes of paper money and other insignia. As we have seen, the image had several variations in its initial evolution. Within the process of the formation of the Star-Spangled Banner, the Cowpens Flag, carried by the Third Maryland Regiment at the Battle of Cowpens in January 1781, signifies a link in the evolution from a solar to a constellational model of the American flag. As in medallion-patterned flags, the stars in the Cowpens design are arranged in a circle on a blue field; but the circle consists of just twelve stars, with the thirteenth identical star in the center (fig. 14; for more on the Cowpens Flag, see chap. 2). The Cowpens design is only a relatively known example of other designs that boasted a distinguishable star within the constellation. A similar design was the Easton (Pennsylvania) Flag, a circle of six-point stars on a blue field with a central star, which may have preceded the Cowpens Flag. The New York Pewterers' Banner, made to celebrate the ratification of the federal Constitution of 1788, included several elements that represented the pewterers and their art, the Constitution, and, in the upper-left corner, an American flag designed similarly to the Cowpens pattern. A flag engraved on David Shaw's powder horn reveals an early and unusual arrangement of the thirteen stars (along with other peculiar ornamentations). The stars on the horn were laid out in two vertical lines of six six-point stars each, with the thirteenth star holding a central position in the middle.

As is evident from the examples above, during the decade following Independence the design of a central star that was similarly shaped yet distinguishable through its pivotal position appeared throughout the republic. While these patterns surely call to mind the representations of the solar monarchism discussed in chapter 2, it is notable that while a single star was centrally positioned in the Cowpens-like examples, it was no longer a domineering sun. At most the central star functioned as a first among peers and not as a monarch among subjects, which in all the abovementioned cases denoted local patriotism, a mute if evident preference toward the state of whoever flew these flags. The various iterations of designs that included a central star may have echoed the solar monarchism, but they did not suggest a longing for kingly rule. Rather, those hierarchical designs actually manifested the difficulty in the intellectual and psychological adjustment of the states in recalibrating their diminished sovereignty in a federal republic.

Nineteenth-century patterns continued to occasionally suggest hierarchy, albeit more vaguely. One example was the Great Star pattern, in which a large central star was surrounded by five smaller stars in each of its angles, five smaller stars between each of the previous five, and so forth, together giving the impression of a large star formed out of the many. Yet Great Star patterns, first proposed by House Representative

FIGURE 21. The Pewterers' Banner (1788). This relatively late example portrays New York, somewhat oddly, as a central seven-point star, with the other stars having seven or eight points. (Photography © The New York Historical)

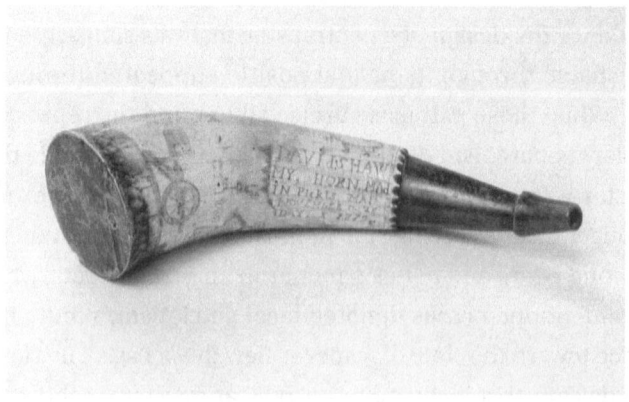

FIGURE 22. David Shaw's powder horn with flag engraving (1779). (Courtesy private collection)

Peter Wendover after the War of 1812 and offered over the years in many varieties, never dominated the vexillological scene, and American flags would soon abandon hierarchical representations altogether.[24] Seen in the broader context, these hierarchical patterns, while not anomalous, do seem the exception. Early American flags tended to convey, and rather consistently, egalitarian constellational models, boasting the indistinguishable state-stars of the American republican federacy.

The Star-Spangled Republic

The ideas related to political astronomy that underlay the Flag Act ("13 stars ... representing a new constellation"), adopted with little ceremony by the obscure Naval Committee of Congress, no longer resonate with modern audiences. Yet from its inception during the Revolution, politically conscious contemporaries seem to have understood perfectly well the motivations behind the design of the new flag, particularly its novel starry symbolism. In a letter that paraphrased the wording of the Flag Act, Benjamin Franklin, who had—not surprisingly for such a Renaissance man as he—a lifelong interest in astronomy, was proud to acquaint the ambassador of Naples with "the Flag of the United States of America [that] consists of thirteen Stripes, alternately red, white and blue; a small Square in the upper angle, next the flag staff, is a blue field, with thirteen white Stars, denoting a new Constellation." Notably, Franklin followed the example of the Flag Act itself in elaborating only on the novel and celestial element of the flag. Benjamin Rush, another savant–scientist–revolutionary politician, proposed in 1777 to introduce "a constellation to be worn on the breast containing thirteen stars as a reward for military exploits," and the Bostonian Patriot James Lovell revealingly remarked in a letter to Abigail Adams that "the rising Constellation which is now in place of the British Union [Jack] is a Device greatly admired in our Colours." Ezra Stiles, president of Yale University, commented that "The Congress have substituted a new Constella of Stars (instead of the Union) in the Continental Colours."[25] The United States was viewed from its outset as a new constellation that replaced an older, corrupt, and European solar-monarchical system. A republican assemblage of stars formed that constellation, an idea still manifested on numerous flagpoles across the land, even if its original meaning has long since been lost and obscured. It would take years, however, (and another, civil, war) before the flag would truly become a democratic symbol of popular identity that entered, literally, into people's homes and backyards. By then, however, its rich symbolic meaning had dimmed and was already fading from collective memory.

The affirmation that the United States was a new constellation represented by state-stars was not fashioned in the private correspondence of the elite and college-educated alone. This language was part and parcel of a public discourse taking place in the democratized public sphere of print. By 1778, Patriots were already extolling "the stars, who support the honor of your flag, your new constellation, the thirteen stars," suggesting that soon after the Stars and Stripes became the nation's official emblem, politically involved Americans were already exploiting the understanding of the United States as a republican assemblage of stars. By the end of the Revolutionary War, American stars had infiltrated popular culture to such an extent that they could present business opportunities. For example, Jane Franklin Mecum suggests in a letter to her brother Benjamin Franklin that it might be "cleaver [sic] to have thirteen stars" imprinted on the soaps her family manufactured for American consumers, in place of the traditional, and now contemptible, crown.[26] The numerous British and Loyalist (as well as friendly French) standards and banners that flew in revolutionary-era camps, battlefields, and shipyards conspicuously did not boast stars. The stars on the American flag were, however, not lost on foreign observers, who left several drawn sketches and paintings that included star-spangled banners. Star-bearing flags, certainly those that boasted a constellation, were a novel and conspicuous innovation of the citizens of the new American federal republic.[27]

The stars on the young United States' numerous flags were a remarkable and saliently graphic representation of the emerging American political consciousness, and the political astronomy that expressed and communicated it. However, regardless of and without reference to the graphic representations on the new American flag, throughout the War of Independence commentators would refer to their political nation, at a time when the united states were still commonly referred to in the plural, as the "new constellation" that would endure the current troubles and "rise to the Zenith."[28] The "new constellation" served as an effective metaphor to justify the unprecedented appearance of a new nation. The newly created United States was the harbinger of modern nationalism, one of the most powerful social forces of the past two centuries. Yet the world of this nascent nationalism was still anchored in the political values of "usage" and tradition.[29] Political astronomy provided a system of thought that, in contrast to traditional republican ideology, was not grounded in the revered and ancient histories of liberty-loving yeomen societies of arms-bearing farmers. Rather, it was a language derived from a star-spangled universe that was justified in cosmic, and thus ahistorical, terms. Political astronomy's ahistoricity was thus a blessing; while the

United States could attempt to anchor itself in history through various connections to revered nations from biblical Israel to ancient Rome and the Anglo-Saxons, the fact that it was newly created was indisputable.[30] That Americans could justify and legitimize their republic through a cosmic and thus timeless order not only bypassed the burden of history but also presented the United States as a congruent polity that was in harmonic agreement with nature, as "natural." Hence, when a group of Native Americans saw the Stars and Stripes for the first time in 1819, "they saw the stars upon the blue, which they knew were from the heavens, they thought God must have put it into the hearts of the people to make such a flag."[31] Even the most peripheral Americans intuitively conversed in political astronomy and interpreted the connection between the stars on the flag and their connection to a cosmic order.

The formal enshrinement of the new constellation on the national flag initiated a starry discourse that would characterize the political rhetoric of the United States thereafter. In this context, five years after establishing the Stars and Stripes, Congress created the Great Seal as the official standard, resolving to place "over the head of the American Eagle . . . a glory, or, breaking through a cloud, proper, surrounding 13 stars, forming a constellation, argent on an azure field." Once again, revolutionaries could go to great lengths to explain the symbolism of the new American constellation. While the rationale of the use of the different colors was set forth (white signified "purity and innocence"; red, "hardiness and valour"; and blue, "vigilance, perseverance, and justice"), "the crest, or constellation," newspapers reports explained, "denotes a new state taking its place among other sovereign powers."[32]

The fact that the Latin motto *e pluribus unum*—out of many, one—was enshrined underneath the Great Seal's thirteen-star constellation underscores why this metaphor was so effective. Although individual members of an assemblage may logically precede the whole, the starry constellation transformed this order. As in the idea expressed in *e pluribus unum*, the constellation of American state-stars formed a more perfect whole than its discrete constituents. Emerging from the "old constellation" of the corrupt European state system, the American Union presented itself to a candid world through its most formal symbols as a new constellation of star-states that was regulated, predictable, harmonious and sublime,

FIGURE 23. The Great Seal, in the 1782 design proposed by William Barton. In this early design the Latin motto is absent, but note the seven-pointed stars on the shield and the medallion pattern on the flag. (National Archives, NAID 595257)

characteristics that could be attributed only to the political constellation as a whole and not to its individual members.[33]

The years surrounding the ratification of the federal constitution and the first years of the operation of the government under its auspices proved particularly important for the establishment of the image of the American constellation. As news began to circulate of the Constitutional Convention about to convene in Philadelphia in May 1787, a writer in the *Newport Herald* articulated the zeitgeist of the Critical Period with his pronouncement that "the political existence of the United States [depends] on the result of the deliberations of the Convention." Aware of the stakes, this author expressed his anger at Rhode Island and its "antifederal position," which ensured that the rogue state's leaders did not send a delegate to the Convention and only ratified three years after its sister states. This state's adamant defiance, the author warned, could lead her to "be dropped out of the union" and would not make the "American Constellation lose one gem thereby." Indeed, the promise in the near future of the addition of states to the constellation "with far superior luster . . . would more than compensate the loss" of the Rhode Island star.[34] With the process of ratification gaining momentum, so were the images of political astronomy gaining prominence in the public sphere, particularly for Federalist advocates of the new Constitution. A song that was "sung in the grand procession, at Portsmouth" to the "new tune—'Union,'" points to the centrality of this celestial language. Written after nine states had ratified, thus making the Constitution valid and operative, the song hailed "the rising of . . . fed'ral Stars." These verses followed:

> Federal States politically join'd,
> With glorious rays our hemisphere adorn;
> As splendid stars in amity combin'd,
> Rise, the auspicious harbingers of morn
>
> . . . .
>
> Hail rad'ant Constellation! Spring of day!
> Ye Stars of magnitude in splendour rise!
> Come, chase the night of Discord far away
>
> . . . .
>
> In perfect concord shall our Council move.[35]

Already an established idiom by 1788, the cosmological language perpetuated attributes that seem to have held a special appeal to Federalists. While the planetary realm harbored balance and order, a constellation of starry states promised, in the words of the song, harmony and "perfect concord." The language of celestial politics claimed cosmic underpinnings for the new and unprecedented form of the American government and the political philosophy of republican federalism. Yet the harmony that the constellational language promised was not one centered on coercion and concentration of power but rather on equality among state-stars, and the republican political firmament was cultivated as a space for equality. This is not to say that the image of political stars comprising a constellation could only express harmony and political tranquility. In similar fashion to the planetary language of power and balance, the constellational image could be applied to describe anxieties related to the relations of part and whole. As Massachusetts counties were preparing to send their delegates to the first Congress under the federal Constitution, an author from Boston emphatically wished that his state would not reflect "delegated light . . . like a dim glimmering star" that would be "scarcely visible in the bright blaze of the federal constellation."[36] Similar concerns regarding the autonomy of the state-stars vis-à-vis the political constellation would be frequently and prominently expressed during the antebellum years as Southern states struggled against what they saw as encroachments of the federal government.

It appears, then, that around the time of the Constitutional Convention the image of the constellation and its entourage of ideas was making deeper inroads into the public sphere and the budding political culture of the United States.[37] One indication of this process was the centrality of the image of the constellation in published and publicly read poems, processions, and material culture. For example, in 1791, a July Fourth celebratory procession in Dover concluded its parade in a townhouse "decorated with figures emblematical of the occasion," with a portrait of George Washington topped "with a constellation of stars" prominently positioned on the head of the house's front pillar.[38] Again, a report that proved right "the many accounts of the flourishing state of the infant manufacturers of America" described a carpet maker from Philadelphia who wove a carpet, hailed as a "master piece of [its] kind," which was designed for the floor of "the Senate chamber of the United States." The carpet visibly represented "thirteen Stars forming a constellation, diverging from a cloud," and was meant to "occupy the space under the chair of the Vice President," who presided over the chamber.[39] The constellation of American stars thus formed a powerful visual image that caught on very early in the life of the United States, making inroads into its material culture. It continued to prevail and flourish as it adapted to the needs of the rapidly expanding Union. As the citizens of the young United States gloried in their new American constellation, they constantly remembered that the cosmos from which they derived their political models "forced [them] to believe" that it was created by a supremely intelligent God.[40]

The American constellation originally consisted of thirteen stars, but it was in no sense a closed group. As we well know, the United States was a sprawling entity that looked to expand as soon as the War of Independence ended in 1783. Indeed, like the federation it represented, the constellation incrementally grew, star by star, for over a century. Those moments of national expansion provided opportunities to elaborate on the enlargement of the federal constellation. As early as 1784, when politically conscious Americans deluded themselves about an imminent Canadian revolt against their formerly shared British "usurper masters," they envisioned Canada as a prospective additional "star in the American constellation."[41]

As in the case of the Canadian star (that, needless to say, did not materialize), Americans missed the mark again in 1788 when predicting that Kentucky would become "the Fourteenth luminary in the American constellation," hoping that it would "reflect upon the original States." Their perennial frustration with Rhode Island's behavior in refusing "to co-operate in this business" of making a federal Constitution in 1787 convinced many that "the American Constellation" would not suffer from the adamant state and that the still-independent state of Vermont, which eventually would become the fourteenth state, "would more than compensate the loss" of Rhode Island's star. When the commissioners of New York and Vermont finally and "amicably adjusted" so "that Vermont [was] dismembered from the state of New York," a reporter rejoiced that "a fourteenth star will be added to the federal Constellation."[42] The early decades of the nineteenth century, a time of continuous growth for the republic, proved right those contemporaries who predicted, like the following writer in Kentucky (itself of course not one of the original thirteen states), that "new states, like stars on our political constellation" would continue "annually acceding to the nation," joining its "beams of liberty."[43] When Arkansas and Michigan joined the Union (respectively in 1836 and 1837) as "sovereign and independent states," a commentator for the *Alexandria Gazette* mused that "the Galaxy of American Glory is brightened, and that star after star is added to that brilliant Constellation which is the pride of the Western World." Referring to the new states as stars, he assured readers that "every star that glitters" would continue to spangle "the azure of the political firmament." The author continued with the prediction, off the mark as the secession of the Southern states would at least temporarily prove, that "forever the banner of our country continue to wave, not a stripe creased nor a star obliterated," but will rather shine "with still increasing effulgence."[44] This author demonstrates the dynamism and power of the language of political astronomy, which not only replicated itself but also drove a process of elaboration and accommodation to new contexts and processes.

Presenting states as stars enabled and encouraged discussion of an "American galaxy" and "political firmament." This tendency was demonstrated time and again, as in a July Fourth celebration in 1836, during which a toast was raised in the honor of the two new states (Arkansas and Michigan), or rather "two planets in [the American] political firmament." The cosmic image was further expanded upon as the words of the toast expressed the wish, "may the sun of Democracy continue to be surrounded by satellites of their order and brilliancy."[45] A hiatus of almost a decade ensued after the joining of Arkansas and Michigan, with the addition of Florida to the Union coming in early 1845, followed by the fateful annexation of the Republic of Texas later that year. With the addition of the Lone Star State, the rhetorical flourishes of political astronomy appeared once more. The citizens of Franklin County, New York, resolved "with joy and pride, the rise of another Star in our political firmament." As in previous cases, they saw this new state-star "shine . . . in glory in our galaxy of states." Not all were content with the growing constellation; one Richmond Whig, for example, whose party was bent on internal improvement rather than expansion, worried that "if additions continue to be made according to the same rate," then "instead of having twenty-six stars glittering, as heretofore, in our political firmament, we are more likely to have thirty-six."

Those inclined toward annexation, such as Alexander Stephens of Georgia, future vice president of the Confederacy, were also keen to advance their stance through political astronomy. In a speech to the House on the Joint Resolution for the Annexation of Texas (joint of the U.S. Congress as well of the Texas legislature), Congressman Stephens addressed the difficulties of adding an independent republic to the Union. The subject, like "great objects in nature, swell out and enlarge as we come nearer to it." Indeed, according to Stephens, "as we approach nearer to it, its surface is far from appearing even and smooth." If, Stephens warned, "the restrictions proposed for Missouri's addition [in 1820] should be imposed upon [Texas]," it may "endanger the harmony and even existence of our present Union." As glad as Stephens was to add "the luster of the 'lone star,' as some gentlemen have been pleased to designate our neighboring Republic," due to its flag (more on that below), he himself felt "much more admiration for the bright galaxy of twenty-six brilliant stars of our own glorious constellation . . . rather than see her shooting from her place, producing disorder and confusion in our well-balanced system." In other words, if Northerners would insist on adding Texas as a free state, Stephens would rather "greatly prefer to let her 'beam on' with increasing splendor" on her own, "as a fixed star in the political firmament." Yet on her own, the Georgian worried, or rather warned, Texas might never reach the status of a star of "first magnitude." Within these spirited discussions of political stars, constellations, and firmaments, it is no wonder that contemporaries wished for a time when the Cuban "beautiful land will add another to the stars that shine in our political firmament."[46] As the republic kept growing, it could be seen as an "animated Colossus . . . crowned with a glittering constellation," with "new stars . . . luminaries" glowing "bright and triumphant . . . daily added to the cluster."[47] By midcentury the issue of territorial expansion was regularly contemplated in celestial terms, further entrenching understandings of the United States as a cosmic polity, albeit one that, in contrast to the unchanging firmament, was constantly reformulating and increasing in size. With the increase of its size and addition of stars, the danger of unbalancing the harmony of the American constellation dangerously increased as well.

On April 4, 1818, President James Monroe signed an act that "Provided for 13 stripes and one star for each state, to be added to the flag on the 4th of July following the admission of each new state." By this time, the flag already held twenty stars, and the official decree stipulated what contemporaries had looked for, namely that additional stars would not ruin the balanced harmony but rather strengthen the American constellation. It is not the intention of this discussion to capture the staggering variety of nineteenth-century American flags.[48] Rather, I wish to point to the American flag culture that developed during that century, which attests to the pervasiveness of the language of political cosmology: Seventeen of the thirty-seven (46 percent) American states that joined the Union after 1776 would explicitly include stars on their flags. New states from Arkansas in the South to Ohio in the North internalized the language of states-as-stars and visually expressed this fundamental notion on the flags that they con-

FIGURE 24. The Lone Star Flag of the Republic of Texas. This flag demonstrates how a potent American political astronomy and flag culture exerted their sway over the independent Texan republic, leading it to adopt a flag that adhered to the idiom of stars and states. (Redrawn by Nat Case)

sciously and deliberately fashioned. Most notable, perhaps, was Texas, "the lone star republic," which was founded as an independent state under the sphere of American political (and flag) culture but eventually attached its star-spangled state banner to the incrementally growing constellation.[49] This dynamism and its ability to project itself outward and keep up with the rapidly expanding American Union of states signaled the efficacy and maturity of nineteenth-century political astronomy.

Arguably even more striking, and entirely overlooked, is the fact that the United States provided starry inspiration not only to the states that joined the American Union but also to numerous new nations and states that established their independence during the nineteenth century and beyond. Scores of new countries across the globe's five continents, from the Philippines and Australia to Brazil and Togo, from tiny island nations such as Micronesia to continental giants such as the Republic of China, took their cue from the American starry idiom and adorned their national flags with celestial phenomena. Republics and monarchies, liberal democracies and authoritarian dynasties, all followed the American lead and fashioned themselves as correlated with heavenly bodies. While some nations made use of the traditional symbol of the sun, such was the American influence that many made use of the distinctly American five-point star to represent their own polities. Particularly striking are confederacies in which each polity is represented by an indistinct star, such as the European Union and the Cook Islands with their Continental-like ring of five-point stars, which adopted the most American of visual images for their national (or, in the case of the European Union, confed-

FIGURE 25. Cook Islands Ensign (1974), demonstrating through the Union Jack its historic ties to the United Kingdom, and a fifteen-star ring symbolizing the Cook Islands. The ring of stars clearly follows the revolutionary Betsy Ross Flag. (Redrawn by Nat Case)

erate) symbol. The modern design of a flag to represent a new nation, of which the American Stars and Stripes led the way, is particularly significant due to the amount of conscious thought that is necessarily put into such symbolism. That a striking vexillological phenomenon on such a massive scale as the use of celestial bodies is so overlooked and understudied can be explained only by the fact that we moderns are thoroughly habituated and thus blind to its uniqueness.

While many nations are chosen, as the revealing title of a study that places nationalism along the paradigmatic lines of biblical chosenness indicates, the flags of many underscore that they perceive themselves as being written in the skies.[50] In this light, the connection between the Stars and Stripes and the complex set of ideas associated with "exceptionalism" seems somewhat ironic. While Americans came to understand themselves in celestial and thus exceptional terms, as a nation that corresponds with the cosmic, they also paved the way for an "exceptionalist inflation" as those of dozens of other nationalities came to present and understand themselves in similar terms. The United States' heavenly image has thus not only shaped Americans' understanding of their nation, but it has also had a powerful global effect on the ways in which numerous communities around the world imagine themselves. The state-as-star and consequent image of the American constellation, born uneventfully in a mundane wartime pronouncement of the Continental Congress, has become remarkable evidence of America's wielding of global soft power.

The global diffusion of this astro-political language should not obscure the fact that it has its roots in the American Revolution and was, and still is, associated with American political culture. One of the hallmarks of this original language was the use of a select set of metaphors upon which discoursers habitually expanded. We have seen how the image of a political constellation was so common that it became a metonym for the United States, the "new constellation." Similarly, the "political firmament" proved a most fruitful image, signifying a celestial space that harbored the American constellation of state-stars. The political firmament was an ethereal locus that showcased the American cosmic polities and displayed "the brilliancy of the star of our Union." State-stars, as well as human stars (as we shall see in the epilogue), could be seen as soaring in the political heavens, but so, at times, could more mundane entities. Cumberland County, New York, for example, was hailed "a bright star indeed in the political firmament."[51] Elite American women such as Letitia Christian Tyler, wife of President James Tyler, believed that a global political firmament could provide an arena for national triumph. In the First Lady's estimate, a global political firmament could host "nations that are now stars of the first magnitude" but would inevitably "shrink into comparative insignificance in the progress of this [American] mighty people."[52] Further expanding on this image, national politicians described the American political firmament as a "welkin dome illuminated only by that sparkling constellation," and "our Union," as "preserv[ing] its azure hue unsullied."[53] At times the innate equality that political astronomy implied could be subverted, as in the case of an author in the *Newburyport (MA) Herald* who in the late 1830s designated six states (Massachusetts, New York, Virginia, South Carolina Kentucky, and Missouri) as "the fixed stars in our political firmament," while "the remaining eighteen have been but twinkling satellites revolving around them."[54] During times in which the crises of the antebellum years seemed temporarily resolved, commentators saw "the portentous clouds which darkened our horizon... disappearing; and the stars which illuminate and adorn the political firmament, still shine, undiminished in number and splendor."[55] Constellations, galaxies, firmaments, luminaries, and stars provided the public and its leaders with a wild field for articulating and evaluating, often lavishing patriotic praise on their ever-dynamic political universe.

The constellation could also provide a venue for concerned citizens to express their anxiety as to their respective states' place within the expanding constellation. A Virginian representative thus asked, "How seemeth Virginia's Star Bright gleaming, as of yore?" He answered his rhetorical question, "Alas! . . . We see it obscured—but feebly twinkling amid the splendour of surrounding orbs!"[56] Even more often commentators articulated their state's unique and favored place in the firmament of political stars. A New Yorker mused on the privileged status of his commonwealth, "that star of the American political constellation," while Pennsylvanians deemed their state "one of the brightest stars in our political constellation." A Marylander raised a toast to his state, which "though disgraced at present by the government of a minority," would—he believed—"shortly appear as a bright luminary in our political constellation." The star of the formerly independent Republic of Texas was "once lone" but transformed into an American state, thus promising that it would "splendidly . . . shine . . . in our political constellation."[57]

Not only states but also prestatehood territories—the yet unorganized expanses of land that were overseen by the federal government—were subject to cosmic descriptions. Musing on the "young territory" of Minnesota, a Massachusetts writer enthusiastically observed that it was "rapidly improving" and wished for it "before many years to take its place in the Union as one of the bright stars which form this political constellation."[58] In the wake of the events of Bleeding Kansas, William Seward commented in a remarkable Senate speech on the process through which United States territories transformed into states. Against the background of the new cosmologies that emerged in the second half of the nineteenth century, which included theories of the evolution of stars and galaxies, Seward described territorial expansion and state formation in terms of political astronomy. He pointed out that territories acquire their eventual character as states through a "majestic and magnificent process," suggesting that new states would become, through influence and projection, free or slave states. Just as "new stars do not form themselves out of the nebular in the recesses of space and come out to adorn the blues expanse above us," so do "free States shape themselves out of the ever developing elements of our benign civilization, and rise to take their places in this great political constellation." Through a teleological view of nature and cosmos, Seward asked his peers not to interfere with the emergence of free states, just as they would not interfere with the creation of new stars. "Let, then, nature and reason and hope have their heaven, appointed way. Resist them no longer."[59]

William Seward's call to let nature have its way had significant implications for the political world, particularly regarding the complex set of ideas involving "American exceptionalism." The repeated use of astronomical images during the decades following the creation of the United States manifests the relatedness of the notion of America-as-constellation and another distinct understanding of the United States, namely as a "redeemer nation." Scholars have long studied this aspect of American history (dating from John Winthrop's famed "city upon a hill") and the various ways in which America was seen as a chosen nation, God's new Israel, and the "last hope of earth." Hence descriptions of an American constellation echoed an already-existing idiom of an American mission to guide a yet-to-be-enlightened world (had not stars guided travelers and navigators for millennia?). An American constellation further implied, however, that the Union was "natural" and in accordance with the cosmos. As opposed to placing the United States in history, for example, as an extension of ancient, biblical, or Anglo-Saxon annals, political astronomy grounded American republicanism in nature, and potentially exempted the United States from the excesses of human history. Hence, one of the attractions of cosmic politics was that it could offer a path to alleviate American anxieties related to the corruption and decline that had snared historical polities in the past, a dreadful moment in historical time that we have come to understand through the scholarship of John Pocock as "Machiavellian." If so, the celestial metaphor was a significant manifestation and addition to the powerful paradigm of "American exceptionalism," the belief that America is unique and uniquely privileged by Providence, and thus not subject to "normal" historical laws.[60]

The echoes of the language of mission and exceptionalism were already evident in early moments of political astronomical elaboration, such as a "very numerous Meeting of the Republican Whig-Citizens" conducted in honor of the British evacuation of Charleston, South Carolina, in 1783. The thirteenth toast was raised to honor "the Thirteen Stars, emblematically adorning the Imperial Pavilion of Confederated America." These celestial bodies had a sacred role to fill, those present at the meeting were told, namely, to "Prove a luminous Constellation, enlightening the Bewildered, and directing the footsteps of the oppressed of the World to the Shrine of Liberty." This pathos-filled appeal to the world's browbeaten, coming from such an unexpected place as the slaveholding and aristocratic South Carolina, presented an eighteenth-century secularized version of the Puritan model of Christian charity, and underscores how a political cosmology integrated with and reinforced a central tenet of American political language. Characteristically, Northerners made even more bluntly millennial appeals than their Southern compatriots, such as, for example, the postrevolutionary Massachusetts writer who prophesized that "the splendor of our American constellation, may go on encreasing—Until sun and stars, shall be no more; and all the kingdoms of this world shall vanish like a scroll."[61] The anxious, millennia-old, and religiously metaphysical apocalyptic tradition, and the observational astronomy that stemmed from the empirical and rational culture of the Enlightenment, had separate if intertwined intellectual genealogies. As we have just seen, however, the two traditions could merge to position the "new American constellation" in a prophetic context. By adding a celestial dimension to their republicanism, American political discoursers considerably expanded their horizon of national expectations. For them, the United States was written in the stars.

Such millennial anxieties and hopes, and their connection to the starry universe Americans observed and of which their knowledge was continually expanding, were innately tied to a religiosity and conception of God that had developed during the revolutionary era. By the middle of the eighteenth century the precepts of natural religion had become part of the mainstream of the British North American scene. Influenced by the movement of the American Enlightenment, which, like its European variant, elevated reason and observation, a religion that was validated on the basis of human reason and experience became prominent.[62] Hence, John Winthrop of Harvard, a teacher of mathematics and one of British America's leading astronomers, declared that celestial observations would not only validate scientific astronomy but also provide deeper insight into the astonishing works of God. Without observation and scientific contemplation, the "just idea of the grandeur of works of GOD" would go unrealized.[63] For Winthrop, the mathematician and descendant of Puritan royalty, a wondrous universe provided proof of an omnipotent and transcendent God. Like Winthrop, American divines and laymen repeatedly marveled at God, who, in the words of a revolutionary-era poem:

> ... bid this universe from nothing spring,
> Can at his Word bid numerous worlds appear,
> And rising worlds the all-powerful Word shall hear.
> His single fiat guide the amazing whole
> And teach the new-born planets where to roll.[64]

During the opening decades of the nineteenth century, as the repeated evangelical revivals of the Second Great Awakening (traditionally periodized 1800–1840) sent shock waves through American communities, the traditional view of the deity was transformed into a more relatable Christo-centric divinity. Nevertheless, even within the altered Second Great Awakening's understandings of God, His role as creator and ruler of a stupendous universe remained a constant. Hence, pupils in early nineteenth-century America were instructed to admire "the Divinity [that] upholds and governs the immense extent of His works, and preserves order, beauty and harmony, throughout the stupendous fabric of the Universe." Similarly, adults worshiped "the wisdom, the goodness and the power of that Being who made, who upholds, and who governs all these [starry] worlds."[65] Northerners could point out that "this earth is but a small speck of creation," which proved the "unbounded wisdom of God ... amazed at the magnitude and magnificence of creation," and thus should "excite in us the warmest gratitude to that Being whose hand [is] upholding so many suns and worlds." Southerners similarly marveled at "our ... vast system" that was "but a small fabric" of the whole of creation. All would agree that the infinite wisdom "necessary to determine how many worlds should exist, to determine their magnitudes their distances from each other, their velocities, their connexions, and dependences," pointed to an "astonishing ... divine omnipotence. ... His power exceeds all description."[66] Whenever Americans observed starry constellations, they perceived what may have been a constellational arrangement that was a human creation; yet they never lost track of the fact that the constellations consisted of real stars, which for them proved the reality of an omnipotent and almighty God. The new, American political constellation that was constructed of state-stars pointed in the same direction: The United States was congruous with the universe and with its godly creator and governor.

Since the republic's inception, George Washington has dominated the American imagination, a truism especially exemplified by Washington's repeated appearances in political astronomical representations. To take one example, in a celebration in a New Hampshire town involving "the largest number of ladies and gentlemen," the soon-to-retire president was commended as one who, like the biblical Joshua, forced "the Sun and Moon of Europe 'to stand still and see our political salvation,'" and since went on to "direct . . . the great federal constellation."[67] That Washington was not only described through, but also himself participated in, the political astronomy of the day indicates yet again the centrality of this idiom to contemporaries' political expression. This language first surfaced in a letter of 1788, in which Washington thanked veterans who had given to him a commemorative medal, predicting that the day would come when "the new Constellation of this Hemisphere shall be hailed and respected in every quarter of the terraqueous globe." It appeared again in yet more revealing texts penned by Washington, such as the draft of what was intended to be his first inaugural address or first annual message. In this formal text, eventually discarded for unknown reasons, Washington rejoiced with "our new Constellation [which] has been received with tokens of uncommon regard."[68]

The language of political astronomy became a staple of public speech and would incessantly surface throughout the antebellum decades in moments of anxiety and glory, as American patriots expected that their republic and "her brilliant constellation [would] be the last which shall be blotted from the political firmament."[69] The language loomed significant particularly during times of crisis, as the Union was consumed by disputes over state autonomy and federal sovereignty. In this parlance: Were the state-stars to revolve in harmony and with little coercion in the political firmament, or would the federal center dictate the orbital limits and course of the American constellation? A celebrated manifestation of the articulation of these tensions through political astronomy emerged as Daniel Webster of Massachusetts and Robert Hayne of South Carolina famously battled in Congress over the "abominable" protectionist tariff. Webster, in his speech of January 20, 1830 (a week before his renowned "second reply"), dreaded the "day, when our associated and fraternal stripes shall be severed asunder, and when that happy *constellation* under which we have risen to so much renown, shall be broken up, and be seen sinking, star after star, into obscurity and night." The Southern senator chose to reply to Webster by employing the symbolic grammar embedded in the nation's flag. Webster, Hayne pointed out sarcastically, "is for marching under a banner studded all over with *stars,* and bearing the inscription *Liberty* and *Union.* I had thought, sir, the gentleman would have borne a standard, displaying in its ample folds a brilliant sun, extending its golden rays from the centre to the extremities, in the brightness of whose beams, the 'little *stars* hide their diminished heads.'" Putting the old solar imagery back on the discursive table, Hayne was reviving the monarchical bogeyman—as well as the Anti-Federalist fears of the late eighteenth century—of a scorching central power, diminishing and enslaving all planets in its sphere with its too-powerful gravitational pull. As opposed to Webster, Hayne's vision was of "twenty-four *stars* . . . in all their undiminished lustre." The clash of the solar versus the constellational political models came into full view, and the rift that defined the fractured politics of the American republic would only grow as the nineteenth century progressed.[70]

The language of political astronomy could present capably and vividly the theory of states'-rights, as well as its opposite of federal supremacy, through images of celestial repulsion, compulsion, and harmony. An author for the *Washington Review* accordingly marveled over the federal government in Washington, which regulates "all our national concerns" but has also "left us twenty four other governments . . . that regulate all the minor concerns of the people, acting within their own sphere." This casual allusion to the planetary language of spheres and orbits set the stage for constellational triumphalism: "Show me," the unnamed author rhetorically asked, "a spectacle more glorious, more encouraging, than this, even in the pages of all history." At this moment he pointed to "a constellation of free States, with no public force, but public opinion,— moving by well-regulated law each in its own proper orbit, around the brighter star in Washington, thus realizing ... the beautiful display of infinite wisdom."[71] This blending of the planetary and the constellational frameworks ("a constellation of free states ... orbit, around the brighter star in Washington") allowed the merging of the two distinct and contradictory idioms of the spirit of the Era of Good Feelings to extol the federal republic. In statements that underscored national purpose and unity, the United States functioned as both a constellation and a solar system, a starry *pluribus* and a solar *unum*. However, as public discourse became increasingly vitriolic during the decades leading up to the Civil War, the sectional conflict witnessed a visible wedge: while Southerners began to emphasize views of the republic-as-constellation, Northerners would underscore understandings of the federation as controlled by a sunlike constitution.

In search of unity as the nation was progressively preoccupied by the North–South conflict, Franklin Pierce was the first incoming president to highlight the flag and its symbolism in his inaugural address. He drew attention in his 1853 speech to the multiplying "stars upon your banner" that were now "nearly threefold their original number," and he hoped to continue to discern "every star in its place upon that ensign." Pierce hoped that not "a single star be lost" from "that radiant constellation which both illumines our own way and points out to struggling nations their course," lest the "luster of the whole is dimmed" or there be "utter darkness."[72] The unity that Pierce strived for proved ever-elusive, however, due to the expansion of the institution of slavery into new states, a process that also could be observed through the lens of political astronomy. While William Lloyd Garrison's famed *Liberator* addressed the newly incorporated state of Florida as "a new star of blood ... to gleam balefully in our political firmament," politicians such as Governor John Dana of Maine, although a Northerner, held otherwise. Dana emphasized the traditional American ideals and institutions that "have been for years the political light of the world." Hence, abolitionists such as Garrison who would dissolve the Union because "in some of the [Southern] confederate States, [exists] an institution, which they regard as inconsistent with man's equality of rights," that is slavery, would do more harm than good as they "would blot out from the political firmament this bright [American] luminary."[73]

The bane of slavery had to be kept from eclipsing the constellation of American stars, yet the Mexican War and the news of the conquest of vast territories in the Southwest promised that slavery would continue to poison national politics. The conquest of Mexican lands could elicit, quite incredibly, fatalistic sentiments from Southerners, who correctly sensed the looming sectional division over the fate of the territories. A Georgian commentator predicted "a great struggle—a period full of danger, and worthy of solemn thought." Describing a time in the "eventual future" in which "all hope of reconciliation is gone," the citizens of slaveholding states "shall be content to triumph or fall with the South. . . . Her final destiny shall be our destiny." Such fatalism, a hallmark of Southern thought ever since the Revolution, predicted the inevitability of a North–South clash in which "our political constellation is darkened by clouds and storms."[74] Political meteorology conjured images of stormy weather that endangered the tranquility and harmony of political astronomy. As the 1856 presidential elections approached, Democrats warned Illinois Republican Abraham Lincoln, "that great high-priest of abolitionism" who was not yet a candidate himself but a significant local Republican: Following the Republican Party's platform, a writer in a New Orleans newspaper alerted, would lead to an American flag with "fifteen glorious stars erased from its national constellation."[75]

Slavery, of course, finally proved the undoing of the Union, and the conflict between the North and the South exacerbated and finally exploded after the Republican victory in the presidential elections of 1860. The stakes were clear even as Abraham Lincoln was preparing to take office, and Southern states held special conventions to calculate their next steps. During those trying weeks, Northerners expressed horror at the sight of "the stars of our political firmament torn from their orbits, and plunging madly about, or tilting one against another." In chapter 2 we saw how contemporaries calculated the balance of federal power through planetary language of orbits and spheres. The image of a constellation of state-stars provided a different angle on the impending crisis, one less concerned with practical solutions for the national quandary and more concentrated on shocking images of collective grievance. The resolution of a meeting of townspeople in Walpole, New Hampshire, should be thus understood, namely, that "if some of the emblematic [Southern] stars, that now float over our heads prove to be nothing but exploding meteors, and shall be struck from our standard, those remaining being fixed stars, will ... become the galaxy of the political firmament." Witnesses to the collapse of the Union took the well-tried constellational language of harmony and fraternity and reshaped it to their current needs by emphasizing disaster and disorder ("emblematic stars ... exploding meteors ... struck from our standard"), yet still promising hope for the future ("fixed stars ... [for] the galaxy of the political firmament"). Northerners could also strike a more appeasing tone, such as those who wished to placate their Southern compatriots with "measures of conciliation [that] will retain every star in our political firmament." Others were distressed at the thought of the "thousands upon thousands" of Americans who would "sink at heart" should it "be impossible to restore to their accustomed positions those stars which have shot madly from our political firmament."[76]

The remarkable aforementioned private letter that the soon-to-be presidential candidate Abraham Lincoln received from an acquaintance attests to the richness that this vocabulary gained as the great crisis of the republic gathered momentum.[77] In this letter, B. F. Lemen extraordinarily expanded the astro-political image of the United States. Writing to Lincoln from Colorado, "the large Observatory in the Rocky Mountains," Lemen wished that "the labored calculations of the political astronomers of the South" fail, and that "the great Southern Comet will not Strike, our American Earth and dash it into fragments." In Lemen's depiction, the South was not a constellation composed of state-stars, but a malign comet bearing a "Fiery appearance [with] nothing more, than a thin and exceedingly light vapor, or gasseous matter." As opposed to the unruly and threatening Southern comet, the American, Northern "Star Spangled Atmosphere" was harmonious and "well regulated in its revolutions ... [and] its universal laws are too well Founded to be over thrown, or blown away by mear gass, or boddies containing no heavier matter than puffs." Lemen went on to convey to Lincoln the binding forces of the American "galaxy," describing the Declaration of Independence as America's "morning, and Evening stars, the Ordinance of Eighty seven, its northern, great Constellation, or Pointers—and it has Liberty and Union, for its Pollar Star." If there are hints of satire in this remarkable exposition, they were eclipsed by the elaborate and meticulous rendition of the American cosmo-political world. Surely Lemen was being playful in this over-the-top description of American politics in astronomical terms, but such playfulness could only become meaningful or even comprehensible within the rich context of political astronomy. Concluding his remarks to the presidential candidate, Lemen noted that it was the regularity and predictability of the American constellation, that is, its Newtonian aspects, which could reassure the letter's author, and possibly Lincoln himself, that the American world, like the star-studded universe, will continue to "roll on in its successive order."[78]

The citizens of the new independent Southern Confederacy, which was eventually founded in February 1861, responded to the Northern constellational harangues in a most effective manner: They reshaped and incorporated the American political astronomy to their own needs and so maintained the American star-ridden symbolic language forged during the previous fourscore years. One of the foci of their heated contentions was the star-spangled national flag. The centrality of the symbolic "battle of the flags" was demonstrated by Senator John Slidell of Louisiana, who addressed the national banner in his seceding speech, combatively promising Northerners "not to give up that flag without a bloody struggle, it is ours as much as yours." The American flag obviously already attracted considerable sentimental attachment, and at least some Southerners hung on to it and claimed it for their own. Admitting that Northern states were more numerous, hence at least "for a time more stars may shine on your banner," Slidell predicted that "our [Southern] children, if not we, will rally under a constellation more numerous and more resplendent than yours."[79] Possibly two similar flags, one Northern and one Southern, could compete for the larger number of stars. Perhaps in response to the rhetoric of Slidell and his likes, the United States' president-elect considered the issue of the flag at a speech he gave in front of Independence Hall in Philadelphia on his way to his inauguration in Washington, DC. When the flag was originally raised at that very spot some fourscore years ago, Lincoln reminded his cheering audience, "it had but thirteen stars." Lincoln wished to call attention to the fact that "each additional star added to that flag has given additional prosperity and happiness to this country." Celebrating the recent addition of the thirty-fourth star, representing Kansas, Lincoln wished optimistically that not only the new Kansas star "placed upon that flag shall be permitted to remain there to our permanent prosperity" but that "additional ones shall from time to time be placed there, until we shall number as was anticipated by the great historian."[80]

Regardless of this still-verbal battle over flags, Southerners understood that clinging to the Star-Spangled Banner did not well serve their rhetorical needs and that they needed a distinct flag of their own. Consequently, the leaders of the Confederate States of America devoted a surprising amount of time to framing a new national banner (surprising in particular when compared to the conception of the American flag as an afterthought back in 1777). During the four years of the Confederacy's existence, the Southern nation would proudly fly a succession of three formal flags, with a fourth, the saltire or St. Andrew's Cross, in effect acting by the end of the war as the unofficial Confederate flag. This flurry of flags began as, in one of its first acts, the Provisional Congress solicited ideas from citizens and officials alike for the design of a new national flag for the seceding states. Congress received numerous suggestions. Remarkably, in the language of the Confederacy's official report, "nearly all the designs submitted to the committee contained a combination of stars." In fact, out of the 120 designs received, 107 (95 percent) included stars for states. The initial design that was adopted as the Confederacy's official flag, the Stars and Bars, thus perpetuated the consensual state-star symbolism of the Stars and Stripes.[81]

The Stars and Bars was first raised over the slaveholding republic's first capitol in Montgomery, Alabama, on March 3, 1861. The flag's formal congressional description was rather sparse as to its starry element, declaring "a circle of white stars corresponding in number with the States in the Confederacy," leaving room for an expansion of states and stars. The Stars and Bars provided, according to the historian Robert Bonner, the new and untested government of the Confederacy a means of "eliciting popular support through a burgeoning body of patriotic poetry, song, and ritual."[82] As the war dragged on, however, the Stars and Bars seems to have lost its initial popularity, which explains the proposals to replace that flag that were circling in Southern newspapers in late 1861 and early 1862. One radical and long-winded scheme planned to replace the Stars and Bars with a flag in which "the sun in his ascending pathway" was presented "in the centre of the broad blue belt, (which represents the zodiac, or track of the sun in the heavens)." The proposal's author may have sensed the attachment of his contemporaries to the symbol of the stars, and he assured readers that "stars as emblems of the States, considered individually and numerically . . . are placed upon the flag," even though the sun remained "the central and most conspicuous figure upon it." His flag, he concluded "may properly be denominated, 'THE FLAG OF THE SUN.'"[83]

Although this sunny scheme went nowhere, Confederates were keen on replacing the Stars and Bars. An official committee to consider a new flag was thus appointed with the assembly of the new Congress in the early months of 1862. The committee reported in April, offering a remarkable proposal that echoed the abovementioned plan published earlier in the *Richmond Dispatch:* The committee proposed that the Confederacy's flag shall have a "red field . . . having in the centre the device of a sun, in its glory . . . the rays of the sun corresponding with the number of the States composing of the Confederacy." Clarifying the proposed flag's symbolism, the committee explained that "the sun manifests the dominion, generosity and the stability of the confederacy." It was wholly unexpected that voices that would champion a symbol that traditionally stood for domination, central sovereignty, and monarchy as did the sun would emerge in the Confederacy, which was founded on the ideology of states'-rights. It is no surprise, then, that the House did not prove partial to a sunny flag that was anathema to the Southern ethos; its members overwhelmingly voted the resolution down (actually postponing it indefinitely).[84]

A year later, and after several iterations, Congress did end up adopting a new flag to replace the Stars and Bars. The new flag would be known as the Stainless Banner, and it would act as the Confederacy's official flag until the Blood-Stained Banner replaced it during the final months of the war. In both these flags the most conspicuous element was a saltire (St. Andrew's Cross) on the model of the battle flag of the Army of Northern Virginia, a red square with the blue St. Andrew's Cross and thirteen stars. The Stainless Banner, its description read, was to be "emblazoned

FIGURE 26. Title page of a musical score, "Stars and Bars Polka Brillante." (Courtesy of the David M. Rubenstein Rare Book & Manuscript Library, Duke University)

with . . . five-pointed stars, corresponding in number to that of the Confederate States."

While all three official flags that the Confederacy would eventually adopt preserved the element of stars as representations of states, the political astronomy that the Confederacy inherited from the United States did not go uncontested. Indeed, during the attempts to replace the Stars and Bars and before the adoption of the Stainless Banner, there were calls to eliminate the stars from the flag altogether. Congressman Ethelbert Barksdale of Mississippi, in particular, wished that the Confederacy would replace the Stars and Bars with the battle flag of the Army of Northern Virginia, without the stars. The Mississippian reasoned that the flags of the United States and the Confederate States of America should be "as distinct as the character of the two peoples." Barksdale thus wished to eliminate the most unmistakable element of constellational political astronomy, the star, from his struggling nation's flag. That calls such as Barksdale's went unheeded demonstrates the potency of political astronomy, a language so entrenched that it not only survived secession but continued to thrive for the entire lifespan of the Confederacy. To paraphrase David Potter's classic formulation, the North and the South were separated not only "by a common nationalism" but specifically by a common political astronomy.[85]

Confederate state flags provide even more proof, if such proof is needed, of the strong hold of political astronomy on Confederate minds. Seceding Southern states were quick to adopt new banners to express their newly gained independence and to declare and convey their sovereign authority. The first sign of the postsecession continuation of political astronomy came even before the adoption of the Stars and Bars as a national flag. In the wake of Mississippi's secession in January 1861, the newly independent republic adopted a flag bearing a single white five-point star on a blue field. Such single-star flags were already recognizable through the independent Republic of Texas's Lone Star Flag, as well as the similar flag of the short-lived Republic of West Florida. The "lone star," and Mississippi's in particular, was greatly popularized through Harry Macarthy's song "The Bonnie Blue Flag" (1861) that, together with "Dixie," became the Confederacy's unofficial anthem.[86] Each stanza of

FIGURE 27. The Stainless Banner, the Confederacy's second official flag. Over time it was criticized, particularly for being easily mistaken for a flag of truce. (Redrawn by Nat Case)

The Star-Spangled Republic

that widely popular song, whose lyrics revolved around the blue-fielded "bonnie blue" flag that bore a single, large, and white five-point star in its middle, concluded with the line, "Hurrah for the Bonnie Blue Flag that bears a single star." The final stanza climaxed reassuringly, "The single star of the Bonnie Blue Flag has grown to be eleven." Following Mississippi, five states adopted flags that incorporated in one way or another the theme of a single star (with an additional state adopting a provisional flag with a lone star).[87]

Political astronomy dominated in the American political imagination both North and South, demonstrating the extent to which Americans shared a political astronomy regardless of geography or conviction. It is also a testament to how ingrained, effective, and elastic this language was, reaching far beyond graphic representations on flags. While that language appealed to Confederates, who inherited the symbolic grammar of political astronomy from the United States from which they broke apart, it was evident that by the era of the Civil War two distinct visions of the cosmological nature of the American Union had emerged. In a wartime debate in the United States Congress on the future of the Western territories of Nevada, Colorado, and Nebraska, House members anticipated that these would "increase the number of stars in the constellation of the Union." Beyond expansion, however, Congress "hoped that by the same time the eleven wayward, wandering stars of the confederacy, now, like the lost Pleiad, separated from their sisters, will be restored to our political firmament, never again to be driven or drawn from their orbit around the central government by any sinister influence." Reflecting the earlier anxious language of dysfunctional political constellations and the ideal image of political Newtonian heavens, these short sentences were packed with celestial images, from the American constellation to the seven Pleiades and the "political firmament," in order to drive their message of hope for a return to celestial harmony.[88]

In the South, however, not binding force but "voluntary cohesion" was believed the right way to hold together "great States" and create harmony. If Southerners, too, imagined the late Union as "the great system of the universe," it was "only by the *benign and gentle influence of attraction* that the bright stars of our constellation can be kept in their orbits." Rem-

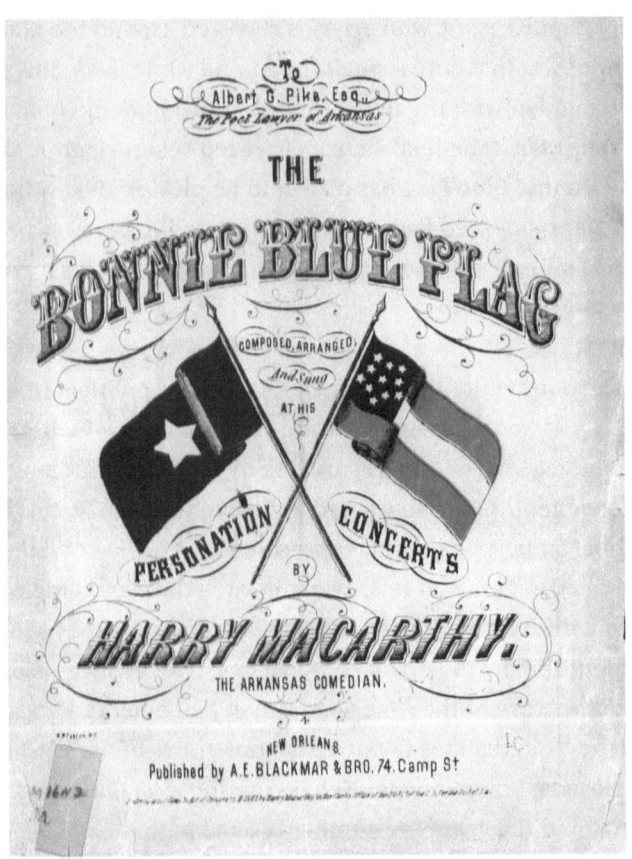

FIGURE 28. Title page of a musical score, "The Bonnie Blue Flag." The Bonnie Blue Flag and the eponymous marching song that commemorated it were hugely popular Confederate staples throughout the war. The stars on the Stars and Bars in this poster resemble a ring arrangement but more likely compose a "great star" with the central star identical in size to other ten stars. (From Harry McCarthy, *The Bonnie Blue Flag* [New Orleans: A. E. Blackmar & Bro., 1861]; Library of Congress)

iniscent of the century-old persuasive and benign gravitational attraction that colonial Americans felt toward the Hanoverian sun kings, as well of as ratification-era Anti-Federalist sensibilities, Southerners believed that if kindness and moderation in maintaining the Confederacy were sustained, "those who attempt to bridle or spur them [Southern states], will, in the end, fare like the rash fool who aspired to direct the chariots of the sun." Gravity, a strict force in the North that kept states from disobedience and scattering, became in the South a gentle, persuasive power that swayed stars into keeping orbit.[89]

To recognize the force and appeal of this language one needs look no further than Jefferson Davis's final speech before the U.S. Senate. On January 10, 1861, just days before he left the U.S. Congress to become the Confederacy's president, Davis described the emergence of the American "constellation which was set in the political firmament, as a sign of unity and confederation." Davis elaborated on the meaning of "that constellation [which] has served to bless our people . . . [and] its light has been thrown on foreign lands." The following sentences, in which Davis powerfully reiterated the familiar contours of the centrifugal view of American cosmo-politics, are worth quoting at length:

> If our Government should fail, it will not be from the defect of the system, though each planet was set to revolve in an orbit of its own, each moving by its own impulse, yet being all attracted by the affections and interests which countervailed each other; there was no inherent tendency to disruption. It has been the perversion of the Constitution; it has been the substitution of theories of morals for principles of government; it has been forcing crude opinions upon the domestic institutions of others, which has disturbed these planets in their orbit; it is this which threatens to destroy the constellation which, in its power and its glory, had been gathering stars one after another, until, from thirteen, it had risen to thirty-three.[90]

The political astronomy of the United States of the Civil War era remained robust and sufficiently supple to accommodate both Federalists and states'-rights advocates, Republicans and Southern Democrats. It provided contemporaries with a language to discuss and articulate the proper relation of the separate state-stars to the constellational and federal whole, of the *pluribus* and the *unum*. During the War of Independence many revolutionaries, and later Anti-Federalists and Southerners, wished to restrain the gravitational pull that cemented the constellation. Federalists and later advocates of a strong Union attempted to avert a universe populated by anarchic, comet-like states, unaffected by the federal constellation's centripetal force. The broadness and elasticity of this discourse also entailed, however, that it could not help in mitigating the ominous and widening fissures that eventually split the American Union. By the Civil War, two opposing political cosmologies had emerged, a Northern and a Southern reading of the heavens in the service of divergent ideological, earthly needs.

Epilogue

THE AMERICAN STAR

> The stars awaken a certain reverence, because though always present, they are inaccessible.
>
> —Ralph Waldo Emerson, *Nature*, 1836

Prior to the advent of the early modern sun king it was not customary, and perhaps even unprecedented, to represent living humans as stars. While humans across time and space have raised their heads and identified deceased leaders or revered predecessors in the night skies, it is far less frequent to encounter examples of people recognizing their living contemporaries as stars. The sun king thus presented a remarkable novelty and spawned an early modern political astronomy, which in turn enabled, after the late eighteenth century, that distinct mode of expounding American politics that this book has traced. We have seen how a revamped European kingship, which developed absolutist aspirations after the sixteenth century, controlled state and society, likening itself to the sun at the heart of a planetary system. Kings were meticulously presented as exhibiting starry characteristics: Like suns they were luminous, radiating, and emitting warmth but also remote, untouchable, and inhabiting a realm of their own. That kings acted as suns, and the fact that they were simultaneously undeniably human, revealed the solar king's two bodies: While monarchy was an institution that regulated the nation and state like a sun controlling its satellites, that sun was a living human being who was incidentally defined in stellar terms.[1]

Over the previous chapters we have followed the ways in which the Revolution in America transformed and republicanized a political astronomy that stemmed from monarchical Renaissance courts. The American political astronomy that became a distinct and noticeable feature of the young American republic took this kingly language and flipped it on its head: Instead of celebrating solar domination, political astronomy in America appealed for equality among state-stars. This novel language saturated the public speech of Americans of all ranks, from politicians to commentators, and from men of science to commoners. Its longest-lasting and most salient feature was visual, as the stars of the "new American constellation" pervaded formal representations of the United States as national symbols and influence the public sphere to this day. Since the revolutionary era, the undistinguished five-point white stars had represented the American states, pointing to the Union's connection to the cosmos throughout the founding era and beyond.[2] Political astronomy provided legitimization of the novel federal confederation and fed into understandings of what would come to be labeled "American exceptionalism." The visual representations that derived from this tradition, first and foremost the American national flag, still characterize and embody the mammoth continental superpower the United States has become.

With the conclusion of the Revolution and the creation of the federal government, however, it became clear that the transition from the king-as-sun to star-for-an-American-state, or from astro-monarchism to celestial republicanism, could not resolve all the tensions that the young nation faced. Yet political astronomy could at the very least help to express the tensions and anxieties that grew out of them. First Anti-Federalists, followed by their ideological successors, the Jeffersonian Republicans, tended to read the political firmament as proving and justifying the autonomy of the respective state-stars. Their Federalist rivals followed a more conservative reading and reverted to a language of augmented central power to counteract the wayward tendencies of the states, reflecting the solar language in which the Constitution replaced the British king as a binding planetary force.[3] Thus even in the republican and antimonarchist culture of the young United States, some Americans still echoed a political language expressed in the solar terms characteristic of kingly courts.

In the American astro-political discourse that emerged out of revolutionary republicanism, celestial bodies, whether suns or stars, commonly stood for impersonal political bodies (usually states) and institutions (often the Constitution), but rarely for men. Identifying men as stars, planets, or the sun was potentially too offensive, a figure with a clear and obvious genealogy from the kingly courts and their associated culture of adulation. But as the historian Eric Nelson reminds us, monarchism was never out of sight during the founding and the creation of the executive branch, and the presidency in particular was shaped for a potent magistrate whose dynamism resembled that of European kings.[4] Nevertheless, during Washington's presidency he avoided titles that might hint at aristocracy, and at the end of his second term, he famously orchestrated his retirement to Mount Vernon as a republican Cincinnatus.[5] The living Washington wished to leave no doubt as to his commitment to limited government and self-effacement, two crucial aspects that differentiated a republic from a monarchy. However, the way in which Americans would cultivate their adoration of first the living Washington and later his memory would deviate from his expressed will, and even stand in stark contrast to it.

Nowhere was this ambivalence more obvious than in the reversion to the quasi-monarchical imagery of the Father of His Nation. Over and over again contemporaries described the retired president in solar terms. Benjamin Banneker, America's "first Black man of science," described the United States' government in his 1795 almanac as spreading its influence "like a cheering sun . . . whilst it is governed by Washington," while a poem from a Harvard College commencement ceremony in 1798 referred to Washington as a "hero [that] shines" and "Columbia's sun" parting "his meridian day."[6] Yet it was Washington's death that sparked the real flurry of solar allegories, and the following decades witnessed luminous references to the dead president that closely resembled the ways in which the Old World monarchs, particularly the eighteenth-century British Hanoverian kings, were portrayed. In the most memorable of eulogies, Richard Henry Lee described Washington as a sun, "moving in his own orbit," imparting "heat and light to his most distant satellites," the American people. Like a massive and radiating sun, "combining the physical and moral force of all within his sphere, with irresistible weight he took his course." Other eulogists saw Washington as "a newly-discovered star," a metaphor befitting the father of a new constellation, "whose benignant light will travel on to the world and time's farthest bounds," sparkling

Epilogue

"in one of the constellations of the sky." This reversion to monarchical and seemingly unrepublican language may have been stimulated by what historians have described as an existential crisis in the new republic that was caused by Washington's death. When this crisis finally passed, America did not succumb to monarchism, as many feared (and as its European rivals hoped), remaining a republic, and as such one that was still seen as amid the stars.[7] Nonetheless, over the following decades early republican authors and speakers continued to portray a sunlike Washington as "bold and striking," his "social affections . . . the luminaries" of the political "sphere." His "soft beams" so comforting that one "wish[ed] the sun would rise no more," while his name continued "shining" amid the "brilliant constellation that never sets."[8] Others described his character as "luminous" and "lending his mingled light of genius, valor and lofty patriotism" to the national history.[9]

While the portrayals of Washington-as-sun continued unrelentingly, his image was simultaneously recast as a generic star rather than the sun. Early modern kings who were repeatedly compared to suns were also referred to as stars (which by the early nineteenth century were generally understood to be distant suns), most memorably by William Shakespeare, who dubbed Henry V "This star of England."[10] One of the most striking representations in this vein was German-born artist Frederick Kimmelmeyer's *The American Star* (1803), a painting that glorifies Washington the soldier and political leader. In the painting, Washington is surrounded by military and national symbols: flags, bugles, cannon round shot, and shields that encircle a pedestal on top of which the likeness of Washington gazes at the onlooker. A bald eagle protected by an American shield hovers above the president, with a glory rising behind him with seventeen (six-point) stars, honoring Ohio as the most recent addition to the Union. The main emblem in this heavily symbolic neoclassical painting, however, was a bold, golden, five-point star above the president. The star ostensibly represented and embodied the dead president above whom it hovered, as indicated by the painting's name. Washington was the American star.

While the living Washington repeatedly spoke and acted as a staunch republican, the dead president's memory would thus repeatedly convey a starkly different political inclination. Indeed, the aforementioned

FIGURE 29. *The American Star*, Frederick Kimmelmeyer, ca. 1803. (The Metropolitan Museum of Art, New York; gift of Edgar William and Bernice Chrysler Garbisch, 1962)

representations of a solar and starlike Washington were not outliers but characteristic of the way in which he was commemorated and enshrined in the national memory. As the historian François Furstenberg notes, Americans attempting to use Washington and his memory as a bond of and for the fragile Union turned him into a "republican king."[11] While significant aspects of the nation's memory of Washington underscored his republicanism, his solar and starry features also were enshrined in memory, and hence monarchical aspects of the first president's image persisted.

George Washington surely held and still holds a unique place in the American national sentiment. He was not, however, the only president upon whom solar imagery was bestowed. Most of the allusions to

Washington-as-sun (or star) came after the first president's death, and these metaphorical titles seem to have allowed authors and speakers to describe future living presidents as suns while they still held office. Early in John Adams's presidency, for example, a poetic author described "glorious Adams" shining in America's "central sphere," identifying the president as "the radiant sphere of liberty."[12] The poet Jonathan Sewall of Portsmouth, New Hampshire, likened Adams to the sun: As

> bright Sol, whom planets odulting [sic] obey
> Darts through clouds those glad beams that enliven creation
> . . . .
> So Adams, 'midst tempest and storms
> . . . .
> Though dire comets may [he] rise
> Let them meet but his eyes.

Leaving no doubt as to his intentions, Sewall concluded by designating the president "Our SUN, Regent, Centre."[13] Unsurprisingly, Jeffersonian Republican partisans were much more skeptical than Federalists of such solar language, which emphasized the concentrated power that was anathema to their country ideology. Consequently, Republicans derided the mutiny within the president's party, mocking Adams as "this sun," asking, "have the federal planets lost their orbits, that they no longer 'exulting obey' old Sol"?[14] In special circumstances, however, such as the deaths of Jefferson and Adams on July 4, 1826, both the Federalist and the Republican deceased presidents were described in stellar, if not solar, language, as "stars in the political firmament; stars which may well be ranked among those of the first magnitude," who have "cast their radiance over the horizon of the political world."[15]

John Adams's son John Quincy, although nominally a Democratic-Republican president, was described in similar fashion to his father as a "Sun in the Firmament, fair and brilliant," his followers hoping that "he ascend till he attains the Zenith of constitutional power."[16] The young Adams's contested election as president brought advocates to describe him as outshining his political rivals, turning them invisible "as are the Stars when the Sun is at meridian height," while Adams radiated "greater brilliancy" than any other of his competitors.[17] Andrew Jackson, who followed Adams as president and brought a new powerful dynamism and populist appeal to the presidency, was consequently scorned by his political rivals, who saw him as "king Andrew." As a powerful president, Jackson, too, was readily described as a sun. In the aptly named newspaper the *Pittsfield (MA) Sun*, a supporter of the president attacked Jackson's rivals, "discontented and evil spirits in the land" who opposed the president. "Unable to strike out this great luminary [Jackson] that has risen to beautify and enlighten our political firmament," the president's enemies could only conspire "to raise a smoldering cloud that shall obstruct his radiance and diminish his luster." The author, identifying himself as one Eastern Argus, could only wish for the approaching hour "when the mists of calumny will break and roll away, leaving the bright orb they have partially obscured more beautiful, luminous and distinct."[18] Even from the vantage point of local and provincial politics, Jackson was imagined as the sun. An author from Portland, Maine (a town that, as the writer emphasized, was the capital of Cumberland District, which gave Jackson the only elector in the New England States), complained that the "old Chief" attached himself to a "mercenary band who are using his popularity for their private ambition." The author, who adopted the pseudonym Noah's Star, warned that unless he separated himself from this cabal "before all the stars in our political firmament desert him," Jackson and his administration would become a "setting sun."[19]

Seeing republican Americans, and particularly those who held the highest office of the land, as celestial bodies indicated a remarkable reversion to a culture that originated in Renaissance and early modern European courts. While the various American images we have traced in previous chapters may have originated from a European tradition of political astronomy, they departed from Old World conventions as they now served as metaphors for republican and impersonal bodies and institutions, such as states or the constitution, or, as in the image of the constellation of stars, represented the entire American Union. However, by addressing presidents (in this case, James Monroe) as in a Fourth of July toast as "the bright sun of our political firmament," Americans made a crucial step in connecting human activities and the heavens.[20] In this alternate branch of astro-politics, which focused on humans and not political bodies, presidents, like kings of yore, were suns or stars. They radiated, illuminated, and shone on their respective spheres and, ideally, controlled their political firmament. Once more we are reminded of the extent to which the American presidency was conceived and understood in the shadow of monarchism.[21]

While presidents were the first Americans to be consistently cast as celestial bodies, once the door to a personal and human-centered political astronomy that equated them with stars was opened, it could not be contained. From presidents it spilled over to other, lesser statesmen. Such minor politicians were not described as suns, nor usually were they even described as individual stars. Rather, authors and public speakers found an image that enabled them, on the one hand, to elevate contemporaries to superhuman heights, but, on the other, avoided describing them in monarchical terms: Expressions such the "constellation of luminaries" in the "political galaxy" or "political firmament" became an effective and popular way to show reverence for politicians without designating them directly as suns, possibly because that language seemed too ostensibly monarchical and was thus preserved exclusively for presidents. Rhetorical allusions to constellations of luminaries lavished praise on various groups of political actors (and consequently, as we shall see, on nonpolitical actors) and thus perpetuated and extended the habit of attaching starry qualities to living humans, as in the case of presidents-as-suns. At the same time, such allusions made this habit less offensive to republican ideology by spreading and decentralizing the view of one monarch-like star while still adhering to republicanism's hierarchical and deferential tendencies.

As early as in 1778, while war with Britain raged and republican ideas were being forged and cemented in the young United States, Benjamin Rush reminded his friend John Adams, who was serving as commissioner to the Court of France, that while "monarchies are illuminated by a *sun* . . . republics should be illuminated by *constellations* of great men."[22] Rush's view was still unquestionably hierarchical, elevating "great men" as the designated leaders of society (in what contemporaries would refer to as a merit-based "natural aristocracy"). It reflects, however, a republican antipathy toward kingship while preserving the political astronomy that was traditionally used to define that institution through the image of the sun king. The conclusion of the Revolutionary War and the swirling in the public sphere of ideas pertaining to political astronomy further enabled Critical Period (1783–89) references to a "constellation of heroes" of the Revolution.[23] These early revolutionary-era examples of designating a group of prominent men of action as positioned in a constellational arrangement signaled the emergence of a novel image that would become a popular vehicle for lavishing praise and elevating select groups of politicians throughout the nineteenth century. Significantly, such images were rarely found before the Revolution. Such was the case among Bostonians celebrating the return of peace, who toasted "the American Constellation of Sages that enlighten the world." Like the new constellation of state-stars that supposedly illuminated the political firmament, the American human stars were said to "enlighten the world."[24] The 1780s, which witnessed the emergence of the image of the "American constellation" of states, thus saw simultaneously also the emergence of human constellations. A self-described Primitive Whig reflected with admiration on the wartime Congress, Washington, state governors, and "all the bright constellation of American Whigs."[25] Throughout the era of the early republic and beyond, contemporaries would continue to invoke—with numerous references—the "constellation of our luminaries," "grand luminaries," and "the bright stars in the brightest constellation in the galaxy of heroes."[26] Authors and public speakers occasionally fancifully articulated the astronomical aspects of the human constellation of stars. They might point out, for example, that "the greater luminaries of this political constellation shine forth their edifying light," while others described their leaders as "Bright stars in the brightest constellation in the galaxy of heroes."[27] Such articulations demonstrate that the astronomical origins of these expressions were obvious and meaningful to contemporaries, and the meaning of the identification of humans as stars should be understood in the wider context of political astronomy.

While the images of human constellations were initially composed of *political* luminaries, other groups of revered and prominent men (but not women, at least initially) soon found themselves clustered and elevated as constellations of stars. Judges from the judiciary branch could, for example, be seen as "mutually reflect[ing] luster on each other," thus

Epilogue

consisting of a "noble constellation."[28] As the nineteenth century progressed, college professors, too, might be deemed "luminaries which have ... appeared in this our firmament," while on other occasions wealthy donors to educational institutions were deemed "luminaries, who ... shine among the stars of heaven."[29] Theologians were likewise "the bright constellation of names which have expressed their profound regard or the truths of revelation," and Freemasons could reminisce on "a constellation of great names ... among the luminaries who gave light to the path of liberty."[30] And in post–Civil War America the artistic scene in metropolitan areas, particularly in New York City, could be seen as hosting "a constellation of artistic luminaries."[31]

Hence, first in the realm of politics and then in other arenas, the "constellation of luminaries" expressed an equality among a cluster of supposed superiors. This image also suggested the now general understanding that the sun is merely a typical star among countless others, and that a human as the sun was an image that was too offensive, with the occasional exception of presidents. Hence, while the human luminaries composing a constellation were stars, and by implication distant suns, they were not the sun. The constellational mode of communicating admiration for uniquely positioned men attributed starry qualities to them that were earlier reserved for one sun only, while simultaneously capitalizing on the pervasive view of the United States as "the American constellation."

Yet it was not the popular image of a constellation of American luminaries that would prove the most important celestial allusion in years to come. Rather it is the isolated star—not sun—representing a towering figure that still captivates twenty-first-century imaginations. "The star" was not a sun because he (and later she) was not supposed to be the raison d'être, the sole reason for being, as the king was to the state, nor the only star in any given social firmament. Nevertheless, the human star was deemed a unique personage with unrivaled qualities soaring above the mundane. While not a monarch, the star took part in a culture reminiscent of courts, one of reverence that appealed to the human inclination for admiration of and supplication to great figures. Such a disposition for admiration and self-deprecation shared much of the reverence and hero-worship sentiment traditionally felt toward monarchs. It thus comes as no surprise that while the image of the sun was reserved for American presidents, the image of the human-as-star first emerged as an image for venerated politicians.

With the securing of American Independence, one of the earliest political leaders described in terms of a star was the most recognized American of his age, Benjamin Franklin. A poem titled "On the Return of Doctor Benjamin Franklin to America" and published in his hometown of Philadelphia, described the overseas feats and achievements of Franklin the diplomat. The poem opens with an astronomical allusion, describing an "arcadian star" rising in the east, and setting "with glory in the west." In the final stanza, Franklin is unequivocally aligned with a star: "Rise a new star 'ith' galaxy of fame, / Confess the greatest and the best: / To latest time let FRANKLIN be its name. / And shine the glory of the west."[32] In this revolutionary-era example it is ambiguous whether Franklin is a star ("a new star 'ith' galaxy of fame") or whether there is merely a star named after the great man ("let FRANKLIN be its name"). It would not be long before stars could not only be men, but men could be stars.

Another early use of the image of the "star politician" demonstrates how, unlike a solar-kingship, the status of the human star was qualified and potentially reversible. In August 1805 the *Aurora (PA) General Advertiser* declared the English-born Thomas Cooper a "bright oriental star, who has so often enlightened our western world with his luminous emanations," that has "risen in the political firmament." In the early nineteenth century, the metaphor of the star was still very much connected to its astronomical origins. Yet for a "Mechanic of Mifflin County," Cooper's devotion to the Republican Party and its ideals were in doubt, and he thus seemed "shorn of his radiant beams." As long as his Republicanism was ardent, Cooper, the political star, reflected his "effulgent rays ... illuminated and animated our republican hemisphere, and dispelled the gloom of night." Yet now "the circumambient clouds of prejudice, self interest, and avarice have so enveloped him, that scarcely a particle of light can penetrate the dense shroud." Cooper, "who shone forth a star of the first magnitude, one of the most splendid primary planets, seems to have lost all his original qualities and to have degenerated into a mere satellite." To conclude this remarkable astro-political diatribe, the Mechanic expressed hope that "the citizens of this country still move in their wonted sphere, supporting their republican pre-eminence with firmness and

Epilogue

dignity."³³ Unlike the ambiguity in the Benjamin Franklin example, for this author Cooper *was* a star, though that status prevailed only so long as he held firm ideologically. Once Cooper's Republicanism languished, he transformed into "a mere satellite."

The ironic description of Thomas Cooper in stellar terms was an outlier, as the star image generally reflected positively on politicians. Such was the case with a Maryland assembly member named Bowles, who upon his decision not to run for another term in office was praised in a local newspaper as outshining "the brightest constellation that has been seen in the political galaxy."³⁴ Representations of politicians as stars increased in the following decades, yet retained a certain elaborate baroqueness that underscored the fact that the human star still operated well within a vibrant and consciously astro-political discourse. A politician was thus not a mere star, but a "star of the first magnitude," or a "meteor . . . whirl[ing] through the political firmament . . . a fixed star," "a new star in the political firmament," or "one of the new stars which have shot into brilliancy in the political firmament."³⁵ While the prefix "super" was not yet attached to politician-stars, those who described them as such were compelled to elaborate on their starry qualities. The adjectives, superlatives, and cosmic attributes given to these antebellum politicians' starry qualities indicate that the designation of "star" was still meaningful in the word's original sense—a "star" was still a metaphor, not yet an idiomatic noun.

By the mid-nineteenth century, the image of the politician-star had become a common idiom in public discourse, mostly (but not exclusively) reserved for actors on the political stage who were deemed particularly successful, virtuous, and notable. The successive deaths of prominent leaders in midcentury particularly drew references to these "bright luminaries," "brightest stars set in the intellectual and political firmament for the guidance of mankind," and noticeably the prominent senators Daniel Webster, John Calhoun, and Henry Clay as stars who "differeth from another star [only in] glory."³⁶ Exploits of military commanders traditionally held a comparable place to that of politicians, as leaders in both real and political combat were men of action, and a life in the military was often seen as a necessary preparation for political leadership. It makes sense, then, that such men of the sword would be described in stellar

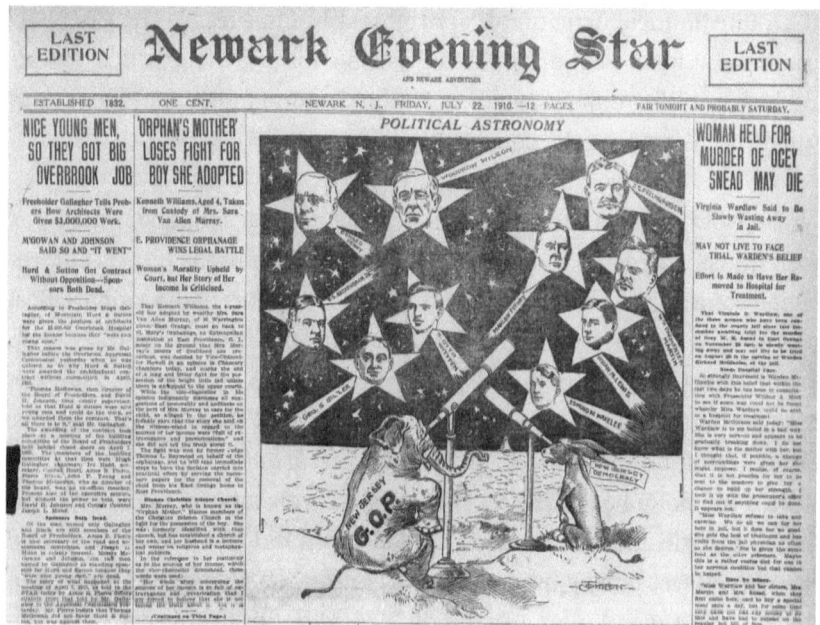

FIGURE 30. *Newark Evening Star*, July 22, 1910. The caricature titled *Political Astronomy* (in a newspaper appropriately titled *Evening Star*) depicts the Democratic and Republican mascots observing New Jersey political stars (or perhaps meteors) through telescopes. This remarkable cartoon demonstrates how early twentieth-century commentators still linked stars, humans, and politics, if in the form of parody. The cartoon's title is the only instance of the contemporary use of the phrase "political astronomy" I have encountered. (Library of Congress, image provided by Rutgers University Libraries)

terms, with virtues that "gleam and . . . twinkle with a star-like radiancy," shining "from their proper sphere . . . expanding and over-arching the firmament of fame."[37] Consequently, the first half of the nineteenth century saw American warriors who would eventually become presidents described as military "stars," often upon their entry into the world of politics. Andrew Jackson, the victor in the Battle of New Orleans, was deemed "among the bright constellation of martial luminaries," who has "just risen above the horizon of the nation's military fame," which was "now seen nearest to the meridian of glory, shining, the most splendid and conspicuous orb."[38] The victor of the Mexican War, Zachary Taylor, who was expected to enter politics, was "this new star in the political firmament." Taylor fulfilled this promise, becoming a political meteor, and his premature death in 1850 was described as "the setting of one

Epilogue

of . . . our political firmament['s] brightest luminaries."[39] The Civil War era brought forth further opportunities to continue the practice, elevating high-ranking officers, such as Union General James McPherson, as "the brightest star in the constellation of genius."[40]

While evolving from the centuries-old image of the sun king, which was then transformed into the sun president, the image of the human star retained some of the traditional qualities and attributes of the monarchical sun, albeit in a more restrained fashion. While both the sun and the stars were heavenly and radiating bodies, the star was not seen as being as dominating as the sun (admittedly, only due to the sun's proximity), nor was it as unique and distinct, for the heavens are strewn with numerous stars. The metaphor of the human star was indicative of and well fitted to a Romantic age that elevated and admired individual greatness and "genius." It was during the nineteenth century, then, that the concept of the genius—the uniquely gifted individual with limitless creative potential—emerged, that the notion of the star percolated out of the political and into other realms.

After politics, the arts were the arena in which human stars shone most brightly. In the opening decades of the nineteenth century, for example, the great writers of the past, from Homer, to Shakespeare, Milton, and Johnson, would be remembered as men of such "individual genius" and "greater brilliancy" that they outshone all other "shining masses which have been enumerated." The great men of literature appeared "like those large insulated stars which properly belong to no constellation, but whose own native light fills up the wide space around them and obscures the lesser luminaries that twinkle in the neighboring regions."[41] While at the beginning of the century it was only the dead and the recognized greats to whom the designation "star" was applied, by its end even a now-forgotten newspaper reporter could be described in similar terms. A report of journalist George Loomis's arrival at Duluth, while earnestly heralding him as a star, playfully paired his celestial description and the city's astronomical nickname: "One of the brightest luminaries that ever shone in the Zenith City journalistic constellation, arrived here last night while hurrying along in his orbit."[42] In a democratic age that would promote individualism over almost any other value, human stars were seen as lofty and remote, floating in the great expanses of space and outshining all others in their vicinity.

The cultural climate of the second half of the nineteenth century was nonetheless one that still tended to present artists in constellational terms rather than as individual stars. New Yorkers hailed their "great city, so well-known as a liberal patroness of the arts and sciences," where "a constellation of artistic luminaries shed around their effulgence."[43] Writing of a benefit gala for an orphan asylum in New York, which by the late nineteenth century had become the nation's foremost artistic hub, a reporter employed the images of both the constellation and stardom: "Dramatic and musical stars diverged from their regular orbits to twinkle in the constellation." The correspondent proceeded to elaborate further astronomical allusions. Referring to the pre-electrical lighting devices used in shows, the stars of the shows (the "constellation") reportedly "mingle[d] with a galaxy of Music footlights and burnt cork luminaries." Astronomical allusions in the realm of the arts—artistic stars and constellations, as well as galaxies of lesser luminaries—were still dynamic and meaningful in the closing decades of the nineteenth century.[44] Within a few decades, however, this situation would change as "the star" became so common an appellation that its original connection to political astronomy would be forgotten and all but obliterated; a meaningful metaphor became simply a bland noun.

While stars could be found across the creative spectrum, it was the performing arts—first the theatrical actors of the nineteenth century and then the twentieth-century cinematic performers—who promoted and brought human stars to the forefront of the attention of mass audiences. All aspects of North American culture were subordinate to English culture throughout the colonial period and into the nineteenth century, and the British theater continued to dominate the American well after political Independence.[45] When the English actress "Mrs. Merry" performed in Philadelphia in the closing years of the eighteenth century, she was readily promoted as an "excellent theatrical Star."[46] Another antebellum "theatrical star" was the English-born James William Wallack (1795–1864), who owned and managed several theaters and acting troupes in New York that would develop many future luminaries of the American stage.[47] The American theater was still embryonic before the

Civil War, consisting mainly of itinerant groups and stock companies. American audiences therefore still looked to European cultural capitals such as Paris to learn about "the theatrical mania" abroad and its "great stars."[48] While itinerant acting troupes brought theatrical entertainment to the hinterland, the stock companies were more significant commercially and artistically. Stock companies had permanent theatrical homes located in metropolitan areas that could support them financially and provide a reliable supply of local crowds. These local and autonomous operations held a cadre of actors, few of whom achieved more than local prominence. Indeed, their characteristic feature was an ability to survive without stars.[49] The American theatrical world would mature after 1870 with the emergence of New York City as the hub of the combination companies, theatrical troupes that performed a single play for the season on a prearranged tour and exhibited an array of "stars."

Nevertheless, by the 1850s the trope of the theatrical star was firmly established and could be applied to the distant "theatrical firmament of California" only a few years after the state achieved statehood. The future home of Hollywood's larger-than-life luminaries, the Golden State already had its "constellation" of "bright and shining" stars as well as "of other luminaries, less planetary in their movements."[50] Even after the Civil War the image of the constellation of stars did not completely give way to the single star; major venues such as New York's Tivoli Theatre ran advertisements for "a Monster Show" with "A CONSTELLATION of Brilliant Luminaries."[51]

Notwithstanding the lingering persistence of the somewhat egalitarian image of a constellation of luminaries (that is, one in which several stars coexist), by the closing decades of the century the image of the individual star was in such common use that it was often deployed without much fanfare. "Stardom" was on the way to becoming more of an idiom than a celestial metaphor when reporters flatly described two of the leading (and aging) actors of the country, Lawrence Barrett and Edwin Booth, as "the two stars" who played their parts exceptionally well.[52] Yet the more significant development of the closing decades of the century was the emergence of a so-called theatrical "star system." The star system was one in which producers (and later, in the movie era, studios) would select, promote, and glamorize promising actors in concerted marketing campaigns. Scholars tend to agree that a theatrical star system of sorts was already in place by the late nineteenth century, and was dependent on the observation, made already in 1867 by the artistic editor of the *London Times*, that great individual performances were the main theatrical attraction of the day: "With all their ardent love for theatrical amusements ... the Americans care much more for the actors than for the merits of the play itself. This predilection is consistently accompanied by a regard less to a perfect ensemble than to the excellence of the 'star' of the evening."[53] The expansion of American theater throughout the 1880s offered novel prospects and venues for new stars to appear, reaching a growing audience and nourishing wider reputations.

Contemporaries recognized and criticized the star system in real time, a system that from early in the twentieth century would define the history of Hollywood's construction of stardom.[54] When Margaret Mather, one of the famed Shakespearean actresses of the 1880s, sued her manager, a sensationalist reporter gave the American public a "peep behind the scenes and a little inside view of the way 'stars' are manufactured." The reporter nostalgically reminisced on the "old-fashioned method" that elevated to greatness actors such as the great Edwin Booth and Charlotte Cushman (1816–1876), who began "at the lowest rung of the ladder and [had] to work up gradually by hard work and patient application to the highest rank." The "new fangled way" of the late nineteenth century, by contrast, seemed to have no interest in hard work and patience but rather relied on "spring[ing] full-fledged into 'stardom' from the head of some managerial Jove."[55] Such deliberate manufacturing of stars coincided and converged with the birth of modern celebrity culture, allowing the description of turn-of-the-century Chicago's "most exclusive social circle" as a "most brilliant constellation of ... social luminaries," in which a Mrs. Kendig was deemed one who shined "for years [as] a star of the first magnitude."[56]

Another notable arena of this budding celebrity culture that was to grow exponentially was that of sports, with the final decades of the nineteenth century witnessing the birth of the star athlete. With the formation of organized sports followed by the emergence of professional sports, it was boxing and baseball that took the lead in producing star sportsmen.[57] Fighters in bare-knuckle matches endured painful and short careers, and one Merwine, as reported in the *Kansas City Times*, was past his "days of . . . pugilistic stardom," and was now, the journalist added tongue in cheek, "the star of a quack medicine combination."[58] A buildup for a baseball match in 1893 promised in celestial language that was taken right out of the political playbook, "an assemblage of . . . athletic luminaries in a grand constellation," although admittedly some players were still "stars that are not in the firmament."[59]

The meteoric rise of late nineteenth-century sport stars notwithstanding, professional actors would remain, at least for the time being, the most prominent stars as cultural astronomy expanded out of the political universe. The preoccupation with the acting star was not confined to America and occurred in tandem on the European continent. The expansion of theatricals in America throughout the 1880s, however, as the historian Benjamin McArthur notes, offered "unequal opportunities for new stars to appear," as they reached vast audiences and nourished wider reputations through a national network of newspapers and magazines in the United States.[60]

In the long run, however, it was not the theatrical but the cinematic stars who would become the brightest and most recognized of all stars, throughout the twentieth century and beyond. The literature on movie stars is rich, particularly studies that examine the emergence of the early movie stars out of anonymity, their hurtling into stardom, and the consequences of the creation of Hollywood's (in)famous star system. The general details of this story, in which within the space of a very few years there was a transition from a cinematic industry completely devoid of stars to one wholly dependent on and constructed around them, are well known, and scholars have toyed with various explanations for this major development.[61] Some have noted the continuity between theatrical and cinematic stardom and how the theatrical star system may have anticipated the cinematic one, but others have disputed that lineage. Yet all acknowledge the complexity of the phenomenon of stardom.[62] Today we live in a world of movie stars, with the cultural rituals of mass audiences enthralled with stars' lives, habits, choices, scandals, and personal biographies a central feature of modern society. Yet the rise of the modern movie star was not inevitable. The existence of a popular cinematic universe without stars in the early twentieth century underscores that a different path in the development of the movies could have been taken. While it may be true that "nothing" like cinematic stardom had ever existed before, as "stage [that is, theatrical] stars were known only to those who could afford to see their plays [whereas] the movies offered amusement to the masses," it should be clear that the notion of the cinematic star had a distinct discursive genealogy that reached all the way back to the halls of early modern European monarchs.[63] It is thus surprising that none of the intricate studies of the emergence of cinematic stardom have asked the simple question, Why "stars"?

Why, indeed, "stars"? Charismatic, beautiful, and talented movie actors have been labeled thus for over a century (and theatrical stars have been so called for at least two centuries), and the tag is universally—and unquestioningly—in use. It seems that the unthinking identification of vastly popular cinematic personalities as stars may have helped to blind us to such a basic question. Contemporary critics who witnessed and commented on the early rise of the movie star, however, may have appreciated the connection of the social phenomenon of stardom with its astronomical roots more than later commentators. Frank E. Wood, America's first dedicated movie critic, who would go on to collaborate with the pioneer filmmaker D. W. Griffith, was among the first to inquire into the phenomenon of cinematic stardom. In an eye-opening column from 1919, Wood noted that "stars have become stars" because they were able to "center the public attention on them." Certain actors' ability to do so was, Wood noted, due to a capacity they shared with real cosmic bodies, namely, "having certain personal qualities of attraction."[64] Stars, whether human or celestial, were characterized by the ability to attract other bodies to their orbits. Yet not all contemporaries recognized the affiliation of the human and celestial star as did Wood. One commentator could thus flatly state that "the star idea is based upon the principle that an artist . . . having achieved great popularity with the public, can be used to great commercial advantage."[65] Nevertheless prominent early film actors such as Douglas Fairbanks were routinely advertised as "The Big Bright Star of the Film Firmament," underscoring that at least during Hollywood's formative decades "stars" were still associated with and understood in terms of celestial stars.[66] Hollywood studios have followed suit. Since the industry's inception the major studios have adopted astronomical images and themes that underscore this cosmic connection: from Paramount's iconic "majestic mountain" with a semi-circular constellation of stars hovering over it, to Universal's floating globe with the sun beaming from behind, to Colombia's classically draped lady raising a glittering and radiating starlike torch in front of a dramatic sky, and the more recent Orion Pictures, which chose that constellation as its namesake and logo.

The unquestioning and pervasive use of the term "star" to designate exceptionally appealing and talented individuals, particularly actors, combined with the dramatic reduction of the visibility of the stars due to the spread of light pollution, would eventually lead to a disconnect between the phrase's origins in early modern political astronomy and its idiomatic, nonpolitical, and broader use. Occasionally, however, references to the astronomical aspects of stardom would surface. In the classic romantic comedy *Singing in the Rain* (1952), Lina Lamont (portrayed by Jean Hagen, 1923–1977) proclaims: "'People'? I ain't 'people.' I am a—'a shimmering, glowing star in the cinema firmament.'" A generation later, upon receiving a Oscar Award in 1979 for lifetime achievement, the great actor Laurence Olivier (1907–1989) demonstrated in his acceptance speech that he was deeply aware of the astronomical roots of the metaphor of human stardom. Addressing "that great firmament" of the American nation, Olivier, a star if there was ever one, appealed to "a beautiful star ... which shines ... dazzling" and brings "the euphoria that happens to so many of us at the first breath of the majestic glow of a new tomorrow."[67] By the second half of the twentieth century, however, such flourishes as Olivier's, which placed human stardom in its wider and historical astronomical context, had become the outlying exception. The human star, once an image that firmly belonged to a rich and meaningful celestial discourse, had become by the late twentieth century an empty idiom whose origins were obscure.

On occasion, however, thoughtful cultural commentators appear to have connected the dots. Celebrating the Statue of Liberty's centennial, ninety-six leading graphic designers and illustrators were invited to reinterpret the iconic image of the Stars and Stripes. The resulting reimagined flags were presented in an exhibition in San Francisco that opened on the Fourth of July, 1986, and were then collected in the album *Stars and Stripes*, published the following year. Some of these reimagined flags echo, like Edwin Church's *Our Banner in the Sky* (1861), the cosmic origins of the stars on the American flag: While Gerard Huerta replaced the well-known straight lines of pentagrams with a picture of a slice of the Milky Way, McRay Magleby replaced the stars with an image of George Washington that created a connect-the-dots style from twinkling stars.[68] Paula Scher (1948–), a renowned graphic designer, produced one of the most memorable designs in the collection, which was later used to illustrate a commemorative CD of President Bill Clinton's first inauguration in 1993. In Scher's monochrome rendition, the flag's stripes were replaced with the recognizable shape of strips of celluloid, alluding to the method for shooting and distributing motion pictures before the digital age. The strips render unspecified and repeating eclectic images, which while referencing the world of film mirror the visual effect of Old Glory's horizontal stripes. What attracts the attention, however, are the images of the floating faces of movie stars on the field of the flag's upper-left corner, which replace the original fifty stars of the American flag. The suspended faces of movie stars from Clark Gable to Elvis Presley (the rock 'n' roll king turned lead actor in scores of films), and from Judy Garland to Elizabeth Taylor, stand in Scher's flag for the original five-point stars. This

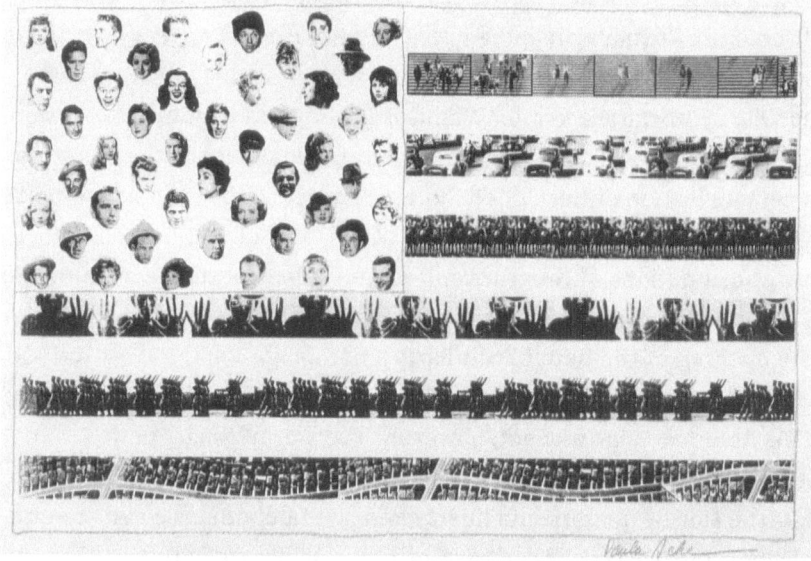

FIGURE 31. *Stars and Stripes,* Paula Scher, 1986. (Courtesy of the artist/Pentagram)

sophisticated commentary on late twentieth-century culture came full circle as Scher replaced the five-point pentagrams with human stars.[69] It is doubtful that Scher was aware of the rich genealogy of political astronomy from which the icon of the movie star emerged. Nevertheless, the famed designer was among the few who not only recognized that human "stars" derived their stellar attributes from the luminous celestial bodies that the English language labels stars but also triangulated that information with the fact that the American flag exhibits stars to represent states. Scher was thus able to bring together political astronomy and the culture of celebrity, making a striking vexillological statement using strips of celluloid and images of Hollywood stars.

American stars, the origins of which we have traced to the early modern European sun kings, stood throughout the first century of the United States for a variety of entities and institutions. The current idiom of human stars originally evolved as part of a rich astronomical discourse of "luminaries," "constellations," and the "political firmament," and participated in a broad array of metaphors and celestial allusions. Providing an evocative system of meaning well into the nineteenth century, by the second half of that century stars were identified with the idea of America to such an extent that they were occasionally enlisted in the contemporary discourse of expansion and empire.[70] In *American Progress* (1872), one of the most iconic paintings of the era, John Gast (1842–1896) created a popular symbolic allegory for Manifest Destiny and westward expansion. The main image of the painting is a large female figure that serves as a personification of the United States, crowned with a golden five-point star, the "star of empire." This trope of the "star of empire" was vital to American notions of progress and played a central role in such public pronouncements as Senator Albert Beveridge's (1862–1911) speech at the opening of the Republican Party's Campaign for the West in 1900, where he marveled how "Westward the Star of Empire takes its Way." This American star was not, however, "the star of kingly power . . . not the star of autocratic oppression." Rather, the American star of empire was the star of "empire and liberty and law, of commerce and communication, of social order and the Gospel." A showcase of the belief in the United States as a "redeemer nation" and of American exceptionalism,

FIGURE 32. *American Progress*, John Gast, 1872. (Library of Congress, LC-DIG-ppmsca-09855)

the star of empire was, in short, the star of American civilization following its course westward.[71]

While this nexus of American geographical expansion, exceptionalism, and stars receded with the closing of the Western frontier at the end of the nineteenth century, it did so only temporarily. John F. Kennedy revived that connection when he declared that his administration would pursue what he designated the New Frontier. By directly linking the heroics of past generations of Americans and their struggles to "build our new west" with exploring the "uncharted areas of science and space," Kennedy rekindled the idea of the star of empire, only now replacing westward movement with a crusade of cosmic proportions. Kennedy hoped that an invigorated space program would encourage Americans to raise their eyes to the stars and would reconstitute a collective political imagination built upon visions of vast expanses, both in outer space and "inside [Americans'] minds."[72]

In retrospect, however, it is clear that by the closing decades of the nineteenth century the most consequential role of the stars would not

Epilogue

be as amorphic allusions to America or symbols of expansion. Rather, the American star would be a human star. Social scientists have analyzed stardom's various aspects, from its psychological implications to its economic efficiency and deficiencies.[73] Critics note how stars became the quintessential objects of mass production and consumption, while others portray stardom as manifesting a glorified version of the American Dream.[74] Stardom continued to evolve in the second half of the twentieth century with the rambunctious "rock star" emerging as a distinct personality, drawing fanatical admiration and followers from the early 1960s. The term "superstar"—which may have caught on after Andrew Lloyd Webber and Tim Rice's megahit rock opera *Jesus Christ Superstar* (opened on Broadway in 1971)—has become a mode of further elevating extremely successful performers or athletes above their starry peers. By contrast, the digital information age has democratized the process of star making, with social networks seemingly lowering the bar for celebrity "influencers," the stars of the day.

With numerous individuals of extraordinary talent in a variety of fields deemed stars (when they rise suddenly, they are "meteors"), stardom has become such a common figure that it is now a hollow cliché. The use of "star" to denote human talent spread as we have seen from politics to theater and to sports, and with the rise of cinema to the rest of the performing arts. Such use was also democratized and applied to female stars, which were formally excluded from politics during the heyday of political astronomy. With their growing pervasiveness, cultural stars soon eclipsed political stars. Cultural stars were still admired but were now also glamourous and envied, whereas late nineteenth-century and twentieth-century politicians were increasingly seen as mundane bureaucratic men in suits. Hence, as "star" was used to designate exceptionally appealing and dazzling individuals, it became a culturally widespread term. With this democratization and spread of the human star, the word inevitably came to be used unquestioningly, its meaning a platitude. This cultural development occurred in lockstep with another striking and encompassing change, namely, the universal urbanization across the globe and the spread of electricity grids. These changes brought about the now ubiquitous nightly glare and sky glow associated with human habitat—namely, light pollution—that brought about a dramatic reduction in the visibility of the night skies. For the first time in history humans have lost sight of the stars, and with it the intimate knowledge of the heavens gained through ages of celestial observation. This literal and psychological disengagement from the stars, brought about through the spread of light pollution, would eventually lead to a disconnect between the human star that originated in early modern political astronomy, and its idiomatic, cultural, and more casual modern use. Ironically, the human star rose in tandem with the exponential accumulation of light pollution, which deprived a mass of humanity of the unmediated experience of night skies and thus deepened the gap between human and celestial stars. As humans lost touch with heavenly stars, cultural stars spread exponentially; with the inflation of human stars, the rich language of political astronomy that accompanied them was in turn forgotten. By the mid-twentieth century human stars were no longer associated with firmaments, orbits, and constellations; neither did they seem connected to comets, propelling and repelling Newtonian forces, or to solar systems. They no longer constituted republics in the sky but rather radiated in lonely solitude. Detached from actual cosmic stars, the reason for deeming "stars" as stars, and with it the use of five-point stars as the visual representation of the five-point "American" star, became unclear.

The five-point star has achieved an unrivaled presence in American visual culture and represents a broad variety of images and entities beyond its original use among the nation's formal symbols. The American star has become such a cultural staple that it can serve impersonal and eclectic purposes, from decorating commercialized merchandise on numerous articles of Americana to adorning sheriffs' badges and ranking products and services (think hotel and Amazon.com star rating systems). The American star also fulfills more somber roles when it stands for and represents fallen servicemen and servicewomen in formal memorial sites, such as in the World War II National Monument, where each star stands for one hundred fallen American soldiers (4,048 in total), and the CIA Memorial Wall, which dedicates a star to each fallen employee who has died in the line of service. In these solemn contexts of fallen patriots, the star is associated once more with humans.

The star comes full circle in the Hollywood Walk of Fame, a landmark of some 2,700 (and counting) metal stars embedded in the sidewalks of

FIGURE 33. Freedom Wall, World War II National Monument, Washington DC. (Courtesy of National Park Service)

FIGURE 34. A Hollywood star. While political stars throughout the eighteenth and nineteenth centuries were exclusively male, the cultural star witnessed a democratization of the gender of human stars, as women became dominant in the performing arts. (Lydia Sigismondi)

Hollywood Boulevard and Vine Street in Hollywood, California. Each star commemorates a performer or professional in the entertainment and media industries, tying together the five-point star—a geometrical form that represents the American states—with the human star. This nexus of the political star-as-American-state, the golden embedded five-point stars on Hollywood sidewalks, and the human "stars" means that these embedded stars represent may resonate, perhaps unconsciously, with

The Star-Spangled Republic

the millions of visitors to the mecca of filmmaking. Whether or not they connect the dots, the crowds are surely not aware of the early modern kingly origins of celebrity culture, which viewed men, first monarchs and then democratic politicians, as stars. This long trajectory, which the present book has charted, and which began in sixteenth-century European courts and took a sharp republican turn during the American Revolution, has come full circle in Hollywood, where celebrity stars are revered in ways reminiscent of modern-day monarchs. Political astronomy still echoes loudly in present-day America. We need only recognize the deep impact that stars made on our predecessors, and how their pale, artificial imitations persist in the imagination of the American republic.

NOTES

Introduction

1. Doreen Bolger Burke, "Frederic Edwin Church and 'The Banner of Dawn,'" *American Art Journal* 14 (1982): 39–46.
2. Robert Y. Hayne quoted in *The Webster-Hayne Debate on the Nature of the Union: Selected Documents,* ed. Herman Beltz (Indianapolis, IN: Liberty Fund, 2000), 183; "Our Own Country," *Washington Review and Examiner,* May 9, 1835.
3. Nicholas Campion is among a handful of scholars who study the political role of astronomy in modern societies and has occasionally used the phrase "political astronomy" (Campion, "Astronomy and Political Theory," *Proceedings of International Astronomical Union Symposium* 260 [2009]: 595–602). The term "political astronomy" would also occasionally pop up in contemporary texts.
4. Clive L. N. Ruggles, *Handbook of Archaeoastronomy and Ethnoastronomy* (New York: Springer, 2014). For astrology, see chapter 1 of this volume.
5. Jacquetta Hawkes, *Man and the Sun* (London: Cresset, 1962), 47–48.
6. Charles Vancouver, *A General Compendium of Chemical, Experimental, and Natural Philosophy, with a complete System of Commerce* (Philadelphia, 1785), 4, 6.
7. Henri Frankfort et al., *The Intellectual Adventure of Ancient Man: An Essay on Speculative Thought in the Ancient Near East* (Chicago: University of Chicago Press, 1946), 60.
8. Thorkild Jacobsen, "The Cosmos as a State," in Frankfort et al., *The Intellectual Adventure of Ancient Man,* 125–84.
9. Hans P. L'Orange, *Studies on the Iconography of Cosmic Kingship in the Ancient World* (1953; New Rochelle, NY: Caratzas Brothers, 1982), 18. Tales, such as that of Prester John, told of a royal hall "with immensely high dome . . . round like the star spangled-sky and revolves like the firmament" (ibid., 19).
10. Jacobsen, "The Cosmos as a State," 125–84. See also Campion, "Astronomy and Political Theory."

11. For an ancient and non-Western example, see Prudence M. Rice, *Maya Political Science: Time, Astronomy, and the Cosmos* (Chicago: University of Chicago Press, 2004).
12. While unique American political astronomy was not "exceptional" in the historiographical sense, it was a distinctly American phenomenon (for exceptionalism, see chapter 3 of this volume).
13. Richard Striner, "Political Newtonianism: The Cosmic Model of Politics in Europe and America," *William and Mary Quarterly* 52, no. 4 (1995): 583–608; Michael Foley, *Laws, Men and Machines: Modern American Government and the Appeal of Newtonian Mechanics* (New York: Routledge, 1990); Scott Breuninger, "'Social Gravity' and the *Translatio* Tradition in Early American Theories of Empire,'" *Southern Quarterly* 43, no. 4 (2006): 70–108.
14. For important relevant studies of newspapers, see Joseph M. Adelman, *Revolutionary Networks: The Business and Politics of Printing the News, 1763–1789* (Baltimore, MD: Johns Hopkins University Press, 2019); Jeffrey L. Pasley, *The Tyranny of the Printers: Newspaper Politics in the New American Republic* (Charlottesville: University of Virginia Press, 2001); and Charles E. Clark, *The Public Prints: The Newspaper in Anglo-American Culture, 1665–1740* (New York: Oxford University Press, 1994).
15. The British Newspaper Archive, https://www.britishnewspaperarchive.co.uk/home/NewspaperTitles.
16. This trend is still evident today, with seven of the top forty highest-circulation newspapers in the United States bearing astronomical titles (*Boston Globe, Newark Star-Ledger, Minneapolis Star Tribune, Indianapolis Star, Kansas City Star, San Jose Mercury News*) (https://www.infoplease.com/culture-entertainment/journalism-literature/top-100-newspapers-united-states).
17. "Prospectus of a New Paper," *Federal Republican*, October 12, 1808.
18. On orreries, see chapter 2 of this volume.
19. "Insurrection of Pittsburg," *Federal Orrery*, October 23, 1794.
20. Many of the insights in this and following paragraphs are from James Geary, *I Is an Other: The Secret Life of Metaphor and How It Shapes the Way We See the World* (New York: Harper Perennial, 2012), 5–16; and Zoltan Kovecses, *Metaphor: A Practical Introduction* (New York: Oxford University Press, 2010), 3–17. See also Philip Wheelwright, *Burning Fountain: A Study in the Language of Symbolism* (Bloomington: Indiana University Press, 1968).
21. *The Rhetoric and Poetics of Aristotle,* introd. Edward P. J. Corbett (New York: Modern Library, 1984), 251.
22. For a similar view of metaphor and political action in the context of the French Revolution, see Mary Ashburn-Miller, *A Natural History of Revolution: Violence and Nature in the French Revolutionary Imagination, 1789–1794* (Ithaca, NY: Cornell University Press, 2011), 14ff.
23. Aristotle, *Politics*; Plato, *The Republic*, bk. 6, 488a–489d.
24. Leonard Barkan, *Nature's Work of Art: The Human Body as the Image of the World* (New Haven, CT: Yale University Press, 1975), 61–115; Cary J. Nederman and Kate L. Forham, *Medieval Political Theory, A Reader: The Quest for the Body Politic, 1100–1400* (Oxford: Routledge, 1993). Thomas Hobbes provided the most memorable image of the state as a body politic: "that great Leviathan called a Common-Wealth, or state." Being the ardent materialist that he was, Hobbes also stated that the

state was "an Artificiall Man" (Hobbes, *Leviathan*, ed. Richard Tuck [Cambridge: Cambridge University Press, 1996], 9, 86).

25. In particular, Brendan McConville has paraphrased Kantorowicz's *The King's Two Bodies*, in his *The King's Three Faces: The Rise and Fall of Royal America, 1688–1776* (Chapel Hill: University of North Carolina Press, 2006). For an excellent example of a study that focuses on a specific metaphor (circulation) in early America, see Joyce E. Chaplin, *The First Scientific American: Benjamin Franklin and the Pursuit of Genius* (New York: Basic, 2006), 78.
26. Drew McCoy, *The Elusive Republic: Political Economy in Jeffersonian America* (Chapel Hill: University of North Carolina Press, 1980).
27. According to Eric Slauter, by the late eighteenth century, the metaphor of the body politic may have become "meaningless" (Slauter, *The State as a Work of Art: The Cultural Origins of the Constitution* [Chicago: Chicago University Press, 2011], 63).
28. Among the histories of "natural" metaphors are Perry Miller's *Nature's Nation* (Cambridge, MA: Harvard University Press, 1967); Henry Nash Smith's *Virgin Land: The American West as Symbol and Myth* (Cambridge, MA: Harvard University Press, 1971); and Leo Marx, *The Machine in the Garden: Technology and the Pastoral Ideal in America* (1975; New York: Oxford University Press, 2000). For a modern collection, see Bernd Herzogenrath, *From Virgin Land to Disney World* (Amsterdam: Brill, 2001).
29. Colleen E. Terrell, "'Republican Machines': Franklin, Rush, and the Manufacture of Civic Virtue in the Early Republic," *Early American Studies* 1, no. 2 (2003): 100–132.
30. Michael Foley, *Laws, Men and Machines: Modern American Government and the Appeal of Newtonian Mechanics* (New York: Routledge, 1990); Richard Striner, "Political Newtonianism: The Cosmic Model of Politics in Europe and America," *William and Mary Quarterly* 52, no. 4 (1995): 583–608. For a study of the cosmic imagination in the English context, see Anna Henchman, *The Starry Sky Within: Astronomy and the Reach of the Mind in Victorian Literature* (Oxford: Oxford University Press, 2014).
31. On the impersonal state, see Quentin Skinner, "The State," in *Political Innovation and Conceptual Change*, ed. Terrence Ball, James Farr, and Russel L. Hanson (Cambridge: Cambridge University Press, 1995), 102.
32. On the prevalence of astronomical knowledge, see chapter 1 of this volume.
33. Arthur Lovejoy's *The Great Chain of Being: A Study of an Idea* (Cambridge, MA: Harvard University Press, 1933) is still the classic on the subject. More about harmony in chapter 1 of this volume.
34. James Daly, "Cosmic Harmony and Political Thinking in Early Stuart England," *Transactions of the American Philosophical Society* 69, no. 7 (1979): 1–41, quote on 29.
35. Kirsten E. Wood, "'Join with Heart and Soul and Voice': Music, Harmony, and Politics in the Early American Republic," *American Historical Review* 119, no. 4 (2014): 1083–116, quote on 1113.
36. *South Carolina Gazette*, December 16, 1783.
37. "Song sung in the Grand Procession, at Portsmouth," *Massachusetts Centinel*, July 2, 1788.
38. James Madison, *Notes of Debates in the Federal Convention of 1787, as Reported by James Madison* (Columbus: University of Ohio Press, 1987), 305.

39. Bos. Centinel, *Independent Ledger* (Philadelphia), July 13, 1776.
40. "Outrages at the South," *Columbian Register* (New Haven, CT), December 22, 1860.
41. Joyce E. Chaplin, "The Other Revolution," *Early American Studies: An Interdisciplinary Journal* 13, no. 2 (2015): 285–308, quote on 287.

1. The American Universe

1. William Barton and David Rittenhouse, *The Memoirs of the Life of David Rittenhouse* (Philadelphia, 1813), 1.
2. Trent MacNamara, "Sky God: Remaking the Heavens and Divinity in the Nineteenth-Century United States," *Religion and American Culture* 32, no. 1 (2022): 30–67, 44.
3. Craig Koslofsky, *Evening's Empire: A History of the Night in Early Modern Europe* (Cambridge: Cambridge University Press, 2011); A. Roger Ekirch, *At Day's Close: Night in Times Past* (New York: Norton, 2006); Nina Edwards, *Darkness: A Cultural History* (London: Reaktion, 2018).
4. Koslofsky points out that, as part of a larger process that he calls "nocturnalization," the rise of public street lighting was swift. While in 1660 no European city had permanently illuminated its streets, by 1700 consistent and reliable street lighting had been established in the main metropolitan centers. In a much more provincial North America, street lighting probably lagged behind (Koslofsky, *Evening's Empire*, 2).
5. Ekirch, *At Day's Close*, 128–29.
6. "The Comet," *Augusta Chronicle and Georgia Advertiser*, January 17, 1824.
7. Ekirch, *At Day's Close*, 326.
8. Ekirch, *At Day's Close*, 138, 236.
9. Trent MacNamara, "The Celestial Commons: Heavenly Space and Earthly Power in the Early United States," *Journal of America History* 111, no. 3 (December 2024): 443–68.
10. I. Bernard Cohen's *Science and the Founding Fathers: Science in the Political Thought of Thomas Jefferson, Benjamin Franklin, John Adams, and James Madison* (New York: Norton, 1995) belonged, on the one hand, to an older school of the history of science that focused on great men and theoretical science but, on the other, broke new ground in its broader vision of what consisted of science and its relation to the wider society. Atlantic historians who have debunked diffusionist notions that scientific knowledge traveled monodirectionally from European centers to colonial peripheries. On natural knowledge in Europe's early modern empires, see Londa Schiebinger, *Plants and Empire: Colonial Bioprospecting in the Atlantic World* (Cambridge, MA: Harvard University Press, 2007); Jorge Cañizares-Esguerra, *Nature, Empire, and Nation: Explorations of the History of Science in the Iberian World* (Stanford, CA: Stanford University Press, 2006); James Delbourgo and Nicholas Dew, eds., *Science and Empire in the Atlantic World* (New York: Routledge, 2007); Joyce E. Chaplin, *Subject Matter: Technology, the Body, and Science on the Anglo-American Frontier, 1500–1676* (Cambridge, MA: Harvard University Press, 2006); Richard H. Grove, *Green Imperialism: Colonial Expansion, Tropical Island Edens and the Origins of Environmentalism, 1600–1860* (New York: Cambridge University Press, 1995); and Antonio Barrera-Osorio, *Experiencing Nature: The Spanish Amer-*

ican Empire and the Early Scientific Revolution (Austin: University of Texas Press, 2006). On the importance of science done in and by actors in borderlands, see Cameron B. Strang, *Frontiers of Science: Imperialism and Natural Knowledge in the Gulf South Borderlands, 1500–1850* (Chapel Hill: University of North Carolina Press, 2018). Historians have also shown how, after the Revolution, American scientific practitioners began to demonstrate a sense of confidence as they realized that they were not mere peripheral collectors corresponding with metropolitan savants but part of a republic of scientific of letters and the equals of their European counterparts (Andrew J. Lewis, *A Democracy of Facts: Natural History in the Early Republic* [Philadelphia: University of Pennsylvania Press, 2011], 9).

11. See, for example, Steven Shapin, *A Social History of Truth: Civility and Science in Seventeenth-Century England* (Chicago: University of Chicago Press, 1994). A recent and important collaborative work on the subject is Conevery Bolton Valencius, David I. Spanagel, Emily Pawley, Sara Stidstone Gronim, and Paul Lucier, "Science in Early America: Print Culture and the Sciences of Territoriality," *Journal of the Early Republic* 36, no. 2 (2016): 73–126, 76. Andrew Lewis provides a prime example of science in the early United States that "highlights the contributions of historical actors not always associated with natural history," including farmers and mechanics, ordinary men and women, the literate but not learned, underscoring the overlooked natural knowledge of Indians and slaves (Lewis, *A Democracy of Facts*, 10).

12. Margaret Rossiter, *Women Scientists in America: Struggles and Strategies to 1940* (Baltimore, MD: Johns Hopkins University Press, 1982); Jennifer S. Light, "When Computers Were Women," *Technology and Culture* 40 (1999): 455–83; Londa L. Schiebinger, *Nature's Body: Gender in the Making of Modern Science* (New Brunswick, NJ: Rutgers University Press, 2004). See also Schiebinger, *The Mind Has No Sex? Women in the Origins of Modern Science* (Cambridge, MA: Harvard University Press, 1989), 195–200; and Tom Shachtman, *Gentlemen Scientists and Revolutionaries: The Founding Fathers in the Age of Enlightenment* (New York: Palgrave Macmillan, 2014). Not satisfied with merely understanding what "science" consisted in and who did it, we have also expanded our understanding of where science happened. In a move reflecting the cultural turn in history, science is now seen as being made and done not only in formal settings (such as laboratories) but also in pubs, coffeehouses, salons, workshops, and the great outdoors (Steven Johnson, *The Invention of Air* [New York: Riverhead, 2008], 59–61; Susan Scott Parrish, *American Curiosity: Cultures of Natural History in the Colonial British Atlantic World* [Chapel Hill: University of North Carolina, 2006]; Anya Zilberstein, "Making and Unmaking Local Knowledge in Greater New England," *Journal for Eighteenth-Century Studies* 36 [2013]: 559–69; David N. Livingstone, *Putting Science in Its Place: Geographies of Scientific Knowledge* [Chicago: University of Chicago Press, 2003]; Katherine Pandora, "Popular Science in National and Transnational Perspective: Suggestions from the American Context," *Isis* 100 [2009]: 346–58; Anne Secord, "Science in the Pub: Artisan Botanists in Early Nineteenth-Century Lancashire," *History of Science* 32, no. 3 [1994]: 269–315; Alan Dugatkin, *Mr. Jefferson and the Giant Moose: Natural History in Early America* [Chicago: University of Chicago Press, 2019]).

13. William Cronon, *Changes in the Land: Indians, Colonists, and the Ecology of New England* (New York: Hill and Wang, 1983); Valencius et al., "Science in Early

America," 79; Richard William Judd, *The Untilled Garden* (New York: Cambridge University Press, 2009); Lewis, *A Democracy of Facts;* Judith Magee, *The Art and Science of William Bartram* (University Park: Pennsylvania State University Press, 2007); Pandora, "Popular Science in National and Transnational Perspective"; Emily Pawley, "Accounting with the Fields: Chemistry and Value in Nutriment in American Agricultural Improvement, 1835–1860," *Science and Culture* 19 (2010): 461–82.

14. See Deborah Jean Warner, "Astronomy in Antebellum America," in *The Sciences in the American Context: New Perspectives,* ed. Nathan Reingold (Washington, DC: Smithsonian Institution Press, 1979), 59; Stephen G. Brush, "Looking Up: The New Perspectives Rise of Astronomy in America," *American Studies* 20, no. 2 (1979): 41–67; and John C. Greene, *American Science in the Age of Jefferson* (Ames: Iowa State University, 1984), 129–57.

15. Alexander MacDonald notes that the focus on astronomy may have stemmed from the inclination of the Puritan clergy in New England to regard the subject as manifesting the work of God (MacDonald, *The Long Space Age: The Economic Origins of Space Exploration from Colonial America to the Space Age* [New Haven, CT: Yale University Press, 2017], 21). See also Donald K. Yeomans, "The Origin of North American Astronomy—Seventeenth Century," *Isis* 68, no. 3 (1977): 414–25.

16. Anthony F. Aveni, "Astronomers and Stargazers Eyeing a Heliocentric Heaven for Planets, Portents, and Horoscopes," *CW Journal* (Winter 2005–6): 56–61, https://research.colonialwilliamsburg.org/Foundation/journal/Winter05-06/telescopes.cfm.

17. Samuel Eliot Morison "The Harvard School of Astronomy in the Seventeenth Century," *New England Quarterly* 7, no. 1 (1934): 3–24; 6, 23.

18. Morison, "The Harvard School of Astronomy in the Seventeenth Century," 3.

19. Yeomans, "The Origin of North American Astronomy—Seventeenth Century," 415.

20. Morison, "The Harvard School of Astronomy in the Seventeenth Century," 17, 24.

21. Yeomans, "The Origin of North American Astronomy—Seventeenth Century," 415.

22. The example of David Rittenhouse in particular demonstrates the importance of the achievements of individuals in colonial Americans to the development and popularization of astronomy in America.

23. Gronim, *Everyday Nature,* 151–52. Gronim brings the example of the transit of Venus of 1769 to demonstrate how middling men used natural philosophy as public performances of their scientific knowledge and to educate the general public through wider publication of their findings.

24. Renee Bergland, *Maria Mitchell and the Sexing of Science: An Astronomer Among the American Romantics* (Boston: Beacon, 2008), 14.

25. Gordon Fraser, *Star Territory: Printing the Universe in Nineteenth Century America* (Philadelphia: University of Pennsylvania Press, 2021), 3. Similarly, if for other reasons, the historian Cameron Strang concludes that imperialism and astronomy developed in the United States in tandem. Imperialism and the encounters it inspired were only recently deemed vital to the practice and application of astronomy, an observational science critical to claiming and organizing the earth's surface in early America. Officials and experts in the early republic measured the heavens to survey international boundary lines, establish the precise location of important spots, navigate between ports, and produce accurate maps. (Strang, *Frontiers of Science,* 161, 131).

26. MacDonald, *The Long Space Age*, 4, 31. Adams further initiated what would later be called the "American Observatory Movement" that spurred the construction of dozens of observatories during the second half of the nineteenth century. For a view of European observatory construction as essential in ensuring the growing social and cultural significance of the mathematical, physical, and cosmological sciences in the nineteenth century, see David Aubin, Charlotte Bigg, and H. Otto Sibum, eds., *The Heavens on Earth: Observatories and Astronomy in Nineteenth-Century Science and Culture* (Durham, NC: Duke University Press, 2010).
27. Fraser, *Star Territory*, 5, 6.
28. Valencius et al., "Science in Early America," 77–78. On circulation of scientific knowledge, see James A. Secord, "Knowledge in Transit," *Isis* 95, no. 4 (2004): 654–72; and Lissa Roberts, "The Circulation of Knowledge in Early Modern Europe: Embodiment, Mobility, Learning and Knowing," *History of Technology* 31 (2012): 47–68. On the development of a mail system, see Joseph Adelman, *Revolutionary Networks: The Business and Politics of Printing the News, 1763–1789* (Baltimore, MD: Johns Hopkins University Press, 2021).
29. Ekirch, *At Day's Close*, 129.
30. Gronim, "At the Sign of Newton's Head: Astronomy and Cosmology in British Colonial New York," 55.
31. Benjamin Franklin, *Poor Richard's Almanac* (New York: Barnes and Noble, 2004), 149.
32. Quoted in T. J. Tomlin, *A Divinity for All Persuasions: Almanacs and Early American Religious Life* (New York: Oxford University Press, 2014), 59.
33. As the historian T. J. Tomlin notes, almanacs played an unparalleled role in reinforcing what Carla Pestana has called British North America's "shared religious culture" (Tomlin, *A Divinity for All Persuasions*, 9).
34. Capp, *Astrology and the Popular Press*, 24.
35. William D. Stahlman, "Astrology in Colonial America: An Extended Inquiry," *William and Mary Quarterly* 13, no. 4 (1956): 551–63, 561.
36. Tomlin, *A Divinity for All Persuasions*, 12.
37. Quote from Fraser, *Star Territory*, 14; Bedini, *Life of Benjamin Banneker*, 226–30.
38. Tomlin, *A Divinity for All Persuasions*, 12.
39. *The New Jersey Almanack for the year . . . 1744 . . . by William Ball* (Philadelphia, 1743).
40. Tomlin, *A Divinity for All Persuasions*, 17, 21.
41. Fraser, *Star Territory*, 32.
42. Bergland, *Maria Mitchell and the Sexing of Science*, 14, 3, 7–8; quote from Samuel Haynes Jenks, *Nantucket (MA) Inquirer*, October 18, 1828.
43. "Choctaw Academy," *Cherokee Phoenix*, August 13, 1828.
44. "Choctaw Academy," *Cherokee Phoenix*, August 13, 1828.
45. "Astronomy," *Cherokee Phoenix*, May 28, 1828; and "Immensity of the Universe," *Cherokee Phoenix*, 1832.
46. The *Native American*, April 7, 1838; Pegasus, "For the Cherokee Phoenix," *Cherokee Phoenix*, January 7, 1829.
47. Thomas W. Kavanagh, *North American Indian Portraits: Photographs from the Wanamaker Expedition* (New York: Konecky and Konecky, 1996), 94.
48. Britt Rusert, *Fugitive Science: Empiricism and Freedom in Early African American Culture* (New York: New York University Press, 2017), 16, 4, 40. This pattern of

inheriting African knowledge in a variety of scientific fields, from mathematics to agriculture and of course astronomy, seems to have been common. Jared Hickman discusses the prevalent idea of Africa as the source of all arts and sciences, particularly of astronomy (Hickman, *Black Prometheus: Race and Radicalism in the Age of Atlantic Slavery* [New York: Oxford University Press, 2016], 207, 170). See also Fraser, *Star Territory*, 9.

49. Fraser, *Star Territory*, 59nn33, 34.
50. Tamara Plakins Thornton, *Nathaniel Bowditch and the Power of Numbers: How a Nineteenth-Century Man of Business, Science, and the Sea Changed American* Life (Chapel Hill: University of North Carolina Press, 2016), 62–63.
51. Fraser, *Star Territory*, 59–60.
52. The *Journal*'s readership was initially supposed to be middling free Black professionals in the North. Fraser notes that the overlap of the celestial, political, and textual on the pages of the *Journal* produced a distinct cosmology: "a mobile, interconnected system governed by a set of predictive laws . . . [that] made sense of the operations of the universe as a site of unfolding freedom" (Fraser, *Star Territory*, 52–53, 67).
53. For political astronomy in the *National Era*, see "McKeesport, Allegheny," *National Era*, July 7, 1853; and "The Conscience of Massachusetts," *National Era*, July 30, 1857.
54. Fraser, *Star Territory*, 49.
55. Floris Barnett Cash, "Kinship and Quilting: An Examination of an African-American Tradition," *Journal of Negro History* 80, no. 1 (1995): 30–41.
56. John Michael Vlach, *The Afro-American Tradition in Decorative Arts* (Athens: University of Georgia Press, 1990), 47.
57. Quote from Robin Bernstein, "Jane Clark: A Newly Available Slave Narrative," *Commonplace: The Journal of Early American Life,* https://commonplace.online/article/jane-clark/.
58. Frederick Douglass, *My Bondage and My Freedom* (New York, 1855), 186.
59. Relieved to see the constellations still in place, Lincoln thus quickly concluded that what he witnessed was not the apocalypse. Quoted in David J. Kent, *Lincoln: The Fire of a Genius* (Lanham, MD: Lyons, 2022), 224.
60. Mary L. Kwas, "The Spectacular 1833 Leonid Meteor Storm: The View from Arkansas," *Arkansas Historical Quarterly* 58, no. 3 (1999): 314–24.
61. Aveni, "Astronomers and Stargazers"; Yeomans, "The Origin of North American Astronomy—Seventeenth Century."
62. See, for example, Vose, *Compendium of Astronomy: Intended to Simplify and Illustrate the Principles of That Science* (Windsor, VT, 1836), 48; and Rev. Amos Pettengill, *View of the Heavens [. . .] Adapted for the Use of Schools* (New Haven, CT, 1826), 8.
63. Noah Webster, "Sketches of American Policy," *State Gazette of South Carolina*, January 19, 1786 (all emphases here and in the following paragraphs of this section are mine).
64. "The Writings of Ms. Mayo," *National Era*, September 19, 1850; "Rebecca," *National Era*, August 9, 1855.
65. *Northern Star* (Rochester, NY), April 20, 1833.
66. See, for example, "Young Ladies' High School," *Northern Star* (Rochester, NY), April 20, 1833; and "Warren Ladies' Seminary," *Northern Star, and Constitutionalist*, December 12, 1835.

67. "Warren Ladies' Seminary," *Northern Star, and Constitutionalist* (Warren, RI), December 12, 1835.
68. "Boarding School for Girls," *National Era*, January 10, 1850; "The Schoolmate," *National Era*, July 7, 1853.
69. "Astronomical Lectures," *Alexandria (VA) Gazette and Advertiser*, March 6, 1824; "Astronomical Lectures," *Northern Star* (Rochester, NY), February 1, 1834; "Astronomical Lectures," *Northern Galaxy* (Middlebury, VT), September 7 1847.
70. See chapter 2 of this volume.
71. Vose, *Compendium of Astronomy*, 15–16.
72. Elijah H. Burritt, *The Geography of the Heavens, and Class Book of Astronomy* (Hartford, CT, 1836), 171.
73. M. R. Bartlett, *Young Ladies' Astronomy: A Concise System of Astronomy [. . .] Designed Particularly for the Assistance of Young Ladies* (Utica, NY, 1825), 14.
74. "Poetry," *Ladies' Garland*, September 10, 1825; Philip Freneau, "The Sun," *Harpers-Ferry (VA) Free Press*, April 17, 1822.
75. *The American Class Book, or, A Collection of Instructive Reading Lessons* (Philadelphia, 1815), 45; *Litchfield (CT) Enquirer*, July 26, 1832.
76. William Guthrie, *A New System of Modern Geography* (Philadelphia, 1794), 16; Vancouver, *General Compendium*, 3.
77. "A Fragment, on the Theory of the Universe, by St. Pierre," *Wheeling (VA) Compiler*, June 16, 1830.
78. For such gendered language, see, for example, Burritt, *The Geography of the Heavens*, 203ff.
79. St. Pierre, "A Fragment, on the Theory of the Universe," *Wheeling (VA) Compiler*, June 2, 1830. See also Vose, *Compendium of Astronomy*, 51; and Bartlett, *Young Ladies' Astronomy*, 63.
80. Burritt, *The Geography of the Heavens*, 171; St. Pierre, "A Fragment, on the Theory of the Universe," *Wheeling (VA) Compiler*, June 2, 1830
81. *Cherokee Phoenix*, August 19, 1829.
82. For accounts of enslaved people, see notes 56–58 in this chapter. For an account in a Native newspaper, see "Grand Phenomenon of the Skies," *Cherokee Phoenix*, December 7, 1833.
83. Charles Ball, *Slavery in the United States* (New York, 1837); Fraser, *Star Territory*, 50. Hickman notes how Ball obsessively charts his escape course in relation to the North Star, which is not only absent but downright deceptive at the most crucial moments (Hickman, *Black Prometheus*, 399).
84. Russert, *Fugitive Science*, 168; Fraser, *Star Territory*, 50; Martin Delany, *Blake; or, The Huts of America: A Corrected Edition* (Cambridge, MA: Harvard University Press, 2017), 134.
85. Hickman, *Black Prometheus*, 195. Hickman additionally notes how the North Star was absorbed into the Judeo-Christian biblical tradition as a shining symbol of the Christian God's constancy.
86. Douglass, *The Heroic Slave*. Hickman notes the ambivalence Madison Washington, the novella's protagonist, feels toward the elusive Polaris, suggesting that Africans were "an ill-starred race" (Hickman, *Black Prometheus*, 203).
87. Hickman, *Black Prometheus*, 184.
88. John Pierpont's *Anti-Slavery Poems* (1843), 34, 38. Hickman further discusses James Russell Lowell's poem "Prometheus" (1843) as central to the White antislav-

ery use of the image of the North Star in the crusade against slavery (Hickman, *Black Prometheus*, 184–87).
89. Hickman, *Black Prometheus*, 213.
90. Astrology may have come under new intellectual pressure already during the sixteenth century, both from humanists and Reformed Christians (Curry, *Prophecy and Power: Astrology in Early Modern England* [Oxford: Polity, 1989], 11). Nevertheless, it would maintain its popularity into the nineteenth century and beyond.
91. Curry's working definition of astrology is "any practice or belief that centered on interpreting the human or terrestrial meaning of the stars" (Curry, *Prophecy and Power*, 1, 4).
92. T. J. Tomlin, "'Astrology's from Heaven Not from Hell': The Religious Significance of Early American Almanacs," *Early American Studies* 8, no. 2 (2010): 288–321, 296.
93. North, "Astronomy and Astrology," 459.
94. Signs of the decline of astrology were already evident in the seventeenth century in European intellectual circles, although evidently it was a slow process that was never entirely completed. For that decline, see the special issue of *Early Science and Medicine* 22, no. 5/6 (2017): 405–516. Born of Mesopotamian roots in the second millennium BC and further developed and then transmitted by the Greeks to generations of Europeans, the study of astrology was split into two major categories, natural and judicial. Natural astrology was concerned with and defined by the correlation (or causal relation) of planetary movements with terrestrial, "natural" phenomena. Large-scale and sweeping events that influenced humanity, such as epidemics or mass social changes and disruption, also fell under the canopy of natural astrology. Judicial astrology, on the other hand, attempted to predict smaller-scale events, which commonly concerned specific individuals, and so could advise their behavior and decision-making. Judicial astrology further divided into nativities (based on a map of the planets' positions at the moment of a person's birth), horary (an attempt to answer specific questions based on a map of the planets' positions at a certain moment), and elections and inceptions (which concerned the beginning of an enterprise). In all cases, astrologers drew a map, called a "figure," "nativity," and later "horoscope," which they then read and interpreted (see Curry, *Prophecy and Power*, 8).
95. Nathaniel Ames quoted in Tomlin, *A Divinity for All Persuasions*, 33.
96. Darrel Rutkin, "Astrology," in *Early Modern Science*, ed. Katharine Park and Lorraine Daston, vol. 3 of *The Cambridge History of Science* (Cambridge: Cambridge University Press, 2008), 541–61, 543.
97. Robert S. Westman, *The Copernican Question: Prognostication, Skepticism, and Celestial Order* (Berkeley: University of California Press, 2011), underlines the extent to which "premodern" modes of thought such as astrology and the occult were not neatly separated from what we consider "science."
98. Gronim, *Everyday Nature*, 47; David Hall, *Worlds of Wonder, Days of Judgment: Popular Belief in Early New England* (Cambridge, MA: Harvard University Press, 1990), 76. For occult traditions in America, see also John L. Brooke, *The Refiner's Fire: The Making of Mormon Cosmology, 1644–1844* (New York: Cambridge University Press, 2008). For notable studies of early modern astrology, see Anthony Grafton, *Cardano's Cosmos: The Worlds and Works of a Renaissance Astrologer* (Cambridge, MA: Harvard University Press, 1999); and Ann Geneva, *Astrology and the Seventeenth Century Mind* (Manchester: Oxford University Press, 1995). For "patriotic

astrology" in early modern Latin America, see Canizeras-Esguerra, *Nature, Empire and Nation*, 64–95.

99. Although historians do not agree over the causes and timing of astrology's decline, they seem to agree that in America it was one aspect of a longer process of the triumph of Newtonian cosmology (see Jon Butler, "Magic, Astrology, and the Early American Religious Heritage, 1600–1800," *American Historical Review* 84, no. 2 [1979]: 317–46; Keith Thomas, *Religion and the Decline of Magic* [New York: Oxford University Press, 1971]; Ann Geneva, *Astrology and the Seventeenth Century Mind: William Lilly and the Language of the Stars* [Manchester: Manchester University Press, 1995]; Peter Eisenstadt, "Almanacs and the Disenchantment of Early America," *Pennsylvania History* 65, no. 2 [1998]: 143–69; Curry, *Prophecy and Power*, 3; and Tomlin, "Astrology's from Heaven Not from Hell," 300).

100. For the standard account of the cultural and technological history of clocks, see David Landes, *Revolution in Time: Clocks and the Making of the Modern World* (Cambridge, MA: Belknap Press of Harvard University Press, 2000).

101. Otto Mayr, *Authority, Liberty, and Automatic Machinery in Early Modern Europe* (Baltimore, MD: Johns Hopkins University Press, 1989). Lewis Mumford noted almost a century ago that the "clock, not the steam engine, is the key machine of the modern industrial age," in Mumford, *Technics and Civilization* (London: Routledge, 1934), 14–15.

102. Mayer, *Authority, Liberty, and Automatic Machinery*, 27–29; Samuel L. Macey, *Clocks and the Cosmos: Time in Western Life and Thought* (Hamden, CT: Archon, 1980), 17; Courtney Weiss Smith, *Empiricist Devotions: Science, Religion, and Poetry in Early Eighteenth-Century England* (Charlottesville: University of Virginia Press, 2016), 70.

103. Understandings of the scientific revolution have been reviewed and revised in the past decades. For a few important studies, see H. Floris Cohen, *The Scientific Revolution: A Historiographical Inquiry* (Chicago: University of Chicago Press, 1994); Margaret J. Osler, *Rethinking the Scientific Revolution* (Cambridge: Cambridge University Press, 2000); Peter Dear, *Discipline and Experience: The Mathematical Way in the Scientific Revolution* (Chicago: University of Chicago Press, 2009); and David Lindberg and Robert S. Westman, *Reappraisals of the Scientific Revolution* (Cambridge: Cambridge University Press, 1990).

104. The seminal work about this process is Thomas S. Kuhn's celebrated *The Structure of Scientific Revolutions* (Chicago: Chicago University Press, 1962).

105. Mayr, *Authority, Liberty, and Automatic Machinery in Early Modern Europe*, 39, 54, 116; Eduard J. Dijksterhuis, *The Mechanization of the World Picture*, trans. C. Dikshoorn (Oxford: Oxford University Press, 1961), 501, 495; George Cheyne, *Philosophical Principles of Religion, Natural and Reveal'd* (London, 1724), 159.

106. In a recent study, Courtney Weiss Smith convincingly demonstrates how the two opposing schools differently understood God's role within the framework of the clockwork universe. Leibniz argued that the divine master-clockmaker designed a perfect clockwork that, due to its infallibility, needed no further intervention. Newton and his followers, by contrast, incorporated the action of a dynamic God inside the universal clock. The Newtonian divine watchmaker was a "maintenance man," an image that affirmed God's constant activity. In other words, the Newtonian clockwork-world was made, driven, and constantly "assisted" by God. Hence, while Leibnitz suggested that the Newtonians made God into a second-

rate mechanic and the world he created a faulty clock, the Englishmen rejected Leibniz's completely mechanized (if not deterministic) clockwork (Weiss Smith, *Empiricist Devotions*). For important studies of natural theology in the context of Newtonianism, see Alexander Koyré, *From the Closed World to the Infinite Universe* (Baltimore, MD: Johns Hopkins University Press), 1957; Steven Shapin, "Of Gods and Kings: Natural Philosophy and Politics in the Leibniz Clarke Disputes," *Isis* 72, no. 2 (1981): 187–215; James E. Force, "Newton's 'Sleeping Argument' and the Newtonian Synthesis of Science and Religion," in *Standing on the Shoulders of Giants*, ed. Norman J. W. Thrower (Berkeley: University of California Press, 1990), 109–27; James E. Force, "Providence and Newton's Pantokrator," in *Newton and Newtonianism: New Studies* (Dordrecht: Kluwer Academic, 2004), 65–92; and John Hedley Brooke, "Science and Religion," in vol. 4 of *The Cambridge History of Science*, ed. Roy Porter (Cambridge: Cambridge University Press, 2003), 741–61. On the other side of the divide, with an interpretation of the Newtonian clockwork universe as leaning toward a nonintervening God, see Jacob, *The Newtonians and the English Revolution, 1689–1720*. For a discussion of Jacob's thesis, see Force's introduction to William Whiston, *Astronomical Principles of Religion, Natural and Reveal'd* (1717; facsimile edition, Hildscheim: Georg Olms Verlag, 1983), 3–8.

107. James Hervey, *Contemplations on the Night. Contemplations on the Starry Heavens*, vol. 2 of *Meditations and Contemplations* (London, 1816), 238, 251–52.
108. "Reflection on the Value of Human Reason," *New York Mercury*, March 14, 1757.
109. Sauter, *The Spatial Reformation*, 2, 4.
110. Charles Vancouver, *A General Compendium; or Abstract of Chemical, Experimental, and Natural Philosophy* (Philadelphia, 1785), 1:6, 3; Nehemiah Strong, *Astronomy Improved: Or a New Theory of the Harmonious Regularity Observable in the Mechanism or Movements of the Planetary System* (New Haven, CT, 1784), 3–4; Cohen, *Science and the Founding Fathers*, 79–88.
111. Charles Vancouver, *A General Compendium of Chemical, Experimental, and Natural Philosophy, with a complete System of Commerce* (Philadelphia, 1785), 4, 6.
112. Vancouver, *A General Compendium*, 3; Nehemiah Strong, *Astronomy Improved: Or a New Theory of the Harmonious Regularity observable in the Mechanism or Movements of the Planetary System* (New Haven, CT, 1784), 3–4.
113. "History, Dignity and Usefulness of Astronomy," *American Recorder*, March 21, 1786.
114. Mayr, *Authority, Liberty, and Automatic Machinery in Early Modern Europe*, 21, 58.
115. Cohen, *Science and the Founding Fathers*, 79–88. For the nexus of the astronomer-watchmaker-orrery constructer, see Barton and Rittenhouse, *The Memoirs of the Life of David Rittenhouse*, 122.
116. MacDonald, *The Long Space Age*, 23.
117. Quoted in John A. Munroe, "The Lyceum in America Before the Civil War," *Delaware Notes* 37 (1942): 65–75, quote on 67.
118. Josiah Holbrook, "Schools, Lyceums, and Lyceum Seminary," (1830), 9; *Text-Book to Accompany Holbrook's Scientific Apparatus* (Hartford, CT, 1853), 57. See Angela G. Ray, *The Lyceum and Public Culture in the Nineteenth-Century United States* (East Lansing: Michigan State University Press, 2005).
119. The concept of deep time would emerge in the mid-nineteenth century with the advent of geology (Martin J. S. Rudwick, *Bursting the Limits of Time: The Recon-*

struction of Geohistory in the Age of Revolution [Chicago: University of Chicago Press, 2005]).

120. Vancouver, *A General Compendium*, 2.
121. William Nicholson, *An Introduction to Natural Philosophy* (Philadelphia, 1788), vii.
122. For the idea of clock and political ideals, see Colleen E. Terrell, "'Republican Machines': Franklin, Rush, and the Manufacture of Civic Virtue in the Early Republic," *Early American Studies* 1, no. 2 (2003): 100–132.
123. Endymion, "Some Desultory Thoughts on the Study of Astronomy," *City of Washington Gazette*, February 10, 1820.
124. Vose, *Compendium of Astronomy*, 49.
125. Benjamin Workman, *Elements of Geography, Designed for Young Students in that Science*, 13th ed. (Philadelphia, 1809), 27.
126. M. A. Davis, "American Uranus: The Early Republic and the Seventh Planet," April 3, 2023, https://ageofrevolutions.com/2023/04/03/american-uranus-the-early-republic-and-the-seventh-planet/.
127. Jefferson to Hopkinson, January 13, 1785, https://founders.archives.gov/documents/Jefferson/01-07-02-0437.
128. John Farrar, "Brewster's Edition of Ferguson's Astronomy," *North American Review* 1 (1818): 209; "The Astronomy of Laplace," *American Quarterly Review* 14 (1830): 258. The use of the title "the Newton of France" was widespread in American circles. See, for example, "Comets," *New York Tribune*, December 14, 1841.
129. "The Comet," *Martinsburg (VA) Gazette*, October 25, 1811. See also *Phoenix (AZ) Gazette*, June 4, 1827.
130. "The Material Universe," *Massachusetts Spy*, February 28, 1827.
131. "Anti-Slavery Convention in New York," *National Era*, July 3, 1851.
132. Koyré, *From the Closed World to the Infinite Universe*, ix.
133. Michael J. Crowe, ed., *The Extraterrestrial Life Debate, Antiquity to 1915: A Source Book* (Notre Dame, IN: University of Notre Dame Press, 2008), 129–30.
134. "Reflection on the Value of Human Reason," *New York Mercury*, March 14, 1757.
135. Vancouver, *A General Compendium*, 2.
136. Vancouver, *A General Compendium*, 2; Hervey, *Meditations and Contemplations*, 106.
137. "History, Dignity and Usefulness of Astronomy," *American Recorder*, March 21, 1786.
138. Jedidiah Morse, *Elements of Geography: Containing a Concise and Comprehensive View of That Useful Science* (Boston, 1795), 22. For similar ideas, see also "Astronomy," *Temple of Reason*, December 20, 1800. The American discussions on the size of the universe and the number of stars may have relied on English tracts from the early eighteenth century, such as George Derham's *Astro-Theology*, copies of which, while not reprinted in America, were available for purchase and found in private libraries (see "Plan for an English Grammar School," *New York Gazette*, August 30, 1773).
139. Sauter, *The Spatial Revolution*, 182.
140. William Donahue, "Astronomy," in vol. 3 of *Cambridge History of Science*, 595; Kuhn, *The Copernican Revolution*, 233–34. This process has been described also as the "Newtonization" of astronomy, among other scientific disciplines (Peter Fong, "Ethics, Politics and Sociology as Newtonian Sciences," in *Newton's Scientific and*

Philosophical Legacy, ed. Scheuder and Debrock [Dordrecht: Kluwer Academic, 1988], 343–53).

141. Brian Greene, *The Elegant Universe: Superstrings, Hidden Dimensions, and the Quest for the Ultimate Theory* (New York: Norton, 2003).
142. "Astronomy," *Temple of Reason*, December 20, 1800.
143. For a full discussion of this view, see chapter 3 of this volume.
144. George Fisher, *The Instructor, or, American Young Man's Best Companion* (New York, 1786), 328.
145. Richard J. Moss, *The Life of Jedidiah Morse: A Station of Peculiar Exposure* (Knoxville: University of Tennessee Press, 1995).
146. David Rittenhouse, *An Oration, Delivered February 24, 1775* (Philadelphia, 1775), 18.
147. Jedidiah Morse, *The Elements of Geography* (Boston, 1795), 22, 23; Morse, *The American Universal Geography* (Boston, 1789), 22.
148. Rittenhouse, *Oration*, 17, 15.
149. "Astronomy," *Temple of Reason*, December 20, 1800.
150. Caleb Bingham, *The American preceptor; being a new selection of lessons for reading and speaking. Designed for the use of schools* (Boston, 1798). For another example of such a text, see Henry Pattillo, *A Geographical Catechism [. . .] with much of the Science of Astronomy* (Halifax, NC, 1796), esp. 24–35.
151. Sereno Wright, *A Short Introduction to Geography: Designed Particularly for the Young Masters and Misses of New England* (Randolph, VT, 1806).
152. Rittenhouse, *Oration*, 21.
153. "A Philosophical Description of Comets," *Essex (MA) Gazette*, September 19, 1769.
154. Morse, *Geography Made Easy* (New Haven, CT, 1784), 8.
155. Jedidiah Morse, *The American Geography* (Elizabeth Town, NJ, 1789), 3.
156. Jedidiah Morse, *The American Universal Geography* (Boston, 1796), 34.
157. Rittenhouse, *Oration*, 25.
158. *The Instructor, or, American Young Man's Best Companion*, 328.
159. Bingham, *The American preceptor*, 5.
160. "Astronomy," *Temple of Reason*, December 20, 1800.
161. "Immensity of the Universe," *Cherokee Phoenix*, November 24, 1832.
162. During the closing decades of the eighteenth century, the pioneering geologist James Hutton was publishing his groundbreaking works on the formation of rocks, which introduced the notion of "deep time," a conception of geological time vastly longer ("deeper") not only from biblical time frames but even from our human ability to intuitively fathom (see Rudwick, *Bursting the Limits of Time*).
163. Daniel Heller-Roazen, *The Fifth Hammer: Pythagoras and the Disharmony of the World* (Princeton, NJ: Princeton University Press, 2011). See also Dominique Proust, "Harmony of the Spheres from Pythagoras to Voyager," *Proceedings of the International Astronomical Union* 5 (2009): 358–67.
164. James Haar, "Musica Mundana: Variations on a Pythagorean Theme" (PhD diss., Harvard University, 1961), 444.
165. The classic study on the subject is Lovejoy, *The Great Chain of Being*.
166. Aviva Rothman, *The Pursuit of Harmony: Kepler on Cosmos, Confession, and Community Account* (Chicago: University of Chicago Press, 2017), 19.
167. Avihu Zakai, *Jonathan Edwards's Philosophy of Nature: The Re-enchantment of the World in the Age of Scientific Reasoning* (London: T&T Clark, 2010), 86–124.
168. Aviva Rothman, "Johannes Kepler's Pursuit of Harmony," *Physics Today* 73 (2020),

https://physicstoday.scitation.org/doi/10.1063/PT.3.4388. Rothman points out that although Kepler's ideas about what might constitute earthly harmony changed over time, he ultimately came to believe that following God's harmonic model in the heavens meant accepting the peaceful coexistence of diverse religious views on earth. M. J. Osler's *Reconfiguring the World: Nature, God, and Human Understanding from the Middle Ages to Early Modern Europe* (Baltimore, MD: Johns Hopkins University Press, 2010) is characteristic in emphasizing the ways that religious thought was integral to the scientific work of many luminaries of the scientific revolution.

169. Hannah Spahn, *Thomas Jefferson, Time and History* (Charlottesville: University of Virginia Press, 2011), 109.
170. Rothman, *The Pursuit of Harmony*, 11.
171. Ruth Tatlow, *Bach's Numbers: Compositional Proportion and Significance* (Cambridge: Cambridge University Press, 2015), 6.
172. Mercy Otis Warren, *Poems, Dramatic and Miscellaneous* (Boston, 1792), 237–38.
173. Bingham, *The American preceptor*, 5.
174. Gordon S. Wood, "Conspiracy and the Paranoid Style: Causality and Deceit in the Eighteenth Century," *William and Mary Quarterly* 39, no. 3 (1982): 401–41.
175. Trent MacNamara, "Sky God: Remaking the Heavens and Divinity in the Nineteenth-Century United States," *Religion and American Culture: A Journal of Interpretation* 32, no. 1 (2022): 30–67.
176. Kirsten Wood, "'Join with Heart and Soul and Voice': Music, Harmony, and Politics in the Early American Republic," *American Historical Review* 119, no. 4 (2014): 1083–116.
177. For "natural knowledge," see Strang, *Frontiers of Science*, 7–8; and Lewis, *A Democracy of Facts*, 5.
178. Joyce Chaplin points out how, already by the mid-eighteenth century, almanacs, usually thought of as propagators of astrological views, could induce Americans to "become champions of nature's regularity" and its "glorious" and "beautiful features" (Chaplin, *The First Scientific American*, 59, 61). For typical science in early America, see Susan Scott Parrish, *American Curiosity: Cultures of Natural History in the Colonial British Atlantic World* (Chapel Hill: University of North Carolina Press, 2006); and Pamela Regis, *Describing Early America: Bartram, Jefferson, Crevecoeur, and the Influence of Natural History* (Philadelphia: University of Pennsylvania Press, 1999).
179. "History, Dignity and Usefulness of Astronomy," *American Recorder*, March 21, 1786.
180. "Astronomical Lecture," *Gazette of Maine*, December 26, 1826.

2. From the Sun King to Republican Solar Systems

1. B. F. Lemen to Abraham Lincoln, Sunday, April 1, 1860, in *Abraham Lincoln Papers: Series 1. General Correspondence. 1833–1916*, https://www.loc.gov/resource/mal.0254100/?sp=1&r=0.252,1.29,0.454,0.27,0.
2. Benjamin Workman, *Elements of Geography, Designed for Young Students in That Science*, 13th ed. (Philadelphia, 1809), 13.
3. In the Western tradition, the Romans were famous for their solar cult. See, for

example, Steven E. Hijmans's recent *Sol: Image and Meaning of the Sun in Roman Art and Religion* (Boston: Brill, 2022). For a general account, see Richard Cohen, *Chasing the Sun: The Epic Story of the Star That Gives Us Life* (New York: Random House, 2010), 3–13. For a classic study of the topic, see H. P. L'Orange, *Studies in the Iconography of Cosmic Kingship* (1953; New York: Caratzas, 1982).

4. Nicholas Copernicus, *On the Revolutions* (1543), II.2.

5. For state building in early modern Europe, see Maija Jansson, ed., *Realities of Representation: State Building in Early Modern Europe and European America* (London: Palgrave, 2007); and Stefan Brakensiek, "New Perspectives on State-Building and the Implementation of Rulership in Early Modern European Monarchies," in *Structures on the Move: Technologies of Governance in Transcultural Encounter*, ed. Fluchter and Richter (Heidelberg: Springer, 2012), 31–41.

6. Antoine De Baecque, *The Body Politic: Corporeal Metaphor in Revolutionary France, 1770–1800*, trans. Charlotte Madell (Stanford, CA: Stanford University Press, 1997). A classic but dated study is Ernst H. Kantorowitz, *The King's Two Bodies: A Study in Medieval Political Theology* (Princeton, NJ: Princeton University Press, 1957). For eighteenth-century biopolitical metaphors in America, see Drew McCoy, *The Elusive Republic: Political Economy in Jeffersonian America* (Chapel Hill: University of North Carolina Press, 1982), 33.

7. Alfonso X of Spain may have been the first European sun king. Yet his representation as such seems far less elaborated than his Renaissance and early modern predecessors (Alejandro García Avilés, "Ministers for a Wise King: The Sun-King and Planetary Imagery at the Court of Alfonso X," *Journal of Medieval Iberian Studies* 11, no. 2 [2019]: 157–92).

8. For quotes and context, see Peter Burke, *The Fabrication of Louis XIV* (New Haven, CT: Yale University Press, 1994), 130, 181, 187; Alain Boureau, "The King," and Anne-Marie Lecoq, "The Symbolism of the State: The Images of the Monarchy from the Early Valois Kings to Louis XIV," both in *Rethinking France*, ed. Pierre Nora, trans. Mary Seidman Trouille (Chicago: University of Chicago Press, 2001), 181–216, 217–68.

9. Samuel Pufendorf, *Of the Law of Nature and Nations: Eight Books* (1672; London, 1728), 735, 737.

10. Burke, *The Fabrication of Louis XIV*; Boureau, "The King"; Lecoq, "The Symbolism of the State."

11. Case's *Sphaera civitatis* seems to have mutated in revolutionary America into strikingly similar representations, such as the "Circle of the Social and Benevolent Affections," *Columbian Magazine*, 1789, 109; reproduced in Sarah Knott, *Sensibility and the American Revolution* (Chapel Hill: University of North Carolina Press, 2009), 196–97). Alexander Hamilton, who remarked that "the human affections, like the *solar* heat, lose their intensity as they depart from the centre; and become languid in proportion to the expansion of the circle on which they act," was centuries later influenced by a similar concentric logic (Hamilton, "On the Adoption of the Federal Constitution," in *The Debates in the Several State Conventions on the Adoption of the Federal Constitution*, ed. Jonathan Elliot [Washington, DC, 1836], 2:347–56, quote on 354).

12. James Daly, "Cosmic Harmony and Political Thinking in Early Stuart England," *Transactions of the American Philosophical Society* 69, no. 7 (1979): 1–41, quote on 11.

13. Daly, "Cosmic Harmony and Political Thinking in Early Stuart England," 11.
14. Subrahmanyan Chandrasekhar, *Newton's "Principia" for the Common Reader* (Oxford: Clarendon, 1995), 1–2.
15. Margaret C. Jacob, *The Cultural Meaning of the Scientific Revolution* (Philadelphia: Temple University Press, 1988), 105. For an evocative essay on the influence of Newtonian ideas on early modern political thought in Europe and America, see Richard Striner, "Political Newtonianism: The Cosmic Model of Politics in Europe and America," *William and Mary Quarterly* 52, no. 4 (1995): 583–603. See also Jorge Cañizares Esguerra, *Nature, Empire, and Nation: Explorations of the History of Science in the Iberian World* (Stanford, CA: Stanford University Press, 2006). Marjorie Hope Nicolson, *Science and Imagination* (Ithaca, NY: Cornell University Press, 1956), remains an important study of the interaction between modern science and other intellectual realms. Michael Hunter, *Science and Society in Restoration England* (London: Cambridge University Press, 1981), provides a systematic assessment of the social relations of Restoration science. For the American context, see Joyce E. Chaplin, *The First Scientific American: Benjamin Franklin and the Pursuit of Genius* (New York: Basic, 2006); James Delbourgo, *A Most Amazing Scene of Wonders: Electricity and Enlightenment in Early America* (Cambridge, MA: Harvard University Press, 2006); and Bernard Cohen, *Science and the Founding Fathers: Science in the Political Thought of Jefferson, Franklin, Adams, and Madison* (New York: Norton 1997). For Atlantic perspectives, see James Delbourgo and Nicholas Dew, eds., *Science and Empire in the Atlantic World* (New York: Routledge, 2008).
16. See Jeffrey R. Wigelsworth, *Deism in Enlightenment England: Theology, Politics, and Newtonian Public Science* (Oxford: Oxford University Press, 2009); and the classic works on Newtonianism: Margaret C. Jacob, *The Newtonians and the English Revolution: 1689–1720* (Ithaca, NY: Cornell University Press, 1976); and Larry Stewart, "Samuel Clarke, Newtonianism, and the Factions of Post-Revolutionary England," *Journal of the History of Ideas* 42 (1981): 53–72. For the ways in which contemporaries adopted the new Newtonian science, see Larry Stewart, *The Rise of Public Science: Rhetoric, Technology, and Natural Philosophy in Newtonian Britain, 1660–1750* (New York: Cambridge University Press, 1992).
17. "A Summer Storm," *New York Journal*, August 31, 1769; "On Time," *New Hampshire Gazette,* March 23, 1759; James Hervey, *Meditations and Contemplations* (Philadelphia, 1750), 106.
18. *New York Journal and Patriotic Register,* October 11, 1797; "Temple of the Muses," *Philadelphia Repository, and Weekly Register,* May 30, 1801.
19. For the infiltration of Newtonian notions into other realms of thought, see Betty Jo Teeter Dobbs and Margaret C. Jacob, *Newton and the Culture of Newtonianism* (Atlantic Highlands, NJ: Humanities Press, 1995), esp. 61–124; Striner, "Political Newtonianism"; and Michael Foley, *Laws, Men and Machines: Modern American Government and the Appeal of Newtonian Mechanics* (New York: Routledge, 1990). For Newtonian notions regarding the English king, see Brendan's McConville evocative *The King's Three Faces: The Rise and Fall of Royal America, 1688–1776* (Chapel Hill: University of North Carolina Press, 2006), 203, 205.
20. Henry St. John Bolingbroke, *Bolingbroke: Political Writings,* ed. David Armitage (Cambridge: Cambridge University Press, 1997), 83.
21. Newtonianism is a larger proposition than the direct impact of Newton's formal works; it was neither a given system nor a definitive synthesis of these works

but, rather, a multifaceted body of ideas that consisted of a simplified summary of Newton's works adapted to multiple geographical and intellectual climates. "Newtonianism" was thus much more than a scientific theory. It was a blend of scientific, political, and religious ideas that echoed and corresponded with, but did not precisely reflect, Newton's original works. For some of the important works on the infiltration of Newtonian notions into other realms of thought, see Dobbs and Jacob, *Newton and the Culture of Newtonianism,* esp. 61–124; Jacob, *The Newtonians and the English Revolution,* 1689–1720; Larry Stewart, "Samuel Clarke, Newtonianism, and the Factions of Post-Revolutionary England," *Journal of the History of Ideas* 42, no. 1 (1981): 53–72; and C. B. Wilde, "Hutchinsonianism, Natural Philosophy, and Religious Controversy in Eighteenth-Century Britain," *History of Science* 18 (1980): 1–24. For the ways in which contemporaries adopted the new Newtonian science, see Stewart, *The Rise of Public Science.* For important studies of natural theology in the context of Newtonianism, see Steven Shapin, "Of Gods and Kings: Natural Philosophy and Politics in the Leibniz Clarke Disputes," *Isis* 72, no. 2 (1981): 187–215; James E. Force, "Newton's 'Sleeping Argument' and the Newtonian Synthesis of Science and Religion," in *Standing on the Shoulders of Giants,* ed. Norman J. W. Thrower (Berkeley: University of California Press, 1990), 109–27; James E. Force, "Providence and Newton's Pantokrator," in *Newton and Newtonianism: New Studies* (Dordrecht: Kluwer Academic, 2004), 65–92; and John Hedley Brooke, "Science and Religion," in vol. 4 of *The Cambridge History of Science,* ed. Roy Porter (Cambridge: Cambridge University Press, 2003), 741–61.

22. This process has been also described as the "Newtonization" of astronomy (see Peter Fong, "Ethics, Politics and Sociology as Newtonian Sciences," in *Newton's Scientific and Philosophical Legacy,* ed. P. B. Scheurter and G. Debrock [Dordrecht: Springer, 1988], 343–53). See also Jacob, *The Cultural Meaning of the Scientific Revolution,* 105; Dobbs and Jacob, *Newton and the Culture of Newtonianism,* esp. 61–124; and Kuhn, *The Copernican Revolution,* 233–34.
23. Vicesimus Knox, *The Spirit of Despotism* (1795; Trenton, NJ, 1802), 210.
24. Ebenezer Pemberton, *The Divine Original and Dignity of Government Asserted* (Boston, 1710), 52.
25. "A Poem on the Death of King George I, And Accession of King George II," *New England Weekly Journal* (Boston), September 4, 1727; "An Ode on the Marriage of the Prince of Wales with the Princess of Sace-Gotha," *American Weekly Mercury* (Philadelphia), September 16, 1736.
26. "The Different Effects of an Absolute and a Limited Monarchy," *Independent Reflector* (New York), December 21, 1752.
27. Pemberton, *The Divine and Original and Dignity of Government Asserted,* 52; Hervey, *Meditations and Contemplations,* 106.
28. *Greenleaf's New York Journal and Patriotic Register,* October 11, 1797.
29. Benjamin Rush, *The Autobiography of Benjamin Rush,* ed. George W. Corner (Princeton, NJ: Princeton University Press, 1948), 46.
30. "The Visitor," *Boston News-Letter,* January 29, 1761.
31. "On Time," *New Hampshire Gazette* (Portsmouth), March 23, 1759; "Ode, On the Total Reduction of Canada," *Boston Post-Boy,* November 16, 1760; "A Poem on the Accession of King George III," *Boston Weekly News-Letter,* August 26, 1762.
32. "A Gratulatory Poem Received from a Friend the Day After the Arrival of His Excellency Governour Burnet," *Boston Weekly News-Letter,* July 18–25, 1728.

33. "Entertainment," *New York Gazette,* May 12, 1768.
34. "Augustus Britannicus, to His Son," *New York Chronicle,* May 29, 1769; "A Gratulatory Poem Received from a Friend the Day After the Arrival of His Excellency Governour Burnet," *Boston Weekly News-Letter,* July 18–25, 1728, quoted in McConville, *The King's Three Faces,* 205, 203.
35. "The Progress of Empire," *Essex (MA) Journal and New-Hampshire Packet,* January 19, 1776. The classic study of the steady rise of the provincial North American assemblies is still Jack P. Greene, *The Quest for Power: The Lower Houses of Assembly in the Southern Royal Colonies, 1689–1776* (New York: Norton, 1963).
36. "Republican Government," *New York Ledger,* August 17, 1861.
37. *A Letter to Doctor Tucker on His Proposal of a Separation between Great Britain and Her American Colonies* (London, 1774), 14.
38. Thomas Pownall, *The Administration of the British Colonies* (London, 1764), 32–33.
39. Thomas Pownall, *The Administration of the British Colonies,* 5th ed. (London, 1774), 1:45. For an insightful analysis of Pownall's theory of empire, see Scott Breuninger, "'Social Gravity' and the *Translatio* Tradition in Early Amerian Theories of Empire," *Southern Quarterly* 43, no. 4 (2006): 70–108. In an original reinterpretation of the American Enlightenment, James Delbourgo emphasizes "the rhetorical career of electricity in the American Revolution" as a counterpoint to prevalent emphases on Newtonian "mechanical constitutionalism." Hence, the revolutionary era may not necessarily have been, as past scholars thought, "a moment when technological languages of politics became prominent." Delbourgo does point out, however, that—as in the case of the political astronomy that this study traces—"electricity lent itself readily to political use because it provided a language of power" (Delbourgo, *A Most Amazing Scene of Wonders,* 131–32).
40. A. B., "An Extract from a Pamphlet Lately Published in England under the Title of 'A Memorial to the Sovereigns of Europe, on the Present State of Affairs between the Old and New World,' Said to Have Been Written by Governor P—w—l.," *Independent Ledger,* June 3, 1782.
41. "Extract of a Letter of N. York," *Salem (MA) Mercury,* April 28, 1787.
42. Reinhart Koselleck, *Futures Past: On the Semantics of Historical Time,* trans. Keith Tribe (New York: Columbia University Press, 2004), 46. For the perceived relation between human and natural law, see Lorraine Daston and Michael Stolleis, eds., *Natural Law and Laws of Nature in Early Modern Europe* (London: Routledge 2008). For the shift from monarchic to republican culture, see Gordon Wood, *The Radicalism of the American Revolution* (New York: Vintage, 1991); and McConville, *The King's Three Faces.* "Seeming wildness" quote from "History, Dignity and Usefulness of Astronomy," *American Recorder,* March 21, 1786.
43. "Sure Bind, Sure Find," *Connecticut Courant,* April 22, 1776.
44. Thomas Paine, *Common Sense* (London, 1792), 16.
45. For the varieties of graphic representations on early American money, see Eric P. Newman, *The Early Paper Money of America* (Iola, WI: Krause 2008). Kirsten Wood notes that to strengthen the early American Union of states contemporaries developed visual representations and a variety of metaphors, likening the Union to a building, a family, a ship, and a physical body (Wood, "'Join with Heart and Soul and Voice': Music, Harmony, and Politics in the Early American Republic," *American Historical Review* 119, no. 4 [2014]: 1083–116). Other historical alternatives included representations of the newly independent American nation as the new home of

Anglo-Saxons who had left Britain to settle a new world to regain their independence; as Roman republicans re-creating a virtuous republic; and the United States as a New Israel bestowed with divine favor (see Eran Shalev, "America's Antiquities: The Ancient Past in the Creation of the American Republic," in *Ancient Models in the Early Modern Republican Imagination,* ed. Velema Wyger and Arthur Weststeijn [Leiden: Brill, 2017], 306–28).

46. The representation of the colonies-turned-states as linked spheres participated in a common discourse that enabled contemporaries to discuss politics (and society more broadly) in terms of universal physical laws and a mechanical language, expressing notions of sociopolitical perfection and harmony. For major studies in this area, see Striner, "Political Newtonianism"; Foley, *Laws, Men and Machines,* 1990; and Wood, "'Join with Heart and Soul and Voice.'"
47. "Our Own Country," reprinted under the title "From the Knickerbocker: Our Own Country" *Washington Review and Examiner,* May 9, 1835. For the image of the American Constellation, see chapter 3 of this volume.
48. *Pennsylvania Ledger,* April 27, 1776.
49. "The Progress of Empire," *Essex (MA) Journal,* January 10, 1776.
50. *Independent Ledger,* June 3, 1782; "Communications," *Vermont Gazette,* October 3, 1794; Edmund Burke, *The Works and Correspondence of the Right Honourable Edmund Burke,* 7 vols., 2nd ed., ed. Charles William, Earl Fitzwilliam, and Sir Richard Bourke (London, 1852), 2:453.
51. *Richmond (VA) Enquirer,* July 13, 1832.
52. "Our Own Country"; Edward Hitchcock, *Utility of Natural History: A Discourse* (Pittsfield, MA, 1823), 31.
53. Noah Webster, "Sketches of American Policy," *State Gazette of South Carolina,* January 19, 1786.
54. Similarly, in 1778 the State of New York adopted a coat of arms (and flag and great seal) with a rising sun, excelsior. James Madison, "Notes," September 17, 1787, in *The Records of the Federal Convention of 1787,* 3 vols., ed. Max Farrand (New Haven, CT, 1911–37), 2:648.
55. Farrand, *The Records of the Federal Convention of 1787* (New Haven, CT, 1911), 1:153, 165.
56. John Adams, *The Political Writings of John Adams,* ed. George W. Carey (Washington, DC: Regnery, 2001), 140–41.
57. "Mr. Cameron's Speech," *The Star,* June 24, 1814.
58. Quoted in Wood, "'Join with Heart and Soul and Voice,'"1019n29.
59. "Our Own Country."
60. Elizabeth R. Varon, *Disunion! The Coming of the American Civil War, 1789–1859* (Chapel Hill: University of North Carolina Press).
61. "To the Lovers of Peace and Friends of Union," *Charleston (SC) Courier,* September 16, 1830.
62. "Virginia Is Opposed to Being Dragged into the Secession Movement," *Daily True Delta* (New Orleans), November 25, 1860.
63. "Republican Feast," *The Enquirer,* March 11, 1808; "In Senate—Wednesday Feb. 6, 1833," *Richmond (VA) Enquirer,* February 14, 1833 (my emphasis).
64. "For the Scioto Gazette," *Scioto (OH) Gazette,* August 7, 1807.
65. "Celebration at Deer Island," *New Bedford (MA) Gazette and Courier,* July 18, 1836.
66. "'Marcus II,' Feb. 27, 1788," in *The Debate on the Constitution: Federalist and*

Antifederalist Speeches, Articles, and Letters During the Struggle over Ratification, vol. 1, ed. Bernard Bailyn (New York: Library of America, 1993), 1:371.
67. "Our Own Country," *Washington Review and Examiner*, 1835.
68. *Virginia Gazette*, April 13, 1830; *Charleston (SC) Courier*, July 18, 1834; *Journal of the Missouri State Convention Held at Jefferson City* (St. Louis, 1861), 99.
69. Henry A. Wise, *New York Daily Tribune*, November 29, 1860.
70. Quoted in Wood, "'Join with Heart and Soul and Voice,'" 1091n28.
71. "Sure Bind, Sure Find," *Connecticut Courant*, April 22, 1776.
72. The context of the quote was a description of the federal Constitution as fixing limits to the exercise of legislative authority, prescribing "the orbit within which [the legislature] must move" ("Mr. Cameron's Speech," *The Star* [Washington, DC], June 24, 1814).
73. *Charleston (SC) Courier*, February 28, 1833.
74. Quoted in Wood, "'Join with Heart and Soul and Voice,'" 1019n30. There were other sunny alternatives, such as the 1782 portrayal of the international system in solar terms in which the American Congress was "a new primary planet . . . taking its course in its own orbit." A new planet, contemporaries knew, "must have an effect upon the orbit of every other planet, and shift the common centre of gravity of the whole system of the European world" (*Independent Ledger*, June 3, 1782).
75. "Jefferson's Birth-Day," *Richmond (VA) Enquirer*, April 23, 1830.
76. "Communication," *The Republican* (Washington, DC), October 25, 1802.
77. Bailyn, *The Debate on the Constitution*, 1:371.
78. "Letters on the Condition of Kentucky," *Richmond (VA) Enquirer*, April 5, 1825.
79. "Meeting at Plymouth," *New Hampshire Patriot and State Gazette*, January 30, 1832. Spherical and orbital language in the context of nullification appeared also in the speech of senator Rives of Virginia (see note 98 below in this chapter).
80. "To the Editors of the Courier," *Charleston (SC) Courier*, April 20, 1841.
81. "P. P. Barbour on the Veto—[. . .] an extract from an address recently delivered by the Hon. Philip P. Barbour of Virginia, at a meeting of the citizens of Amherst Court-house and its vicinity," *Frankfort Argus*, September 12, 1832.
82. "For the Courier," *Charleston (SC) Courier*, July 18, 1834.
83. John Adams to H. Niles, February 13, 1818, https://founders.archives.gov/documents/Adams/99-02-02-6854.
84. "Concluded from Yesterday's Gazette," *Federal Gazette and Baltimore Daily Advertiser*, December 1, 1798.
85. *Federalist*, no. 9, in Bailyn, *Debates*, 1:340.
86. "To the Printer of the Daily Advertiser," *Daily Advertiser* (New York), January 31, 1789.
87. "Mr. Breckenridge vs. Mr. Jefferson," *Gazette of the United States*, February 23, 1802.
88. John Adams, *The Political Writings of John Adams*, ed. George W. Carey (Washington, DC: Regnery Gateway, 2001), 140–41.
89. James Burgh, *Political Disquisitions* (London, 1774), 3.
90. "Old Sedition Act," *Washington Gazette*, February 22, 1821.
91. "Threatened Invasion of Switzerland," *National Gazette*, October 23, 1832.
92. "To the Friends of Free Government," *The Reporter* (Washington, DC), June 15, 1811.
93. "Political Pamphlet," *New York Herald*, April 24, 1813.
94. Charles Jared Ingersoll, "To his Constituents," *Palladium of Liberty*, September 30, 1813.

95. *Martinsburg (VA) Gazette,* November 10, 1814 (my emphasis).
96. Merlin, "The Influence of Government," *National Gazette and Literary Register,* September 23, 1820.
97. William Cabell Rives, "Speech of Mr. Rives, of Virginia, on the Bill Further to Provide of [*sic*] the Collection of Duties on Imports: Delivered in Senate, February 14, 1833" (Frankfort, KY: F. P. Blair).
98. The staying power of such spherical and orbital understandings of political movement are evident in the speech of modern jurists and judges who describe separation of powers in this cosmo-mechanical language. Modern constitutions that self-consciously draw on the American model, such as that of South Africa, explicitly refer to "spheres of government" in framing their political system.
99. Nathaniel Bowditch, quoted in Tamara Plakins Thornton, *Nathaniel Bowditch and the Power of Numbers: How a Nineteenth-Century Man of Business, Science, and the Sea Changed American Life* (Chapel Hill: University of North Carolina Press, 2016), 119. Bowditch himself left room for cosmic change, yet change that was as regular and predictable as Laplace's planetary motions.
100. Plakins Thornton, *Nathaniel Bowditch and the Power of Numbers,* 120.
101. Calhoun, "Fort Hill Address," July 26, 1831, in *John C. Calhoun: Selected Writings,* ed. H. Lee Cheek (Washington, DC: Gateway, 2003), 321–22, 327.
102. Jackson, "Veto Message Regarding the Bank of the United States," July 10, 1832, quoted in *The Statesmanship of Andrew Jackson,* ed. Francis Newton Thorpe (New York, 1909), 175.
103. "Next Tuesday," *Bellows Falls (VT) Gazette,* September 3, 1841.
104. Ekirch, *At Day's Close,* 10; John North, *Cosmos: An Illustrated History of Astronomy and Cosmology* (Chicago: University of Chicago Press, 2008), 442.
105. Sara Schechner Genuth, *Comets, Popular Culture, and Birth of Modern Cosmology* (Princeton, NJ: Princeton University Press, 1997), 29–31.
106. Genuth, *Comets, Popular Culture, and Birth of Modern Cosmology,* 135.
107. See, for example, the ambiguous reactions to the comet that appeared in the 1769 summer skies of the colonies: "To the Printer of the Essex Gazette," *Essex (MA) Gazette,* November 14, 1769; and "A Philosophical Description of Comets," *New York Gazette,* September 11, 1769.
108. *Political Repository* (Philadelphia), January 15, 1799, 4.
109. "A Philosophical Description of Comets," *New York Gazette,* September 11, 1769.
110. *Delaware Gazette,* October 10, 1789.
111. Junius Americanus, "To the People of England," *Boston Evening Post,* December 3, 1770.
112. "The Celebrated Mr. Samuel Johnson's Character of Junius," *Pennsylvania Packet,* April 20, 1772, supplement page 1.
113. "A Dialogue between Orator Puff and Peter Easy, on the proposed Plan or Frame of Government," *Pennsylvania Ledger,* November 2, 1776; *Royal Pennsylvania Gazette,* May 26, 1778.
114. *Boston Evening-Post and the General Advertiser,* May 3, 1783; "A Plain Dealer," *Pennsylvania Packet,* July 5, 1781.
115. "Unlucky," *Freeman's Journal* (New York), April 14, 1784, 2.
116. Cited in Jack Rakove, *The Beginning of National Politics: An Interpretive History of the Continental Congress* (New York: Knopf, 1979), 335.
117. Adams, *The Political Writings of John Adams,* 140–41; Publius IX in *The Debate on*

the Constitution: Federalist and Antifederalist Speeches, Articles, and Letters During the Struggle over Ratification, ed. Bernard Bailyn, 2 vols. (New York: Library of America, 1993), 1:340.
118. "To the Printer of the Daily Advertiser," *Daily Advertiser*, January 31, 1789 (my emphasis).
119. "Charleston, S.C . . . written by Mrs. Gardner, and spoken by her on Monday evening last," *Pennsylvania Packet*, May 29, 1789.
120. "Foreign Intelligence," *Gazette of the United States*, September 24, 1794.
121. Quoted in McCoy, *The Elusive Republic*, 200.
122. "Mount Ararat and New Jerusalem," *New Hampshire Gazette*, November 1, 1825. For the history of Ararat, see Eran Shalev, "'Revive, Re-new and Reestablish': Mordecai Noah's Ararat and the Limits of Biblical Imagination in the Early American Republic," *American Jewish Archives Journal* 62, no. 1 (2010): 1–20.
123. "Remarks of Mr. Mann of New York," *Albany (NY) Argus*, March 10, 1835.
124. A.C., "Democratic Meeting in Powhatan," *Richmond (VA) Enquirer*, March 9, 1847.
125. "Political World," *Charleston (SC) Courier*, March 26, 1847.
126. Jefferson Davis in "Deferred Debate in Senate of the United States, Thursday, March 14," *Richmond (VA) Whig*, March 22, 1850.
127. *Alexandria (VA) Gazette*, October 14, 1851.
128. "Outrages at the South," *Columbian Register*, December 22, 1860.
129. *Daily True Delta* (New Orleans), December 9, 1860.
130. "Speech of Hon. J. R. Doolittle, of Wisconsin, in the Senate of the United States, February 24, 1860," *National Era*, March 15, 1860.
131. "Hon. J. T. Paulding on Coercion," *Macon (GA) Telegraph*, May 15, 1861.
132. William B. Wedgwood, *Reconstruction of the Government of the United States of America: A Democratic Empire Advocated, and Imperial Constitution Proposed* (New York, 1861). Interestingly, Wedgwood was actually bringing into this discussion of the dangers of secession the example of the biblical Israelite nation and its lost "eleven stars," that is, tribes. On the myth of the lost tribes in the context of antebellum America, see Eran Shalev, *American Zion: The Bible as a Political Text from the Revolution to the Civil War* (New Haven, CT: Yale University Press, 2012), 118–50.
133. *Philadelphia Inquirer*, January 21, 1861.
134. *Daily True Delta* (New Orleans), December 9, 1860, and November 25, 1860.
135. "From the Metropolitan Record," *Daily Constitutionalist* (Georgia), June 29, 1864.
136. "The New Constitution," *Southern Literary Messenger*, February 18, 1852, 122.
137. Quoted in Robert E. Bonner, *Colors and Blood: Flag Passions of the Confederate South* (Princeton, NJ: Princeton University Press, 2002), 53.
138. "The Confederate Flag," *Richmond (VA) Daily Dispatch*, January 2, 1862.
139. "A Passing Show," *New York Herald*, January 1, 1882.

3. The American Constellation

1. "A Passing Show," *New York Herald*, January 1, 1882.
2. Benjamin Rush, *The Autobiography of Benjamin Rush*, ed. George W. Corner (Princeton, NJ: Princeton University Press, 1948), 46.
3. David Rittenhouse, *An Oration, Delivered February 24, 1775* (Philadelphia, 1775),

14–15. Significantly, Rittenhouse was the most important of contemporary American orrery-builders and among the first to depict in painting the star-studded American flag (Brooke Hindle, *David Rittenhouse* [Princeton, NJ: Princeton University Press, 1964], 85, 87). For a reproduction of Rittenhouse's painting, see William R. Furlong and Byron McCandless, *So Proudly We Hail: The History of the United States Flag* (Washington, DC: Smithsonian Institution Press, 1981), 138.

4. For this distinction, see Ernst Kantorowicz, *The King's Two Bodies: A Study in Political Theology* (Princeton, NJ: Princeton University Press, 1957).

5. By the 1840s the view of the solar system as a representation of monarchical hierarchy was transformed to conform with current political understanding. Hence the Scottish thinker Robert Chambers could understand the earth's physical and metaphysical situation as "nothing at all singular or special," and as "a member of a democracy" of other similarly positioned planets (Chambers, *Vestiges of the Natural History of Creation* [London, 1844], 27).

6. Thomas Paine, *Common Sense* (London, 1792), 16; *Pennsylvania Ledger*, April 27, 1776.

7. Bos. Centinel, *Independent Ledger*, July 13, 1776.

8. Sylvia Sumira, *Globes: 400 Years of Exploration, Navigation, and Power* (Chicago: University of Chicago Press, 2014), 132, 141, 150.

9. Quotes from *Independent Gazetteer*, April 3, 1784; and *Pennsylvania Packet*, November 9, 1784. These newspaper advertisements are quoted in Plakins Thornton, "The 'Use of the Globes': Mathematical Geography, the Mercantile Imagination, and Global Commerce in Postrevolutionary America," paper presented to the Program in Early American Economy and Society, October 7, 2016. Plakins Thornton further quotes a London globe-maker who explained to the American Philosophical Society that he had "deferred sending the globes till the Geography &c had received the latest additions, and discoveries" (Wm Jones to John Vaughan, June 24, 1799, APS Archives, Record Group IIA). Plakins Thornton notes that celestial globes, which were vastly popular in nineteenth-century America, had to be updated constantly in tandem with the new constellations of the Southern Hemisphere. See also Elly Dekker and Peter Van der Krogt, *Globes from the Western World* (London: I. B. Tauris), chaps. 3–6; and Sumira, *Globes*, 26, 132, 141, 144, 150, 195, 199.

10. Elijah Burritt, *The Geography of the Heavens* (1833; New York, 1858), 8.

11. "Internal Improvement," *Vermont Gazette*, April 13, 1830.

12. Flag Act quoted from "Philadelphia, April 17, In Congress," *New York Gazette and Weekly Mercury*, April 28, 1783; Woden Teachout, *Capture the Flag: A Political History of American Patriotism* (New York: Basic, 2009), 29. See also Marc Leepson, *Flag: An American Biography* (New York: St. Martin's Griffin, 2006), 22.

13. Scot M. Guetner, *The American Flag, 1777–1924: Cultural Shifts from Creation to Codification* (Vancouver, British Columbia: Fairleigh Dickinson University Press 1990), 27.

14. Woden Teachout points out that the nine may have referred to the forty-fifth edition of the *North Briton* newspaper, in which publisher John Wilkes lambasted King George (Teachout, *Capture the Flag*, 30).

15. Quote in Guenter, *The American Flag, 1777–1924*, 28.

16. Benjamin H. Irvine, *Clothed in Robes of Sovereignty: The Continental Congress and the People out of Doors* (New York: Oxford University Press, 2011), 145–46, 242–43.

17. Arnaldo Testi, *Capture the Flag: The Stars and Stripes in American History* (New York: New York University Press, 2010), 17.
18. In some sketches of flags the stars consisted of three crossing lines, which created a two-dimensional six-point star (David Martucci, "The 13 Stars and Stripes: A Survey of the 18th Century Images," *North America Vexillology Association News* 167 [April–June 2000], http://www.vexman.net/13stars/#Sedeen).
19. *Harmon Stebens Powder Horn* (engraving detail), image in Furlong and McCandless, *So Proudly We Hail*, 129.
20. For an early examination of the symbolic genealogy of the American flag, see Sir Charles Fawcett, "The Striped Flag of the East India Company, and Its Connexion with the American 'Stars and Stripes,'" *Mariner's Mirror* 23 (October 1937): 449–76. See also Moeller, *Shattering an American Myth: Unfurling the History of the Stars and Stripes* (Mattituck, NY: Amereon, 1976), 9; Furlong and McCandless, *So Proudly We Hail*, 99; and Leepson, *Flag*, 31–35. Kevin Keim and Peter Keim, *A Grand Old Flag: A History of the United States Through Its Flags* (New York: DK, 2007), 40–42, point out the connection between the symbol of the star and contemporary astronomy.
21. Teachout, *Capture the Flag*, 30.
22. For the use of celestial language in colonial Spanish America, see Jorge Cañizares Esguerra, "New World, New Stars: Patriotic Astrology and the Invention of Indian and Creole Bodies in Colonial Spanish America, 1600–1650," *American Historical Review* 104, no. 1 (1999): 33–68.
23. For the plurality of flags, their symbolism, and antecedents during the Revolution, see Teachout, *Capture the Flag*, 25; Leepson, *Flag*, 7–20, 35–36; Testi, *Capture the Flag*, 16–17; and Moeller, *Shattering an American Myth*, 19–112. For a nineteenth-century interpretation of the symbolism of the American flag, see Schuyler Hamilton, *History of the National Flag of the United States of America* (Philadelphia, 1853), 85–93. Although nowhere did the decree of 1777 stipulate that the thirteen stars should constitute a circle, the Neoplatonic perfect form, the circular presentation of the state-stars was one of the popular forms, ensuring that no star—or state—overpowered or encroached upon another. For the optional arrangements of the stars on early flags, see Teachout, *Capture the Flag*, 30; Testi, *Capture the Flag*, 17; and Guetner, *The American Flag, 1777–1924*, 31–32.
24. R. C. Ballard Thruston, *The Origin and Evolution of the United States Flag* (Washington, DC: Government Printing Office, 1926), 16.
25. Teachout, *Capture the Flag*, 7–8; Testi, *Capture the Flag*, 25. Quoted in Jared Sparks, ed., *The Diplomatic Correspondence of the American Revolution* (Boston, 1829), 1:470. Benjamin Rush to John Adams, October 21, 1777, in *Letters of Benjamin Rush*, vol. 1: *1761–1792*, ed. Lyman Henry Butterfield (Princeton, NJ: Princeton University Press, 1951), 162; James Lovell to Abigail Adams, April 16, 1778, in *The Diplomatic Correspondence*, ed. Smith, 9:423. Stiles quoted in Furlong and McCandless, *So Proudly We Hail*, 101–2.
26. *Pennsylvania Packet*, September 26, 1778; *Letters of Benjamin Franklin and Jane Mecum*, ed. Carl Van Doren (Princeton, NJ: Princeton University Press, 1950), 246.
27. For graphic representations of revolutionary-era American flags by foreigners, see Martucci, "The 13 Stars and Stripes," items no. 17, 18, 22, 23, 24, 29, 30, 35, 35.1, 35.2, 35.3, 37–41, for German, British, French, and Italian examples.

28. *New Jersey Gazette*, February 17, 1779.
29. For the language of "usage," see J. G. A. Pocock, *Politics, Language, and Time: Essays on Political Thought and History* (Chicago: University of Chicago Press, 1989). The question as to whether nationalism is a modern or premodern phenomenon has not been settled. While primordialists propose that nations and thus nationalism is a perennial and ancient phenomenon, advocates of modernization theory believe that nationalism is a recent social phenomenon that required the socioeconomic structures of modern society to emerge. In either case, however, it is quite obvious that the American Revolution, followed by the French example, brought about a categorical change in the meaning and scale of national movements. For primordialism, see Anthony Smith, *The Antiquity of Nations* (London: Polity, 2004); for the most prominent advocacies of a modern understanding of nationalism, see Ernest Gellner, *Nations and Nationalism*, 2nd ed. (London: Blackwell, 2006); and Benedict Anderson, *Imagined Communities: Reflections on the Spread and Origin of Nationalism*, rev. ed. (London: Verso, 2016).
30. For the early American historical imagination, specifically Americans imagining themselves as Romans and Israelites, see Eran Shalev, *Rome Reborn on Western Shores: Historical Imagination and the Creation of the American Republic* (Charlottesville: University of Virginia Press, 2009); and Eran Shalev, *American Zion: The Bible as a Political Text from the Revolution to the Civil War* (New Haven, CT: Yale University Press, 2012).
31. Thomas W. Kavanagh, *North American Indian Portraits: Photographs from the Wanamaker Expedition* (New York: Konecky and Konecky, 1996), 94.
32. "Extract from the Journals of Congress," *Essex (MA) Journal*, August 20, 1784; *Pennsylvania Evening Herald and the American Monitor*, August 6, 1785.
33. In coming decades, the image of the constellation became so common and recognizable that Americans could alter its common scale of reference, identifying cities and counties as "luminaries," and political constellations within constellations. Take, for example, the author who wished "the Star of Cumberland, Maine . . . [to] become the center of a political system in old New-England, around which her sister luminaries shall ere long form a brilliant constellation" ("Anniversary Celebration at Au Sable Forks, Essex Co. N.Y.," *Albany [NY] Argus*, February 3, 1829).
34. "Salem," *Newport (RI) Herald*, April 5, 1787.
35. "American Poetry," *Massachusetts Centinel*, July 2, 1788. See also a similar song describing how "Freedom's constellation decks the West." "Ode, On the Dissolution of the First Congress," *Federal Gazette and Philadelphia Evening Post*, March 2, 1791.
36. "Boston," *Herald Freedom and the Federal Advertiser*, January 1, 1789.
37. For the political culture of the early republic, see the following excellent studies: David Waldstreicher, *In the Midst of Perpetual Fetes: The Making of American Nationalism, 1776–1820* (Chapel Hill: University of North Carolina Press, 1997); Irvine, *Clothed in Robes of Sovereignty*; and Simon P. Newman, *Parades and the Politics of the Street: Festive Culture in the Early American Republic* (Philadelphia: University of Pennsylvania Press, 1999).
38. "Dover," *New York Packet*, July 28, 1791.
39. "Carpet Manufactory," *Daily Advertiser*, June 14, 1791.
40. "On the Plurality of Worlds," *The Repository*, February 5, 1805.
41. *New Jersey Gazette*, July 19, 1784.
42. "American Intelligence," *Pennsylvania Mercury and Universal Advertiser*, Septem-

ber 11, 1788; *Newport (RI) Herald*, April 5, 1787; *Columbian Centinel*, October 16, 1790.
43. "To the Electors of the 3rd Congressional District of Kentucky," *Argus of Western America*, April 9, 1819.
44. "The Twenty-Six States," *Alexandria (VA) Gazette*, June 15, 1836.
45. "Celebration at Deer Island," *New Bedford (MA) Gazette and Courier*, July 18, 1836.
46. "Franklin Country," *Plattsburgh (NY) Republican*, November 1, 1845; "Another State Wanted," *Richmond (VA) Whig*, October 21, 1845; "Speech of Mr. Stephens," *Augusta (GA) Chronicle*, February 17, 1845; "Island of Cuba," *New York Herald*, September 6, 1848.
47. *Alexandria (VA) Gazette and Daily Advertiser*, November 1, 1819.
48. For a sample of this rich vexillological variety, see Thruston, *The Origin and Evolution of the United States Flag*.
49. Congress Flag Act of April 14, 1818. Ironically, a mere year later the Missouri Crisis (1819-20) proved that the addition of states to the Union was the greatest threat to its integrity.
50. William R. Hutchison and Hartmut Lehmann, eds., *Many Are Chosen: Divine Election and Western Nationalism* (Philadelphia: Fortress, 1994).
51. "At a Meeting of the Citizens of Providence," *Providence Patriot*, December 29, 1832; "Celebration at Portland," *Albany (NY) Evening Journal*, October 3, 1837.
52. "Reply from Mrs. Tyler, wife of Ex-President Tyler, to the Duchess of Sutherland," *Charleston (SC) Courier*, February 1, 1853. Ironically, it would be Tyler's granddaughter and namesake who would be the first to hoist the Stars and Bars after its approval over the Confederacy's Capitol Building (Deveraux D. Cannon, *The Flags of the Confederacy: An Illustrated History* [Gretna, LA: Pelican, 2005], 13).
53. "Speech of Mr. Bradford," *American Mercury*, June 4, 1832.
54. *Newburyport (MA) Herald*, March 10, 1837.
55. "In Senate," *Richmond (VA) Enquirer*, March 12, 1833.
56. "Speech of Mr. Segar of Northhampton," *Richmond (VA) Enquirer*, March 17, 1838.
57. *New York Journal*, January 27, 1810; *Philadelphia Inquirer*, April 3, 1833; "Selected Toasts; At Baltimore," *Washington Examiner*, July 20, 1818; *Augusta (GA) Chronicle*, May 17, 1849.
58. *Pittsfield (MA) Sun*, May 20, 1852.
59. "Speech of the Hon. W. H. Seward, in the United States Senate," *Albany (NY) Journal*, May 4, 1858.
60. Ernest Lee Tuveston, *Redeemer Nation: The Idea of America's Millennial Role* (Chicago: University of Chicago Press, 1968). For earlier Spanish readings of stars as revealing God's special design for the New World, see Canizeras-Esguerra, *Nature, Empire, and Nation*, 78-83. For American exceptionalism, see Joyce Chaplin, "Expansion and Exceptionalism in Early American History," *Journal of American History* 89, no. 4 (2003): 1431-55; and Dorothy Ross, *The Origins of American Social Science* (New York: Cambridge University Press, 1991), 22-52.
61. *South Carolina Gazette and General Advertiser*, December 16, 1783; Pax Fidelitas, "The Miscellany," *Massachusetts Centinel*, May 4, 1785.
62. Caroline Winterer, *American Enlightenment: Pursuing Happiness in the Age of Reason* (New Haven, CT: Yale University Press, 2016), 175.
63. John Winthrop, *Two Lectures on the Parallax and the Distance of the Sun, as Deducible from the Transit of Venus* (Boston, 1769), 14.

64. "June," "*Ames' Almanac for 1786,*" in *The Essays, Humor, and Poems of Nathaniel Ames*, ed. Samuel Briggs (Cleveland, OH, 1891), 393.
65. Benjamin Workman, *Elements of Geography, Designed for Young Students in That Science*, 13th ed. (Philadelphia, 1809), 13; "The Speculator" no. 6, *Edwardsville (IL) Spectator,* March 4, 1826.
66. "An Undevout Astronomer Is Man" [The Monitor no. XCII], *Portland (ME) Gazette*, December 28, 1812; "On the Greatness of God," *Monticello (MS) Republican*, April 1, 1820.
67. *New Hampshire Gazette,* Mach 4, 1797. For biblical representations of Washington, see Shalev, *American Zion*, 6–20.
68. George Washington to Joseph Barrell, June 8, 1788, in *The Writings of George Washington from the Original Manuscript Sources, 1745–1799*, 39 vols., ed. John C. Fitzpatrick (Washington, DC: Government Printing Office, 1931–44), 29:510. Compare with Ezra Stiles, who mused that "Navigation will carry the American flag around the globe . . . and display the thirteen stripes and new constellation at *bengal* and *canton,* on the *indus* and the *ganges,* on the *whang-ho* and the *yang-tse-kiang*" (Stiles, *The United States Elevated to Glory and Honor* [New Haven, CT: 1783], 52). Tellingly, Washington directly proceeded to connect the American Constellation with the Stars and Stripes, arguing that "an energetic government will give to our flag still greater respect" (Washington, "Proposed Address to Congress," April 1789, in *The Writings of George Washington,* ed. Fitzpatrick, 30:305).
69. "Toasts," *Carolina Centinel,* July 19, 1823.
70. Daniel Webster quoted in *The Webster–Haynes Debate on the Nature of the Union: Selected Documents,* ed. Herman Belz (Indianapolis, IN: Liberty Fund, 2000), 24; Robert Hayne quoted ibid., 183.
71. "Our Own Country," *Washington Review and Examiner,* May 9, 1835.
72. Page numbers are from *Inaugural Addresses of the Presidents of the United States from George Washington 1789 to Richard Milhous Nixon 1969* (Washington, DC: Government Printing Office, 1969), 105–8.
73. "Another Slave State," *The Liberator* (Boston), May 4, 1838; "Governor Dana's Message," *The Age* (New York), May 19, 1848.
74. *Augusta (GA) Chronicle,* October 27, 1847, 2. For Southern fatalism, see Shalev, *Rome Reborn on Western Shores,* 110–12.
75. "Is Disunion Probable?," *New Orleans Daily Creole,* September 17, 1856.
76. "Outrages at the South," *Columbian Register,* December 22, 1860; "Mass Meeting at Walpole," *New Hampshire Sentinel,* May 9, 1861; "The Issue—What Is It?" *Plattsburgh (NY) Republican,* April 13, 1861.
77. See chapter 2 in this volume.
78. B. F. Lemen to Abraham Lincoln, Sunday, April 1, 1860, http://memory.loc.gov/mss/mal/maltext/rtf_orig/mal006f.rtf.
79. John Slidell of Louisiana, "On the Occasion of His Withdrawal from the U.S. Senate," February 4, 1861, in Thomas Ricaud Martin, *The Great Parliamentary Battle and Farewell Addresses of the Southern Senators on the Eve of the Civil War* (New York: Deale, 1905, as reprinted by Bibliolife), 219–20.
80. Abraham Lincoln, "Speech at the Flag-raising before Independence Hall, Philadelphia, Pennsylvania, February 22, 1861," in *Selected Works of Abraham Lincoln,* 9 vols., ed. Roy P. Basler (New Brunswick, NJ: Rutgers University Press, 1953), 4:242–43.

81. Robert E. Bonner, *Colors and Blood: Flag Passions of the Confederate South* (Princeton, NJ: Princeton University Press, 2002), 6, 52, 97; John M. Coski, *The Confederate Battle Flag: America's Most Embattled Emblem* (Cambridge, MA: Belknap Press of Harvard University Press, 2006), 15.
82. Bonner, *Colors and Blood*, 5.
83. "The Confederate Flag," *Richmond (VA) Daily Dispatch*, December 10, 1861, and January 2, 1862.
84. Cannon, *The Flags of the Confederacy*, 14–21.
85. Barksdale quote in Cannon, *The Flags of the Confederacy*, 17; David M. Potter, The *Impending Crisis, 1848–1861* (New York: Harper and Row, 1976), 484.
86. Coski, *The Confederate Battle Flag*, 2–3.
87. South Carolina adopted a flag that included a different cosmic element, a moon. For Confederate state flags, see Cannon, *The Flags of the Confederacy*, 34–48. For the sentimental power of the Bonnie Blue Flag, see Bonner, *Colors and Blood*, 30–33.
88. "The Territories in Congress," *New York Herald*, March 10, 1863.
89. *Macon (GA) Telegraph*, May 15, 1861 (emphasis added). For similar language regarding the eighteenth-century Hanoverian kings, see Brendan McConville, *The King's Three Faces: The Rise and Fall of Royal America, 1688–1776* (Chapel Hill: University of North Carolina Press, 2006).
90. Jefferson Davis, "Remarks on the Special Message on Affairs in South Carolina, Jan. 10, 1861," in *Southern Pamphlets on Secession, November 1860–April 1861*, ed. Jon L. Wakelyn (Chapel Hill: University of North Carolina Press, 1996), 135.

Epilogue

1. The idea of the king's two bodies—the body politic and the body natural—was originally developed in Ernst H. Kantorowicz, *The King's Two Bodies: A Study in Medieval Political Theology* (1957; Princeton, NJ: Princeton University Press, 2016).
2. See chapter 3 of this volume for the early variety of star shapes and the eventual domination of the pentagram.
3. For the continuities between colonial and national tensions, and the political center and its provincial peripheries, see Jack P. Greene, *Peripheries and Center: Constitutional Development in the Extended Polities of the British Empire and the United States, 1607–1788* (New York: Norton, 1986). In order to alleviate Anti-Federalist fears, Alexander Hamilton resorted to the solar image, to which both parties could relate: "The human affections, like the *solar* heat, lose their intensity as they depart from the centre; and become languid in proportion to the expansion of the circle on which they act. On these principles, the attachment of the individual will be first and for ever secured by the State governments" (Hamilton, "On the Adoption of the Federal Constitution," in *The Debates in the Several State Conventions, on the Adoption of the Federal Constitution, As Recommended by the General Convention at Philadelphia in 1787*, 4 vols., ed. Jonathan Elliot [Washington, DC, 1836], 2:354).
4. Nelson, *The Royalist Revolution*.
5. For the role of the Cincinnatian ideal in late eighteenth-century America, see Eran Shalev, *Rome Reborn on Western Shores: Historical Imagination and the Creation of the American Republic* (Charlottesville: University of Virginia Press, 2009), 217–40.

6. Benjamin Banneker, *Banneker's New-Jersey, Pennsylvania, Delaware, Maryland, and Virginia Almanac [. . .] for . . . 1795* (Baltimore, MD: S. and J. Adams, [1794]), 22; "Astronomy," *Salem (MA) Gazette*, August 6, 1798.
7. Richard Henry Lee, *Funeral Oration on the Death of General Washington* (Boston, 1800), 7; "Eulogy on Washington," in *The American Orator* (Charleston, SC, 1819), 225. Fisher Ames in *A Selection of Orations and Eulogies*, ed. Atherton, 71. François Furstenberg, *In the Name of the Father: Washington's Legacy, Slavery, and the Making of a Nation* (New York: Penguin, 2006), 7.
8. "The Memory of Washington," *Village Register and Norfolk County Advertiser*, November 22, 1822.
9. "Noble Sentiment," *Rhode Island American and Providence Gazette*, January 17, 1832.
10. William Shakespeare, *Henry V*, epilogue.
11. Furstenberg, *In the Name of the Father*, 65.
12. "Astronomy," *Salem (MA) Gazette*, August 6, 1798.
13. "Song . . . sung at the celebration of President Adams's Birthday," *New Hampshire Gazette*, November 6, 1799.
14. "Song . . . sung at the celebration of President Adams's Birthday."
15. "Death of Mr. Adams and Mr. Jefferson," *New Hampshire Observer*, July 22, 1826.
16. *Salem (MA) Gazette*, August 12, 1823.
17. "To the Voters of Virginia," *Constitutional Whig*, July 13, 1824.
18. "President Jackson," *Pittsfield (MA) Sun*, August 2, 1829.
19. Noah's Star, "Portland," *Portland Advertiser and Gazette of Maine*, April 22, 1834.
20. "Independent Cadets," *Essex (MA) Register*, July 8, 1824.
21. This thesis was convincingly elaborated by Eric Nelson, *The Royalist Revolution*; and Brendan McConville, *The King's Three Faces: The Rise and Fall of Royal America, 1688–1776* (Chapel Hill: University of North Carolina Press, 2006).
22. Benjamin Rush to John Adams, October 21, 1778, in "Excerpts from the Papers of Dr. Benjamin Rush," *Pennsylvania Magazine of History and Biography* 29, no. 1 (1905): 15–30, quote on 20; original emphasis.
23. James Littlejohn, "The Friend. No. V," *New Haven (CT) Gazette*, April 27, 1786. I could not locate a similar use of a constellation of great men before 1780 in a search in the extensive Early American Newspapers (Readex) digital database.
24. *Massachusetts Spy*, May 16, 1783.
25. "Primitive Whig," *New Jersey Gazette*, January 9, 1786.
26. "Fourth of July at North Canaan," *Connecticut Courant*, July 30, 1842.
27. *Connecticut Herald*, July 28, 1835; "Fourth of July at North Canaan," *Connecticut Courant*, July 30, 1842.
28. "Letter II," *Pennsylvania Evening Herald and the American Monitor*, October 1, 1785.
29. "The 4th of July," *Washington Examiner*, July 9, 1817. Interestingly, Mr. Anderson, the president of Washington College, was said to have outshined all other luminaries. "Abbot Lawrence's Public Bequest," *Boston Courier*, August 27, 1855.
30. Christian Spectator, "Christianity vs. Infidelity" *American Advocate*, March 5, 1834; A Brother, "The Masonic Celebration," *The Transcript*, October 21, 1852.
31. "The Galle Musee in America," *New York Herald*, November 26, 1870. Italian medieval writers Boccaccio, Dante, and Petrarch were described in the same publication a few years later as literary "luminaries" in a "brilliant literary constellation" ("Memorial to Boccaccio," *New York Herald*, July 15, 1879).

32. *Pennsylvania Packet,* September 16, 1785.
33. A Mechanic of Mifflin County, "From the Republican Argus," *Aurora (PA) General Advertiser,* August 17, 1805. The image of the star could be completely ironic, such as in the case of attacks on Stephen Douglass for his stance on slavery: "A new luminary appears in 1854 in the political firmament of the Senate of the United States, and unfolds the astounding fact to a benighted people that slavery was never abolished or prevented by Congressional enactment from one inch of American soil" (Edward Coles, "To Senator Douglass," *Daily National Intelligencer,* February 18, 1854).
34. "We the People," *Hagerstown (MD) Gazette,* July 21, 1812.
35. Meteors were now representing sudden striking appearances that were positive, as opposed to ominous in the past. For examples, see *Charleston Courier,* July 2, 1844; "Where Will I Go," *Alexandria (VA) Gazette,* June 14, 1843; "Where Will I Go," *Alexandria (VA) Gazette,* June 18, 1846; and "By the Southern Mail," *New York Herald,* March 19, 1845. See, among many other examples, "Convention Nominations," *Charleston (SC) Courier,* March 26, 1847; "For the Whig," *Richmond (VA) Whig,* July 25, 1848; "Public Meeting," *Floridian and Journal,* August 10, 1850; *Richmond (VA) Whig,* October 29, 1852; "Our National Jubilee," *Charleston (SC) Courier,* July 6, 1853; and Edward Coles [of Philadelphia], "To Senator Douglass," *Daily National Intelligencer,* February 18, 1854.
36. "Public Meeting," *Floridian and Journal,* August 10, 1850; *Richmond Whig,* October 29, 1852; "Our National Jubilee," *Charleston (SC) Courier,* July 6, 1853.
37. "Elogium," *Commercial Advertiser* (New York), October 1, 1819.
38. "Oration . . . By George Shannon Esq.," *Reporter* (Philadelphia), March 6, 1815.
39. "News of the Day," *Alexandria (VA) Gazette,* June 18, 1846; Taylor's eulogy in "Public Meeting," *Floridian and Journal,* August 10, 1850.
40. "The Death of General James B. McPherson," *Memphis (TN) Daily Avalanche,* March 4, 1866.
41. "The Correspondent," *Western Herald & Steubenville (OH) Gazette,* April 27, 1822.
42. "A Former Duluth Editor," *Duluth (MN) Daily News,* April 6, 1888.
43. "The Gallie Musee in America," *New York Herald,* November 26, 1870.
44. "The Orphan Asylum Benefit at the Academy of Music," *New York Herald,* December 5, 1883.
45. For the budding cultural scene in the early years of the United States, see Kenneth Silverman, *A Cultural History of the American Revolution: Painting, Music, Literature, and the Theatre in the Colonies and the United States from the Treaty of Paris to the Inauguration of George Washington, 1763–1789* (New York: Columbia University Press, 1987).
46. "For the Gazette of the United States," *Gazette of the United States,* December 16, 1796; Paul McDonald, *The Star System: Hollywood's Production of Popular Identities* (London: Wallflower, 2000), 16–19.
47. "Theatrical Communication," *Evening Post,* September 25, 1818.
48. "Theatricals in Paris," *Southern Patriot,* February 13, 1840.
49. Benjamin McArthur, *Actors and American Culture, 1880–1920* (Iowa City: University of Iowa Press, 1979), 3–8.
50. "Dramatic and Musical Invasion" *Daily Placer Times and Transcript* (San Francisco), April 3, 1854.
51. "Memorial to Boccacio," *New York Herald,* July 28, 1879. For an example of a

contemporary use of the constellation trope in the arts, see *The Sun* (New York), April 27, 1883, advertising "the Brightest Luminaries in the Piano and Organ constellation."
52. "Amusements," *Sunday Oregonian*, September 10, 1887. For a similar use, see "The Passing Show," *Boston Daily Journal*, March 1, 1890.
53. "What They Are Doing at the Theatre," *Watson's Art Journal* 8, no. 3 (1867): 42.
54. Quote in McArthur, *Actors and American Culture*, 11. For the theatrical "star system," see McDonald, *The Star System*, 16–19. See also Andrew Harris, *Broadway Theatre* (London: Routledge, 2017), 1–15.
55. "Gleams from Gotham," *New Haven (CT) Evening Register*, June 28, 1888.
56. "Chicago Society Shocked," [from the *Chicago Times Herald*], *Kansas City (MO) Star*, December 6, 1896.
57. For the professionalization of sports, in particular baseball and boxing, see Steven A. Riess, "Professional Baseball and Social Mobility," *Journal of Interdisciplinary History* 11, no. 2 (1980): 235–50; Matthew Von Vogt, "Baseball in the Frame of Gilded-Age America," in *Playing Games in Nineteenth-Century Britain and America*, ed. Ann R. Hawkins et al. (Albany: State University of New York, 2021), 69–86; and Kristin Flieger Samuelian and Mark Schonfield "Bodies in Play: Boxing, Dance, and the Science of Recreation," in *Playing Games in Nineteenth-Century Britain and America*, 41–68.
58. "General Sporting News: Merwine Thompson to Blossom out Again," *Kansas City (MO) Times*, August 12, 1888.
59. "A Baseball Iliad," *Daily Picayune* (New Orleans), April 25, 1893.
60. McArthur, *Actors and American Culture*, 11.
61. McDonald, *The Star System;* Richard Dyer, *Stars* (London: BFI, 1992); Richard deCordova, *Picturing Personalities: The Emergence of the Star System in America* (Champaign: University of Illinois Press, 1980).
62. Jennifer M. Bean, "Stardom in the 1910s," in *Flickers of Desire: Movie Stars of the 1910s*, ed. Jennifer M. Bean (New Brunswick, NJ: Rutgers University Press, 2011), 1.
63. William J. Mann, *The Biograph Girl* (quote in Bean, *Flickers of Desire*, 1).
64. Frank E. Wood, "Why Is a Star," *Photoplay*, October 1919, 70.
65. "The Star Idea Versus the Star System," *Motion Picture Magazine*, August 1919, 107.
66. *Nevada Daily Mail*, November 20, 1917.
67. "Sir Laurence Olivier receiving an Honorary Oscar," Oscars, YouTube, https://www.youtube.com/watch?v=TSgvp0l1n2s.
68. Delphine Hirasuna, ed. *Stars & Stripes: Ninety-Six Top Designers and Graphic Artists Offer Their Personal Interpretations of Old Glory* (San Francisco: Chronicle, 1987), 64, 82.
69. Samuel Antupit's design similarly made use of the faces of film stars; his, however, were placed on top of silver stars, perhaps alluding to their ruling of the "silver screen" (Hirasuna, *Stars & Stripes*, 98).
70. Clifford Geertz, *The Interpretation of Cultures* (New York: Basic, 1973).
71. Albert J. Beveridge, "The Star of Empire," in *God's New Israel: Religious Interpretations of American Destiny*, ed. Conrad Cherry (Chapel Hill: University of North Carolina Press, 1998), 146–62, quote on 146. For the idea of redeemer nation, see Ernest Lee Tuveson, *Redeemer Nation: The Idea of America's Millennial Role* (Chicago: University of Chicago Press, 1968).
72. John F. Kennedy, "Democratic National Convention Nomination Acceptance

Address," https://www.jfklibrary.org/learn/about-jfk/historic-speeches/acceptance-of-democratic-nomination-for-president.

73. For the sociology of superstardom, see Loek Groot, "Roger Caillois, Games of Chance and the Superstar," *Diogenes* 48, no. 2 (2000): 33–42. For an economic analysis of superstardom, see Alan B. Krueger, "The Economics of Real Superstars: The Market for Rock Concerts in the Material World," *Journal of Labor Economics* 23, no. 1 (2005): 1–30; Timothy Perry, "A Competitive Model of (Super)Stars," *Eastern Economic Journal* 39, no. 3 (2013): 346–57; and Sherwin Rosen, "The Economics of Superstars," *American Economic Review* 71, no. 5 (1981): 845–59.

74. Dyer, *Stars*, 35.

INDEX

Italicized page numbers indicate illustrations.

abolitionism, 49–50, 60–61, 118, 134, 155–56
absolutism, 77–78, 82, 86, 118, 134, 167
actors. *See* cinematic stars; theatrical star system and constellation of luminaries
Adams, John, 34, 58, 95–96, 102–4, 110, 172
Adams, John Quincy, 34, 172–73, 201n26
Addison, Joseph, 65
Aeneid (Virgil), 9
African Americans: astronomical education of, 40; astronomical/scientific knowledge of, 39–41, 202n48; Banneker as "first Black man of science," 37, 39, 169; fugitive science and, 39; Leonid meteor shower and, 42–43, 48; newspapers' copy sharing and public readings by, 41; North Star and, 20, 28, 48–50, 72; political astronomy and, 41, 202n48; Turner's interpretative system for cosmos, 41. *See also* enslaved people; slavery
African Free School, 40
Alexandria Gazette on new states as stars in Union constellation, 143–44
Alfonso X (Spanish king), 210n7
almanacs, 35–37, 44, 51–52, 71, 124, 201n33, 209n178

American Bibliography (Evans), 36
American constellation ("new constellation"), xi, 3, 4, 11, 15, 22–23, 88, 115, 117–66, 168, 173, 176. *See also* American flag; constellation of state-stars; state-stars
American Dream, 190
American Enlightenment, 151
American exceptionalism, 4, 147, 150–51, 168, 188–89
American flag: addition of more stars for new states, 22, 115, 131, 142–45, 155, 170; Betsy Ross Flag, 131, *133*, 147; Civil War and, 127, 158; colors of British flag and, 129; constellation imagery of, 2, 93, 134–35; Continental Colors, 128, *129*; Cowpens Flag, 93, *93*, 134–35; creation of, 126–42; Easton (Pennsylvania) Flag, 135; equality of stars on, 93, 125–26, 131, 136, 168, 176; over Fort Sumter at start of Civil War, 1–3, *2*; General Schuyler's Flag, 131, *133*; hierarchical designs abandoned, 135–36; iconic status of, 126–27; liberty pole as motif, 127; medallion patterns, 131, *133*, 134, 219n23; Native Americans understanding design upon

229

American flag (*continued*)
  first viewing, 39, 139; omnipresence of, 126, 137; original meaning of stars on, 1–3, 126, 127, 129, 132, 137; Plan of Fort Harmar showing (1786), 131, *132;* political astronomy and, 130, 132, 133, 137, 145–46, 168; reimagined flags for San Francisco exhibition (1986), 186–87, *187;* on Shaw's powder horn, 134, *136;* snake as motif, 127; variations and inconsistencies in early flags, 130–36
American Geography, The (Morse, 1789), 64
American government. *See* American Union
American Observatory Movement, 201n26
American Preceptor, The (school lesson booklet), 65
American Progress (Gast's painting), 188–89
American Recorder (newspaper), 55
American Revolution: change from British sun imagery to stars, 3–4, 22, 118–21, 124–25, 134–35, 168; clock imagery and, 58; comet imagery and, 109; cosmic imagery and, 3, 88; electricity imagery and, 213n39; global effect of, 23, 147–48; harmony and, 70, 81; king-as-sun imagery republicanized after, 118–21; momentous decisions of Americans after, 14; nationalism and, 127, 138, 147, 220n29
American Star (newspaper), 7
American Star, The (Kimmelmeyer's painting), 170, *171*
American Union: as artificial human creation, 12–13; Civil War language and, 73; equal to European counterparts in scientific knowledge, 199n10; as God's chosen nation, 150; harmony and, 90, 94, 96, 139, 153; as "new constellation," xi, 3, 4, 11, 15, 22–23, 88, 115, 117–66, 168, 173, 176; as newly discovered planet, 93–94; as planetary system, 3, 21, 73–75, 89–91, 94–99, 107, 110–16; political astronomy for legitimation of unprecedented creation, 15, 17, 73–75, 90–91, 96, 114, 139, 168; as solar system, 61, 74–75, 82, 90–91, 95, 97–98, 101–2, 106, 121, 154; as source of liberty and happiness, 15; states' entry into, 22, 98–99, 115, 131, 142–45, 155, 158–59, 163, 170; sun imagery applied to, 87, 96, 98–99; sun imagery unsuitable to state-stars composing, 121; unshakeability of, 61; variety of metaphors for, 213n45. *See also* constellation of state-stars
American Universal Geography (Morse, 1796), 66
American Zion (Shalev), 19
Ames, Fischer, 110
Ames, Nathaniel, 51
anarchy, 9, 16, 98, 106–7, 165
ancient Greece and Rome: astrology and, 204n94; constellations named for mythological figures, 123; cosmic harmony and, 15, 68; metaphors from, 11; newly independent America recreating Roman republic, 214n45; Ptolemaic worldview, 35–36, 50, 68, 80, 123; solar cult of Rome, 210n3. *See also* Aristotle
anthropomorphism, 21, 45–46, 63, 78, 80, 82, 85, 177. *See also* king-as-sun imagery
Anti-Federalists, 95, 154, 164, 168, 223n3
antimonarchism, 22, 133–34
Anti-Slavery Poems (Pierpont), 49–50
Antupit, Samuel, 226n69
apocalyptic tradition, 151
Ararat (Grand Island, NY), as failed Jewish "city of refuge," 111
archaeoastronomy, 5
Argus, Eastern, 173
Aristotle, 11, 33, 47, 50, 60, 80
Arkansas, entry into Union, 98–99, 143–45
Army of Northern Virginia battle flag, 160, 162
Articles of Confederation, 89–90, 109–10
artists as luminaries, 176, 181–82
asteroids, 71, 73
Astraea (star-maiden daughter of Zeus), 80
astrology, 5, 31, 37, 50–52, 132, 204n90, 204n94, 204n97, 205n99
astronomical politics, 45–48, 77, 112, 141, 173
astronomy: John Quincy Adams and, 34; in American eighteenth- and nineteenth-century education, 44; ancient cultures

and, 5; astrology and, 51; Banneker as "first Black man of science" publishing almanacs on, 37, 39, 169; Black knowledge of, 40–41, 202n48; in early America, 31–48; female education and, 45–48; imperialism and, 200n25; maritime communities' navigation and, 33, 38, 40, 200n25; mathematical, 51; Nantucket and, 37–38; Native Americans' knowledge of, 38–39, 139, 199n11; Newtonization of, 212n22; politicians' predictions about, 34, 158; printed texts and almanacs spreading knowledge of, 34–37, 44, 46–48, 51–52, 124; theological language and, 44; widespread knowledge of, 14, 20, 27, 29, 32–33, 40, 71, 139

Astronomy Improved: The Harmonious Regularity Observable in the Mechanism or Movements of the Planetary System (Strong), 55, 67

astro-political discourse, 2–3, 22, 44, 73–74, 113, 120, 147–48, 157, 168–69, 173–74, 178

athlete stars, 183–84, 190

Aurora (PA) General Advertiser on Thomas Cooper, 177

Australia's flag, 146

autonomy: of state-planets, 94, 96, 114, 115; of state-stars, 121, 129, 142, 153

bald eagle symbol, 115, *133*, 139, 170
Ball, Charles, 48
Ball, William, 37
Bank Wars, 101
Banneker, Benjamin, 37, 39, 169
Barbour, Philip P., 101–2, 125
Barksdale, Ethelbert, 161–62
baroque movement, 70
Barrett, Lawrence, 182
Bartlett, M. R., 46
Barton, William, 139
Battle of Brandywine (1777), 130
Battle of Cowpens (1781), 93, 134
Berkshire Star (newspaper), 7
Berlin, Isaiah, 11
Betsy Ross Flag, 131, *133*, 147
Beveridge, Albert, 188
Bibb, Henry, 49
Blake; or the Huts of America (Delany), 49

"blazing stars." *See* comets
Blood-Stained Banner (Confederate official flag), 160
body politic, 12–13, 69, 77, 80–81, 83, 94, 121, 197n27
Boethius, 68
Bolingbroke, Lord, 84
Bonner, Robert, 159
Bonnie Blue Flag, The (song), 162–63, *164*
Booth, Edwin, 182, 183
Bowditch, Nathaniel, 60
Bowles (Maryland assembly member), 178
boxing matches, 183–84
Bradford, Sarah Hopkins, 49
Brazil's flag, 146
Breckinridge, John, 103
Britain: Canada's rumored revolt against, 143; Civil War, 12; cultural superiority to colonies and early America, 181–82; Elizabethan world, 79–80, *81;* flag as influence on American flag, 129; horological revolution of, 53; newspaper titles in, 7; stars not on flag of, 138; sun-kings and, 3, 80, 82–87; theater and stars of stage, 181–84; Union Jack, 126–27. *See also* American Revolution; colonial America; *specific rulers and dynasties*
Brown, William Wells, 49
Burke, Edmund, 94
Burritt, Elijah, 46

Calhoun, John C., 106–7, 111, 178
California, performing arts in, 182
Campion, Nicholas, 195n3
Canada's rumored revolt against Britain, 143
Case, John, 80, *81,* 210n11
celebrity culture and constellation of luminaries, 183, 190
celestial cycles, 68
celestial globes, 124, 218n9
Chambers, Robert, 218n5
chaos: American political system and, 95, 109; Civil War and, 157; constitution as way to counter, 90; political commentary using language of, 74, 107; in political metaphors, 74

Chaplin, Joyce, 19, 209n178
Cherokee Phoenix (Native newspaper), 48, 67
Chester County Militia Color's version of American flag, 130
Cheyne, George, 54
Church, Edwin, 1–2, *2*, 24, 187
CIA Memorial Wall, 191
cinematic stars, 184–86, 190–93
city upon a hill, 16, 150
Civil War: American flag over Fort Sumter, 1–3, *2;* American flag's adoration during, 127; astro-political images anticipating, 73–74, 111–13, 148, 156–57; "battle of the flags" and, 158; comets and, 73, 114, 157, 165; discord and chaos of, 157; inevitability of, 156; military officers likened to stars, 180; political astronomy and, 19, 148, 158, 161–63; republic-as-constellation vs. solar constitution in lead up to, 155; revived image of thirteen interlocked spheres, 113–15, *115*. *See also* Confederate States of America; secession
Clark, Jane, 42–43
Clay, Henry, 178
clockwork universe, 13, 16, 28, 53–58, *57*, 67, 83, 205n106. *See also* mechanical language
coat of arms, 126, 131, 214n54
cognitive science on metaphors' use, 11
coins, 91, *92*
college professors as luminaries, 176
colonial America: almanacs' importance in, 35–37, 44, 51–52, 71, 124, 201n33, 209n178; British flag and, 126–27; flags associated with resistance to British governance, 127–28; king-as-sun imagery and, 82, 85–87; knowledge of universe's size and, 62; mechanical universe and, 54–55; names of newspapers in, 7; newspapers and journals reporting on nature and astronomy, 35; planetary imagery applied to colonies, 89–90; science as inconsequential in, 32; unraveling of solar metaphor during Revolutionary era, 87–88
Colorado, entry into Union, 163

Columbia studio's astronomical icon, 186
comets: astrology and, 52; British and Europeans rejecting traditional view of, 108; Civil War language and, 73, 114, 157, 165; disturbing harmony of cosmos, 107–11, 113; early American imagery of, 110–11; maritime communities' knowledge of, 33; "Miss Mitchell's Comet," 38; Newtonian physics and, 108; Revolutionary-era imagery of, 109; traditionally signaling downfalls and unwelcome events, 108, 111; widespread knowledge of, 14. *See also* Leonid meteor shower (1833); meteors
Common Sense (Paine), 121–22
Compendium of Astronomy (Vose), 46
Compromise of 1850, 111
Confederate States of America: Army of Northern Virginia battle flag as possible flag of, 160, 162; *The Bonnie Blue Flag* (song), 162–63, *164;* "Dixie" (unofficial anthem), 162; flags of, 113–14, 159–63, *161–62, 164;* founding of, 158; keeping stars on flag, debate over, 162; political astronomy and, 158, 161–66; Stainless Banner (official flag), 160–61, *162;* Stars and Bars (official flag), 159–62, *161, 164*, 221n52; state flags of Confederate states, 162–63; states' rights and, 18, 72, 94, 113–14, 153–54, 160, 165. *See also* Civil War
Constellation, The (newspaper), 7
constellation of state-stars, 115–66; in accordance with cosmos, 150; anxiety of citizens for their state's place in expanding constellation, 148–49; blending of planetary and constellational frameworks, 154–55; equality and democracy of imagery, 93, 125–26, 131, 136, 168, 176; expansion as new states join Union, 22, 115, 131, 142–45, 155, 170; first years of United States establishing image of, 137–42; mission to guide yet-to-be-enlightened world, 150; as part of political culture, 118, 142, 168, 220n33; replacing sun-king imagery, 22, 118–21, 124–25, 134–35, 167–68; solar system imagery clashing with, 154; territories' process to become states and, 149–50,

Index

232

156. *See also* American constellation ("new constellation"); American flag constellations, 10; almanacs keeping track of, 37; Lacaille's identification of new constellations, 123–24; of luminaries, 23, 174–76, 181–84, 190; widespread knowledge of, 14, 31. *See also* constellation of state-stars

Constitution: John Adams advocating to prevent chaos of "comets" in new country, 110; analyzing political power as interaction among heavenly bodies and, 215n272; as-sun metaphor, 9, 10, 21, 90, 96, 99–100, 103, 152, 168; cosmic harmony and, 16, 110; cosmic stability and, 90; political astronomy and, 141; ratification of, 16, 100, 135, 140–41; as "work of art," 12

Constitutional Convention (1787), 30, 94–95, 140, 142

Continental Colors, 128, *129*, 137

Continental Congress, 93, 120, 124, 126–27, 147

Cook Islands, flag of, 23, 146, *147*

Cooper, Thomas, 177–78

Copernicus, Nicolaus, and Copernican astronomy, 33, 35, 69, 77–79, 83–84; America referring to itself as sun in, 87, 93, 99; Newtonian worldview complementing, 84; political universe imagery from, 90; revolution concept in politics from, 89

Cornish, Samuel, 40

corruption, 16, 113, 137, 139, 150

cosmic evolution, theory of, 98

cosmos: in American politics and political imagination, 4–6, 89, 119, 121–22, 138, 147–48, 163; ancient understandings of, 5–6; as divine creation, 14; intergalactic space as corollary of democracy, 125; Mesopotamian civilization and, 5–6; in modern US political discourse, 3, 4, 25, 35; multiple galaxies composing, 122; vastness of, 61–67, 72, 122, 207n138. *See also* astronomy; harmony; political astronomy; *specific cosmic features*

Cowpens Flag, 93, *93*, 134–35

Critical Period (1783–1789), 109–10, 140, 175

Crowe, Michael, 62

Cumberland County (NY) as bright star in political firmament, 148

currency. *See* money

Cushman, Charlotte, 183

Daly, James, 15, 80–81
Dana, John, 155
Dante, 121, 224n31
Davis, Jefferson, 111, 165
deep space, 63, 67
deep time, 207n119, 208n162
Delany, Martin, 49
Delbourgo, James, 213n39
Democratic-Republicans, 101, 105, 172
democratization: of astronomical knowledge, 71; of human star, 190
Democrats, 18, 111, 156, 165, *179*
De revolutionibus (Copernicus), 77
Dickerson, John, 104
Dickinson, John, 95
digital information age, star making in, 190
discord: Civil War and, 157; as dissonance in harmonic framework, 16, 100; political astronomy making harder to negotiate in, 18–19; political harmony and, 70
disunion, 96, 110–12
diurnal cycles, 28–29, 37, 68
divine design, 14, 15. *See also* God's greatness
"Dixie" (Confederacy's unofficial anthem), 162
Donne, John, 69
Doolittle, James, 112
Douglas, Stephen, 225n33
Douglass, Frederick, 43, 49
Dunster, Henry, 33
Dürer, Albrecht, 75–77, *76*
dysfunction. *See* fears of anarchy and dysfunction

eagle symbol, 115, *133*, 139, 170
earth's smallness in universe, 64–65
Easton (Pennsylvania) Flag, 135
eclipses, 52, 104, 107
education: African Free School, 40; astronomical schooling using planetarium

Index

233

education (continued)
  or orrery, 56–57, 57; female education, 45–48; Kentucky Native schools, 38; on universe, 59, 65–67
egalitarianism, 22, 32, 122, 125, 133–34, 136, 168, 176, 182
electric lights. *See* light pollution
Elizabeth I (English queen), 80, *81*
Elusive Republic, The (McCoy), 12
Emerson, Ralph Waldo, 167
England. *See* Britain
Enlightenment, 33, 52, 55, 70, 75, 84, 123, 124, 151, 213n39
enslaved people: knowledge of astronomy and nature, 14, 32, 199n11; North Star and, 20, 28, 48–50, 72; political astronomy and, 18; as stargazers, 40–43; telling time by moon and stars, 31. *See also* abolitionism; slavery
e pluribus unum (Latin motto, "out of many, one"), 139–40, 155, 165
equality: state-stars on flag and, 93, 125–26, 131, 136, 168, 176. *See also* egalitarianism
Era of Good Feelings, 155
ethnoastronomy, 5
European discourse of sun-king, 3, 76–77; cinematic stars' concept as descendant of, 185; as roots of American cosmic concepts, 4, 6, 14, 21, 99, 118, 120–21, 167, 173. *See also* king-as-sun imagery
European federalism, 104–5
European theater and actors, 182, 184
European Union, flag of, 23, 146–47
Evans, Charles, 36
exceptionalism. *See* American exceptionalism

Fairbanks, Douglas, 185
fears of anarchy and dysfunction, political astronomy's power to cope with, 4, 16–17, 60–61, 113, 141, 148–49, 151, 163, 168, 223n3
Federal Galaxy (Vermont newspaper), 7, *8*
federal government. *See* American Union; federalism
federalism: John Adams's defense of, 103–4; astronomical politics and, 45, 112, 119–20, 141; European, 104–5; explained through cosmic worldview, 4, 21, 74–75, 94–95, 100; as major issue in early America, 17; orbit metaphor and, 102–3; sun and, 94, 100, 115
Federalist Papers, The: no. 9 (Hamilton), 102–3; no. 15 (Hamilton), 103
Federalists, 17, 58, 105, 110, 141, 165–66, 168
Federal Orrery (Federalist newspaper), 8–9, *9*, 58
Ferguson, James, 35–36
First Amendment, 104
First Party System, battles of, 8. *See also* Federalists; Jeffersonian Republicans
fixed stars, 29, 52, 59–67, 71, 103, 110, 148, 157, 178
Flag Act (1777), 93, 124, 126, 127, 133, 137, 219n23
flags, 145–53; in colonial America, 126–27; Confederate, 159–63; new foreign countries modeling flags from American cosmological idiom, 22–23, 146–47; new states using stars on their flags, 22, 145–47. *See also* American flag; Confederate States of America
Florida: entry into Union, 144, 155; West Florida, Republic of, 162
Foley, Michael, 13
foreign countries modeling flags from American cosmological idiom, 22–23, 146
Fort Harmar's Plan showing American flag (1786), 131, *132*
Fort Sumter attack (Charleston 1861), 1–2
Fourth of July: celebrations on, 142, 144; new stars for new states added to flag on, 145; toast to Monroe as "bright sun," 173; toast to Revolutionary statesmen and soldiers as "planets and suns," 94
France: French Revolution and nationalism, 220n29; stars not on flag of, 138; sun king as absolutist monarch, 86. *See also* Louis XIV
Franklin, Benjamin, 36, 95, 127, 137, 177–78
Fraser, Gordon, 33–34, 202n52
Freedom's Journal, 40–41, 202n52
Freedom Star. *See* North Star

French and Indian War, 86
Freneau, Philip, 58
fugitive science, 39, 50
"Fugitive Slave's Apostrophe to the North Star, The" (Pierpont's poem), 49–50
fugitive slaves following North Star. *See* North Star
Furstenberg, François, 171

Galileo, 33
Garrison, William Lloyd, 155
Gast, John, 188–89
gender, 32, 47
General Compendium (Vancouver), 55
General Schuyler's Flag, 131, *133*
geocentric solar system, 27, 33, 35, 68, 76–77
Geography of the Heavens, and Class Book of Astronomy, The (Burritt), 46
geometrization of space, 61
George II (British king), 85, 86
George III (British king), 86, 94
Georgius Sidiu (initial name of Uranus), 59
globalization: universal urbanization and, 190; of US political astronomy, 23, 147–48
Globe, The (newspaper), 7
globes including terrestrial and celestial discoveries, 124, 218n9
Goddess of Liberty, 127
God's greatness: cosmic harmony as God's plan, 68, 152; cosmic political models created by, 142; as divine clockmaker, 52, 205n106; linked to astronomy, 14, 44, 74, 151–53, 200n15; Newtonianism and, 54; North Star and, 203n85; orbits, both physical and political, under control of, 105; revealed through astrology, 51, 52
Grand Union Flag, 128. *See also* Continental Colors
gravity, 55, 81–82, 88, 93, 164–65, 215n74
Great Chain of Being, 15, 68
Great Seal, 127, 129, 139, *140*
Great Star pattern, 135–36
Great Union Flag, 128. *See also* Continental Colors
Griffith, D. W., 185

Gronim, Sarah, 33, 35, 200n23
Guthrie, William, 47

Hagen, Jean, 186
Hamilton, Alexander, 102–3, 110, 210n11, 223n3
Hancock, John, 109
Hanoverian monarchs (Britain), 82–83, 85, 86, 164, 169
harmony, 13; American Revolution and, 70, 81; American Union and, 90, 94, 96, 139, 153; balance of political parties creating, 112; Confederate view on way to create, 163; constellation of state-stars and, 125; cosmic, 16, 60, 63, 67–70, 98, 102, 106, 110, 114, 122; harmony-music-astronomy nexus, 68; Kepler and, 69, 209n168; kingly harmony in constitutional system, 84; mechanical language to express, 214n46; monarchical political structure and, 81; *musica mundi* (music of the spheres), 68; political harmony, 15–17, 70, 98; return to cosmic harmony after Civil War, 163; secession as collapse of cosmic harmony, 17; transcendental celestial harmony, assumption of, 18
Harmony of the World, The (Kepler), 69
Hawkes, Jacquetta, 5
Hayne, Robert, 2, 154
heavens: as divine creation, 14; order and significance of, 51; sky as traditional location of, 31
heliocentrism, 21, 27, 35–36, 53, 57, 62, 68–69, 72, 76–80, 84, 87, 122. *See also* Copernicus, Nicolaus, and Copernican astronomy; solar system; sun
Henry V (Shakespeare), 80, 170
Henry VIII (English king), 78
Heroic Slave, The (Douglass), 49
Herschel, William, 59, 98
Hershel (planet). *See* Uranus, discovery of
Hervey, James, 54
Hickman, Jared, 49, 50, 203nn85–86, 204n88
hierarchical relationships in planetary system, 21, 45–47, 63, 72, 87, 121, 174
historians' use of metaphors, 12
historical consciousness, 6, 19–20

Hobbes, Thomas, 12, 15, 196n24
Holbrook, Josiah, 56–57
Holbrook School Apparatus Manufacturing Company, 56
Hollywood's use of astronomical images, 182, 185
Hollywood Walk of Fame, 191–93, *192*
horological revolution, 53
horoscopes, 204n94
Horton, George Moses, 40
Huerta, Gerard, 187
human body: astrology and, 51; harmonic balance and, 69. *See also* body politic
human stars (men as stars), 148, 169–93; athletes, 183–84; celebrities, 180, 190; cinematic stars, 184–86; at close of nineteenth century "stars" allusion pointing to, 189–90; cultural stars eclipsing political stars, 190; current-day cliché of term "star," 24, 25, 181, 190; in digital information age, 190; enlightening the world, 175; fallen servicemen and servicewomen represented by stars, 191, *192*; Franklin as star, 177–78; history of, 23, 167; individual with unrivaled qualities as star, 176; military officers as stars, 179–80; politicians, 177–80; presidents, 172, 174, 179; reverence and hero-worship bestowed on, 176; rock stars, 4, 190; solitude of, 191; superstars, 4, 5, 190; theatrical star system and constellation of luminaries, 181–84; Washington as star, 169; writers, 180–81
Hutton, James, 208n162

imperialism and astronomy, 188–89, 200n25
Independent Ledger article seeking support for new American constellation, 123
individualism, 176, 180–81
Industrial Age, clock as key machine of, 205n101
Instructor, The: or, American Young Man's Best Companion (unnamed compiler), 66
itinerant acting troupes, 182

Jackson, Andrew (freed enslaved man), 48–49
Jackson, Andrew (president), 101, 107, 111, 173, 179
Jacobinism, 9
Jacobsen, Thorkild, 6
James VI (Scottish King)/James I (English king), 80
Jefferson, Thomas, 59, 73, 96, 106, 172
Jeffersonian Republicans, 110, 168, 172
Jeffersonians, 17, 58
Jesus associated with North Star, 50
Jesus Christ Superstar (rock opera), 190
Johnson, Mark, 10–11
Johnson, Samuel, 109
judiciary: functioning as sun, 100–101; in its own orbit, 103; in noble constellation, 175–76
July Fourth. *See* Fourth of July
Junius Americanus (Arthur Lee), 108–9
Jupiter, 59

Kansas, entry into Union, 158–59
Kansas City Times on boxing matches, 184
Kantorowicz, Ernst, 12, 23
Kendig, Mrs., 183
Kennedy, John F., 189
Kentucky, entry into Union, 98, 143
Kepler, Johannes, 33, 69
Kimmelmeyer, Frederick, 170, *171*
king-as-head of body politic, 77, 80–81, 121–22
king-as-sun imagery, 3, 6, 75–80, *76*, *81*, 188; Alfonso X (Spanish king) as first European sun king, 210n7; American colonials and, 82; based on dominance, heat, and light, 82–87; bifurcated into political body and into human body, 23, 167, 223n1; British use of, 82–87, 118; Confederacy's flag echoing, 114; constellation of state-stars replacing, 22, 118–21, 124–25, 134–35, 167–68; dethroned by vastness of universe, 63, 168–71, 180; early modern king embodying modern state, 23, 78–80; European origins of, 4, 6, 14, 21, 99, 118, 120–21, 167, 173; heliocentrism and its tensions with planetary imagery, 84–85; Pufendorf

and, 78; republicanism and, 118–21, 134, 168, 175. *See also* Louis XIV
King Lear (Shakespeare), vii
King's Two Bodies, The (Kantorowicz), 12
Koselleck, Reinhart, 89
Koslofsky, Craig, 198n4
Koyré, Alexander, 61
Kuhn, Thomas S., 205n104

Lacaille, Nicolas-Louis de, 123–24
Lakoff, George, 10–11
Laplace, Pierre-Simon, 60, 106
Laws, Men and Machines (Foley), 13
Lee, Arthur (Junius Americanus), 108–9
Lee, Richard Henry, 169
Leibnitz, G. W., 54, 206n106
Lemen, B. F., 73–74, 157–58
Leonid meteor shower (1833), 42–44, *42*, 48, 60
Leviathan (Hobbes), 12
Lewis, Andrew, 199n11
Liberator on Florida's entry into Union, 155
liberty caps, 127
liberty pole, 127
light and brightness, 10, 29–30, 64, 82–87, 102, 105, 108, 198n4
light pollution, effect on visibility of night skies, 4, 23, 29–30, 71, 108, 186, 190–91
Lincoln, Abraham, 43–44, 60, 73, 156–59, 202n59
literary stars of early America, 35, 180–81
London Times on theatrical star system, 183
Lone Star Flag, 145, 146, *146*, 162
Loomis, George, 180–81
lost tribes of biblical Israel, 217n132
Louis XIV (French king, Sun King), 78, 79–80, *79*, 85, 134
Louisiana Purchase, 110
Lovell, James, 137
Lowell, James Russell, 204n88

Macarthy, Harry, 162–63, *164*
MacDonald, Alexander, 200n15
Machiavelli, 90
Madison, James, 16, 95, 105
Magleby, McRay, 187

mail delivery system in early America, 35
Maine, called "Eastern Star," 71
Manifest Destiny, 188–89
Masons, 70, 131, 176
mathematical astronomy, 51
Mather, Margaret, 183
Maximilian I (Holy Roman emperor), 75, *76*
McArthur, Benjamin, 184
McConville, Brendan, 85, 86–87, 197n25
McCoy, Drew, 12
McPherson, James, 180
Mécanique celeste (Laplace), 60
mechanical language, 102–6; Adams' imagery of Union functioning like mechanical clocks, 34, 58, 102–4; applied to government pre–Civil War, 21, 105–6; clocks and, 53, 58–59; explicitly planetary, 103; to express sociopolitical perfection and harmony, 214n46; modern judges using to describe separation of powers, 216n98; universe as great machine, 53–54. *See also* clockwork universe
Mecum, Jane Franklin, 138
medieval thought: clocks and, 56; Great Chain of Being and, 15, 68; harmonic tradition and, 68; mathematical astronomy and, 51; metaphors, use of, 12
Meditations and Contemplations (Hervey), 54
Memoirs of the Life of David Rittenhouse, 27
Mercury (Roman god), 7
"Mercury" in early newspaper titles, 7–8
Mesopotamian civilization, 5–6, 204n94
metaphorical language: architectural metaphors for early republic, 12; Aristotle's definition of "metaphor," 11; astrology and, 52; clock and, 58; as empty clichés, 24, 25, 181, 190; history of, 10–14; political astronomy's power from, 16, 17, 48, 60; prevalence in early United States, 31; shift from organic to cultural political, 13; state-as-art metaphor, 12; unraveling of solar metaphor during Revolutionary era, 87–88. *See also* king-as-sun imagery; *specific cosmic bodies and systems*

Meteoric Shower of Nov. 13, 1833 (Vollmy), 42
meteors, 10; disturbing harmony of cosmos, 107–11; Leonid meteor shower, 42–44, *42*, 48, 60; in metaphors of political destruction, 9, 16; Native American knowledge of, 39; sightings of, 35; Southern state-stars as, 157; talented individuals' rise as, 190, 225n35; Taylor as president who died prematurely likened to, 179–80
Mexican War, 156
Michigan, entry into Union, 98–99, 143–44
Milky Way, 30, 66, 187
Miller, Perry, 14
Mississippi: *The Bonnie Blue Flag* (song), 162–63, *164*; secession flag of, 162–63
"Miss Mitchell's Comet," 38
Missouri, entry into Union, 106, 144, 221n49
Mitchell, William, and daughters Maria and Phebe, 38
monarchy: constitutional monarchy, 84; founding of United States and, 169; monarchical absolutism, 77–78, 82, 86, 118, 134, 167; planetary relations used to describe, 21, 48; solar monarchism's loss of relevance, 63, 168–71, 180; stars used to describe, 170; unsubstantiated as institution in nature, 122; Washington and, 169–71
money: republican solar system and, 134; Revolutionary America's image of new political creation on, 91, *92*
Monroe, James, 145, 173
moon, 29, 31, 37, 47, 223n87
Morison, Samuel Eliot, 33
Mormon Utah territory, 118
Morning Star (newspaper), 7
Morse, Jedidiah, 64–66
movie studios and stars, 184–86, 190–93
Mumford, Lewis, 205n101
musical references, 15–16, 70. *See also* harmony
musica mundi (music of the spheres), 68
My Bondage and My Freedom (Douglass), 43

Nantucket, 37–38
Narrative (Jackson), 48–49
National Era (African American publication), 41
nationalism, 127, 138, 147, 220n29
Native Americans: astronomical and natural knowledge of, 38–39, 139, 199n11; astronomical instruction in Kentucky Native schools, 38; Leonid meteor shower and, 48; newspapers, 38–39; political astronomy and, 18, 139; understanding American flag's design upon first viewing, 39, 139; vastness of universe and, 67
natural philosophy/knowledge, 33, 35, 52, 63, 71, 199n11, 200n23
natural religion, 151
Naval Committee of Congress, 126, 137
navigation, 31, 40, 48–49, 120, 222n68
Nebraska, entry into Union, 163
Nelson, Eric, 169
Neptune, discovery of, 98
Nevada, entry into Union, 163
Newark Evening Star on New Jersey political stars, 178–79
Newburyport (MA) Herald on six states as fixed stars, 148
New England symbols on flags, 127
New Frontier of Kennedy era, 189
New-Hampshire Mercury (newspaper), 7
Newport Herald on Constitutional Convention (1787), 140
New Science of eighteenth century, 36, 68, 84
newspapers: copy sharing and public readings of, 41; early America, astronomy coverage in, 35, 44, 47; titles of, 6–9, *8–9*, 196n16. *See also specific titles*
New Star (newspaper), 7
new states: American flag adding more stars for, 22, 115, 131, 142–45, 170; entry into Union, 22, 98–99, 115, 131, 142–45, 155, 158–59, 163, 170; flags with star-related symbols adopted by, 22, 145
New System of Modern Geography, A (Guthrie), 47

Newton, Isaac, 33, 36, 54, 120
Newtonianism and Newtonian physics, 6, 13, 53–54; associating United States with, 14–15, 75; astrology and, 205n99; comets and, 108; constitutions holding state-planets together in worldview of, 90; Copernican worldview complementing, 84; eighteenth-century astronomy and, 59, 207n140; God and universal clock in terms of, 205–6n106; gravity and, 55, 81–82, 88, 93, 164–65, 215n74; king-as-sun imagery and, 83–84; machinelike predictability of, likened to American politics, 102, 158; meaning of "Newtonianism," 211–12n21; political astronomy and, 18, 71, 163; universe as great machine and, 53–54

New York: African American education in, 40; coat of arms of state with rising sun, 214n54; constellation of luminaries and stardom imagery of, 181 82

New York Herald's fictitious dialogue on stars on American flag, 117–18

New York Manumission Society, 40

New York Pewterers' Banner, 135, *136*

night skies of preindustrial world, 28–31, 48, 120, 123

Noah's Star (pseud.), 173

Northerners: astro-political images anticipating Civil War, 73–74, 111–13, 156–57; constitution-as-sun imagery of, 152; on free vs. slave status of territories seeking statehood, 145; on God's infinite wisdom in governing the universe, 152; political astronomy and, 18, 21, 151, 157–58. *See also* Civil War

North Star, 20, 28, 48–50, 72, 203n85

North Star (Douglass's newspaper), 49

nullification, 101, 215n79

observatories, 34, 201n26

Ohio, entry into Union, 98, 145, 170

Olivier, Laurence, 186

"On the Return of Doctor Benjamin Franklin to America" (poem), 177

orbits, 10, 21, 55, 61, 68, 82, 83; federalism and, 102–3; harmony and, 106, 156; judiciary in its own orbit, 103; stars attracting other bodies to, 185

orderliness of universe, 6, 62, 68, 70, 74, 98, 106. *See also* orbits; spheres and spherical movements

Orion Pictures' astronomical icon, 186

orreries, 8–9, 55–58, *57*, 218n3

Our Banner in the Sky (Church's painting), 1–2, *2*, 24, 187

Paine, Robert Treat, 58

Paine, Thomas, 90, 121–22

paper money, heliocentric design on, 91, *92*

Paramount studio's astronomical icon, 186

patriarchal hierarchy of solar system, 47

Pawnees, 39

Pennsylvania Ledger on Paine's astro-political language, 121–22

Pewterers' Banner, 135, *136*

Philip IV (Spanish king), 78

Philippines' flag, 146

Pictorial Quilt (Powers), 41–42, *43*

Pierce, Franklin, 155

Pierpont, John, 49–50

Pittsfield (MA) Sun on Andrew Jackson's rivals trying to obstruct his radiance, 173

planetarium, 56–57, *57*. *See also* orreries

planets: almanacs on alignment of, 37; American flag design not using, 93; American Union consisting of states as, 3, 21, 73–75, 89–91, 94–99, 107, 110–16; astronomical politics and, 45; blending of planetary and constellational frameworks, 154–55; colonies compared to, 89–90; discovery of new planets, 59, 71, 93–94, 98; hierarchical relationships in cosmos, 21, 45–47, 63, 72, 87, 121, 174; maritime communities' knowledge of, 33; in metaphors of political system on verge of destruction, 16; viewed in preindustrial America, 29, 48; widespread knowledge of, 14. *See also* orbits; solar system; state-planets; *specific planets by name*

Plato, 11, 68

Index

239

Pocock, John, 150
Polaris. *See* North Star
political actors: human-as-star imagery associated with, 177–80; likened to constellations of luminaries, 174, *179;* military backgrounds of, 178–79. *See also* judiciary; presidents
political astronomy: adaptable to new contexts and processes, 18, 143–44; African Americans and, 41, 202n48; American flag and, 130, 132, 133, 137–42, 145–46; centrality and pervasiveness in early American speech, 4, 10, 13, 17, 139, 153, 168, 196n12; compared to history, 19–20, 138; conditioning of political astronomers, 44–48; contemporary echoes of phrase, *179*, 193; creation of United States and, 14–17, 94, 96, 114, 120, 139, 168; critical in making sense of fundamental political concepts, 4, 13, 14, 16, 119; defined, 3; distorting to promote some state-stars to fixed-star status, 148; European tradition of, 4, 6, 14, 21, 99, 118, 120–21, 173; facilitated by widespread knowledge of astronomy, 14, 20, 27, 29, 32–33, 40, 71, 139; forgotten language of, 191; global effect of US use of, 23, 147–48; as metaphorical mode of thinking, 10; most recent astronomical knowledge's effect on, 93; newspaper titles and, 6–9, *8–9;* redefined by shift from sun/monarch to stars/states, 22, 118–21, 124–25, 134–35, 167–68; republicanism and, 22, 150, 173, 174; studied previously in terms of ancient or indigenous societies, 6; US harmony with cosmos and, 4, 14, 71; Whiskey Rebellion described in terms of, 9. *See also* astro-political discourse; metaphorical language; *specific cosmic systems and celestial bodies*
political firmament, 4, 10, 17, 40, 87, 96, 99–100, 102, 107–13, 116–17, 121, 125, 141–49, 153–57, 163, 168, 174, 188
political harmony. *See* harmony
politics. *See* astronomical politics; Northerners; political actors; political astronomy; Southerners; *specific political parties*

Politics (Aristotle), 11, 80
Poor Richard's Almanac, 35–36
Potter, David, 162
power: momentous decisions following American Revolution, 14; planetary language and, 121; political astronomy's explication of, 4, 13, 105; soft power of United States, 23, 147. *See also* king-as-sun imagery; monarchy; presidents
Powers, Harriet, 41–42, *43*
Pownall, Thomas, 87–88
preindustrial societies, 28–31, 36–37, 48
presidents: military stars becoming, 179; monarchism and, 169, 180; as stars, 172, 174; as suns, 91–92, *92*, 99, 172–74, 176
Prester John, 195n9
Principia (Newton), 33
print culture of early America, 34–37, 44, 51–52, 71, 124, 201n33, 209n178
professional sports and celebrity culture, 183–84, 190
Protestantism, 36, 51, 52, 86, 200n15, 204n90; Second Great Awakening (1800–1840), 152
Ptolemaic worldview, 35–36, 50, 68, 80, 123
Publius (pseud. of Alexander Hamilton), 110
Pufendorf, Samuel, 78
Pythagoras of Samos, 68–69

quilts, 41–42, *43*

Rebellious Stripes (banner of Sons of Liberty), 128, *128*
relativity, 64–65
religion: astrology and, 51, 52; natural, 151; Puritan model of Christian charity, 151. *See also* Protestantism
Renaissance, 75, 77, 108, 119, 137, 168, 173
republicanism: astronomical politics and, 45, 112; as benevolent and benign form of government, 92; constellations of luminaries and, 174; cosmic harmony and, 70, 122; early American republic and, 12–13; king-as-sun imagery and, 118–21, 134, 168, 175; legitimation explained through planetary images and cosmic worldview, 4, 14, 90–91, 96, 151; mon-

archy vs., 168–69; political astronomy and, 22, 150, 173, 174; star politician and, 177–78; state-stars and, 131, 133, 137–38, 168; vastness of universe and, 63–64; of Washington, 171

Republican Party, *179;* 1860 presidential election, 73, 156; Campaign for the West (1900), 188; Civil War and, 156; Cooper and, 177–78; political astronomy and, 165. *See also* Jeffersonian Republicans

Republican Star (newspaper), 7

Revolutionary War. *See* American Revolution

revolution as astronomical image, 10, 55, 57, 68, 73, 89, 157. *See also* spheres and spherical movements

Rhode Island's antifederal position, 140, 143

Richmond Dispatch on proposals for Confederate flag, 160

Richmond Enquirer's Fourth of July toast, 94

Rights of All, The (newspaper), 40

Rittenhouse, David, 27, 33, 56, 64–66, 120, 200n22, 218n3

Rives, William, 106, 111, 215n79

rock stars, 4, 190

Romantic age, 180

Rome. *See* ancient Greece and Rome

Romeo and Juliet (Shakespeare), 78–79

Rome Reborn on Western Shores (Shalev), 19

Rothman, Aviva, 69, 209n168

Rush, Benjamin, 86, 119–20, 137, 174–75

Russert, Britt, 39

Russwurm, John, 190

saltire (St. Andrew's Cross), 128, 159–60

satellites, 45, 59, 99

Saturn, 39, 59, 64

Scher, Paula, 187–88, *187*

science, early American history of, 31–32, 71, 198n10; Banneker as "first Black man of science," 37, 39, 169. *See also* astronomy

scientific revolution, 53, 209n168

secession, 17, 74, 97, 98, 112, 143, 162, 217n132. *See also* Civil War

Second Great Awakening (1800–1840), 152

Sedition Act of 1798, 104

Segar, Mr. (of Northampton), 117

separation of powers, 102, 215n72, 216n98

Sewall, Jonathan, 172

Seward, William, 149–50

Shakespeare, William, vii, 78–79, 80, 170

Shaw, David, powder horn of, 135, *136*

shooting stars. *See* comets

Short Introduction to Geography and Astronomy, A (school lesson book), 65

Singing in the Rain (movie), 186

single-star flags, 162–63, *164*

Sirius (dog-star), 64–65

sky watching, 32–33

Slauter, Eric, 12, 197n27

"Slaveholder's Address to the North Star" (Pierpont's poem), 50

slavery, 106, 155–56, 225n33. *See also* abolitionism; enslaved people

Slavery in the United States (Ball), 48

Slidell, John, 158

Smith, Courtney Weiss, 205n106

snake as flag motif, 127

soft power of United States, 23, 147

solar monarchy. *See* king-as-sun imagery

solar system: addition of new planets as new states added to United States, 98; American Union likened to, 61, 74–75, 82, 90–91, 95, 97–98, 101–2, 106, 121, 154; Confederacy's flag using imagery of, 114; geocentric, 27, 33, 35; instability of, 59–61; mid-eighteenth century charting of, 61; Old Regime political cultures and, 21, 22, 118–21, 124–25, 134, 168; outmoded imagery after Civil War, 115; political, 74, 82, 114; predictable and self-correcting structure of, 106–7; in universe of infinite size, 61–67, 176, 180; Washington and solar imagery, 23, 169–70. *See also* geocentric solar system; heliocentrism; king-as-sun imagery; planets; sun; *specific planets and other celestial bodies*

Sons of Liberty's Rebellious Stripes, 128, *128*

South Carolina: flag with moon, 223n87; threats of secession, 97

Southerners: astro-political images anticipating Civil War, 73–74, 111–13;

Southerners (*continued*)
  on God's infinite wisdom in governing the universe, 152; political astronomy and, 18, 21, 73, 112, 165–66; republic-as-constellation imagery of, 152; state banners and political astronomy, 162–63. *See also* Civil War; Confederate States of America
space program of 1960s, 189
Sphaera civitatis (Case), 80, *81*, 210n11
spheres and spherical movements: colonies orbiting in proper sphere, 88; crystalline spheres, 33, 68; government and elected representatives keeping to their sphere, 105–6, 107, 215n272; harmony and, 81, 96–97, 100, 106; judiciary's sphere, 103; music of the spheres, 16; new planet moving in own proper sphere, 98; of Ptolemaic universe, 80; separation of powers and, 102; spheres of influence, 4, 21, 101, 103; state and federal governments in own sphere, 101; thirteen interlocked spheres revolving around uniting center, 91, *92*, 113, 115, *115*, 156, 214n46
sports and celebrity culture, 183–84, 190
Stainless Banner (Confederate official flag), 160–61, *162*
Star, The (London newspaper), 7
Star, The, pervasive as newspaper name, 7–8
stardom, 23–25, 181–86, 190; "star," modern society's use of term, 3, 4, 25. *See also* human stars
stargazing, 33, 41, 50, 123
"star of empire" trope, 188–89
Star of Freedom (newspaper), 7
Star of Raleigh (North Carolina newspaper), 8
stars: anthropomorphism of, 78, 177; bifurcated into political body and into human body, 23, 167, 223n1; disconnect between political astronomy's use of term and modern age's use, 186, 188, 191; equal and undistinguished, 93, 125–26, 131, 136, 168, 176; fallen servicemen and servicewomen represented by, 191, *192*; five-point star as omnipresent in American visual culture, 8, 24, 130, 146, 161–63, 187–88, 191–92; light of, 29–30; mid-eighteenth century interest in, 61–62; number of, 65–67, 207n138; as suns of other systems, 66–67. *See also* fixed stars; human stars; state-stars

Stars and Bars (Confederacy's official flag), 159–62, *161*, *164*, 221n52

Stars and Stripes. *See* American flag

Stars and Stripes (Scher's graphic design), 187–88, *187*

Star-Spangled Banner, 93, *93*, 118, 126–42, 159. *See also* American flag

state banks vs. federal bank, 101

state-planets, 3, 21, 73–75, 89–91, 94–99, 107, 110–16

states' rights, 18, 72, 94, 113–14, 153, 154, 160, 165

state-stars: on Confederate flags, 159; emerging as city upon a hill, 15; equal, interchangeable, and unidentifiable, 93, 125–26, 131, 136, 168, 176; new states as stars, 22, 115, 131, 142–45, 155, 170; new states employing stars on their flags, 22, 145–47; as novel political system, 22, 120, 126, 132, 168; origin of symbolism of, 131; political astronomy and, 138, 168; replacing Old Regime of sun-king, 22, 118–21, 124–25, 134–35, 167–68; shape of, 130. *See also* American constellation

Statue of Liberty's centennial, 186–87

stellar astronomy. *See* stars

Stephens, Alexander, 144–45

Stiles, Ezra, 33, 137, 222n68

stock companies of actors, 182

Stonehenge, 5

Strang, Cameron, 200n25

Striner, Richard, 13

Strong, Nehemia, 55, 67

sun: almanacs telling time of rising and setting, 37; American interpretation of constellation with sun as center, 2; American Union as, 93, 96, 99–102, 115; anthropomorphized, 21, 45–46, 63, 80, 85; as center of solar system, 21, 27, 35–36, 53, 57, 75–80, 82; as Confederacy's

Index

242

flag symbol, 114, 160; Constitution as, 9, 10, 21, 90, 96, 99–100, 103, 168; countless other suns in infinite universe, 61–67, 176, 180; dethroned from privileged position by vastness of universe, 63, 168–71, 180; federalism and, 94, 100, 115; gender associated with, 47; judiciary functioning as, 100–101; as marker of time's passage, 29; metaphors based on dominance, heat, and light, 82–87; presidents as, 91–92, *92*, 99, 172–74, 176; in Vose's astronomy textbook, 46; Washington as, 23, 169–72. *See also* king-as-sun imagery

Sun, The, as popular newspaper title, 7

sun-king imagery. *See* king-as-sun imagery; Louis XIV

superpower, United States as, 168

superstars, 4, 5, 190

Swiss cantons, 104–5

Taft, William Howard, 126

"tailed stars." *See* comets

tariff of abominations, 97, 154

Taylor, Zachary, 179–80

Teachout, Woden, 218n14

telescopes, 33, 34, 65–67, *179*

Testi, Arnaldo, 129

Texas: entry into Union, 144–45; Lone Star Flag, 145, 146, *146*, 162

theatrical star system and constellation of luminaries, 23, 181–84, 190

theologians as luminaries, 176

Third Maryland Regiment, 93, 134

Thirty Years' War, 69

Thornton, Tamara Plakins, 40, 124, 218n9

time: moon indicating passage of, 31; sun indicating passage of, 29. *See also* clockwork universe; mechanical language

Time-Piece (Jeffersonian newspaper), 58

Togo's flag, 146

Townshend Acts (Britain, 1767), 86

transit of Venus, 200n23

Triumphal Chariot of Maximilian I, The (Dürer's woodcut), 75–77, *76*

Tubman, Harriet, 43, 49

Tucker, Dr., letter to (England), 87, 88

Turner, Nat, 41

Tyler, John, 97, 148, 221n52

Tyler, Letitia Christian, 148

"Union" (song), 141

"United Forever" envelope, 114–15, *115*

United States. *See* American flag; American Union

Universal studio's astronomical icon, 186

universe. *See* cosmos

Uranus, discovery of, 59, 71, 93–94, 98

Vancouver, Charles, 55, 58

van Gogh, Vincent: *Starry Night*, 29–30, *30*

Vermont as fourteenth state, 143

Virgil: *Aeneid*, 9

Vollmy, Adolf, *42*

Vose, John, 46

Wallack, James William, 181

Walpole (NH) town meeting on Southern stars as exploding meteors, 156

War of 1812, 105, 136

Warren, Mercy Otis, 70

Warren Ladies' Seminary, 45–46

Washington, George: American flag and, 127; appearances in political astronomical representations, 142, 153, 170, *171*; at Constitutional Convention, 95; on Continental Colors, 128; family coat of arms' use of stars, 131; in Magleby's graphic design with twinkling stars, 187; monarchy and, 169–71; political astronomy and, 73, 153, 222n68; public adoration of, 169; solar imagery and, 23, 169–72; as star, 170–72

Washington Review using planetary language of spheres and orbits, 154–55

Webster, Daniel, 154, 178

Webster, Noah, 94–95

Wedgwood, William B., 217n132

Weekly Aurora (newspaper), 7

Wendover, Peter, 136

Western Sun (newspaper), 7

West Florida, Republic of, 162

Whigs, 17, 104, 107, 111, 119, 144, 150, 175

Whiskey Rebellion (1794), 9

Index

Wilkes, John, 218n14
Willard, Joseph, 33
William III (British king), 82, *83*
Winthrop, John, 150–52
Winthrop, John, Jr., 33
women: female education and astronomical politics, 45–48; Maria Mitchell as most famous female astronomer of nineteenth century, 38; science and, 32; solar system, gender of bodies in, 47

Wood, Frank E., 185
Wood, Gordon, 70
Wood, Kirsten, 15–16, 213n45
World War II National Monument, 191, *192*

Young Ladies' Astronomy (Bartlett), 46
"Young Ladies' High School" (Rhode Island), 45

zodiac, 37, 51, 160

RECENT BOOKS IN THE SERIES

Jeffersonian America

The Gendered Republic: Reimagining Identity in the New Nation
CRAIG THOMPSON FRIEND AND LORRI GLOVER, EDITORS

The Scientist Turned Spy: André Michaux, Thomas Jefferson, and the Conspiracy of 1793
PATRICK SPERO

Sacred Capital: Methodism and Settler Colonialism in the Empire of Liberty
HUNTER PRICE

Empire of Commerce: The Closing of the Mississippi and the Opening of Atlantic Trade
SUSAN GAUNT STEARNS

Black Reason, White Feeling: The Jeffersonian Enlightenment in the African American Tradition
HANNAH SPAHN

Replanting a Slave Society: The Sugar and Cotton Revolutions in the Lower Mississippi Valley
PATRICK LUCK

The Celebrated Elizabeth Smith: Crafting Genius and Transatlantic Fame in the Romantic Era
LUCIA MCMAHON

Rival Visions: How the Views of Jefferson and His Contemporaries Defined the Early American Republic
DUSTIN GISH AND ANDREW BIBBY, EDITORS

Revolutionary Prophecies: The Founders and America's Future
ROBERT M. S. MCDONALD AND PETER S. ONUF, EDITORS

The Founding of Thomas Jefferson's University
JOHN A. RAGOSTA, PETER S. ONUF, AND ANDREW J. O'SHAUGHNESSY, EDITORS

Thomas Jefferson's Lives: Biographers and the Battle for History
ROBERT M. S. MCDONALD, EDITOR

Jeffersonians in Power: The Rhetoric of Opposition Meets the Realities of Governing
JOANNE B. FREEMAN AND JOHANN N. NEEM, EDITORS

Jefferson on Display: Attire, Etiquette, and the Art of Presentation
G. S. WILSON

Jefferson's Body: A Corporeal Biography
MAURIZIO VALSANIA

Pulpit and Nation: Clergymen and the Politics of Revolutionary America
SPENCER W. MCBRIDE

Blood from the Sky: Miracles and Politics in the Early American Republic
ADAM JORTNER

Confounding Father: Thomas Jefferson's Image in His Own Time
ROBERT M. S. MCDONALD

The Haitian Declaration of Independence: Creation, Context, and Legacy
JULIA GAFFIELD, EDITOR

Citizens of a Common Intellectual Homeland: The Transatlantic Origins of American Democracy and Nationhood
ARMIN MATTES

Between Sovereignty and Anarchy: The Politics of Violence in the American Revolutionary Era
PATRICK GRIFFIN, ROBERT G. INGRAM, PETER S. ONUF, AND BRIAN SCHOEN, EDITORS

Patriotism and Piety: Federalist Politics and Religious Struggle in the New American Nation
JONATHAN J. DEN HARTOG

Becoming Men of Some Consequence: Youth and Military Service in the Revolutionary War
JOHN A. RUDDIMAN

Amelioration and Empire: Progress and Slavery in the Plantation Americas
CHRISTA DIERKSHEIDE

Collegiate Republic: Cultivating an Ideal Society in Early America
MARGARET SUMNER

www.ingramcontent.com/pod-product-compliance
Lightning Source LLC
Chambersburg PA
CBHW020932180426
43192CB00036B/649